AND GOD SAID TO ANGEL

Spiritualism, Advocacy, History, Mysticism, and More

THE UNION PATH

You may order this book through booksellers or by contacting Realm of Union Publishers, a subsidiary of Realm of Union Foundation.

ISBN: 978-1-9594-1627-2 (sc)
ISBN: 978-1-9594-1628-9 (hc)

Library of Congress Control Number: 2024920406

Realm of Union
FOUNDATION

Angel Fereshteh Bailey
Realm of Union Publishers
Realm of Union Foundation
2485 Rivermont Ave., #3354
Lynchburg, VA 24503

DEDICATION

THIS BOOK IS GOD'S GIFT

TO HUMANITY

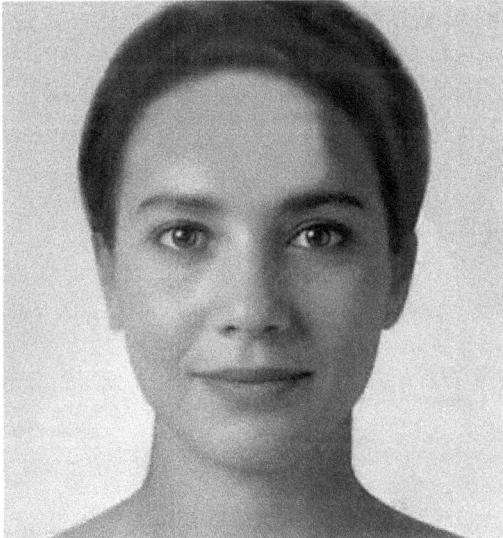

In 1993, Time Magazine hired a computer company to analyze a mix of races and other attributes to determine what the mixture would look like. The programmers developed this image of a young woman. When I first saw it, I thought, "So, humanity is also a woman like Iran and Virginia, where I grew up most of my life." Soon, I realized there is a need for feminine energy to grow and balance masculine energy. No question, we need this balance for the Realm of Union wave to come and roll naturally. So, let it flow.

CONTENTS

INTRODUCTION

A lexander Solzhenitsyn said, "If only there were evil people somewhere, insidiously committing evil deeds, and it were necessary only to separate them from the rest of us and destroy them. But the line dividing good and evil cuts through the heart of every human being. And who is willing to destroy a piece of his own heart?"

That is certainly the most profound statement that belongs to the Realm of Union.

Solzhenitsyn was a great man who was from Russia and adored by many, including my doctoral advisor at the Sorbonne, Professor Jean Claude Simon, who was one of the leading scholars and engineers in the field of computer pattern recognition and the winner of the 1998 K. S. Fu Prize, "for his contributions to the automated recognition of handwritten words and his lifelong leadership in Pattern Recognition." Professor Simon and many of his colleagues worked extremely hard to support Solzhenitsyn because they truly honored him for his contributions to a better understanding of humanity.

When I was in Paris working with Professor Simon, I remember meeting at his home with another great scientist, Professor Rosenfeld, from the University of Maryland, strategizing to find the best way to support Solzhenitsyn and free him from the cases of abuse of the Realm of Disunion because of his political ideas and standing. Another attendee in our meeting was a young computer scientist who later became a renowned expert in the development of the Bible Code.

These scientists cared about humanity and worked hard to make the world a better place for all. They wanted the Realm of Union to win over the Realm of Disunion, but they just couldn't see how the Realm of Union could ever triumph over the Realm of Disunion when most people seemed to be addicted to the Realm of Disunion and its attributes.

This book is here from God to humanity, to inform us that Solzhenitsyn's statement is correct and appropriate for the twentieth century. However, now that the Age of Disunion is ending and the Age of Transformation is unfolding, we must try to see both the Realm of Union and the Realm of Disunion and give the Realm of Union a chance.

The Realm of Disunion is the true enemy of humankind, always waiting to bind every person. However, the Realm of Union is also here waiting to bring us Divine Light and Love that can dissolve the Realm of Disunion and let us all live with God in His Realm of Union. His Heaven on Earth!

The key to living a fulfilled, happy life in the Realm of Union, where God dwells, and Truth resides to set us free, is to empower union attributes rather than disunion attributes daily, so that the Realm of Union can grow stronger in and around us, dissolving the Realm of Disunion for us.

We must stay positive rather than negative. That is the only way to remain in the Realm of Union with God, where there is no disunion. The Realm of Disunion cannot exist in Divine presence. When we allow evil thoughts, words, and deeds to occupy our lives to the point of disabling us to find a way to get closer to the Realm of Union and preferably stay there for good, then it is like empowering disunion attributes rather than union, knowing all along that the Realm of Disunion can take us away from God and His precious Realm of Union.

Hence, the only way to get free of disunion is to stop empowering disunion and its attributes. That does not mean we can't think about or discuss them to better understand them. It just means not to occupy ourselves with the Realm of Disunion to the point of forgetting about the Realm of Union. To pay attention to the Realm of Union passing us by and wishing to embrace us so that we may witness it and properly interact with it to receive our divine instructions daily. Otherwise, how is God going to work with us to dissolve the Realm of Disunion for us in and around us?

The main reason for this is that it is only in the Realm of Union that we can easily obtain the Divine Light, His pure energy, and the Divine Love,

His full support, to become holy enough to be in the Divine Presence, where there is no disunion. It is then that we can live through our Divine Selves, witnessing the Divine Logos and interacting with it to continue to get to know God and His wish to be known by man, every one of us, and the rest of His creation.

Remember that God dwells in the Realm of Union, not Disunion, and in the Realm of Union, there is no disunion because His presence alone dissolves the Realm of Disunion. And since He honors our free will, when we use disunion attributes, He departs to allow us the freedom to choose Him, because He doesn't want a bunch of zombies!

Judaism emphasizes the 613 mitzvot to remain holy and pure. Christianity says, "Follow Jesus and His way to reach the Father through the Holy Spirit." Islam says, "Follow the Divine Will rather than your own will."

Buddhism warns against antithetical concepts. It emphasizes mindfulness of our thought processes regarding not only good and evil but also success and failure, rich and poor, and even the duality between enlightenment and delusion. We are encouraged to distinguish between the opposing terms so that we may choose union rather than disunion, yet recognize that the meaning of each depends on the other.

Zoroastrianism says, "Think Good. Say Good. Do Good and live a happy life."

When we create stories to convince people that they are not strong enough, good enough, or insightful enough to choose between good and evil, we are empowering the negative rather than the positive. The Realm of Disunion rather than Union.

Stories can make or break us. They are not just entertainment. They teach us what is important in life. They give us models of how to live in a complicated, confusing world. In the past, the most important stories for most people were religious. Today, however, the bottom line is, "Will it sell?"

The story of good versus evil sells because it is simple and easy to comprehend, yet from a religious standpoint, it can be dangerously deceptive. It can keep us from looking deeper and from trying to discover causes. Once we identify something as evil, we tend not to explain it or look for its reasons. We are only interested in going against it.

We all love the struggle between good (us) and evil (them), the plots of the James Bond, Star Wars, and Indiana Jones films. In such movies, it is quite obvious who the bad guys are. They are ruthless and remorseless, so we must stop them by any means necessary, lest they spread shallowness and other similar disunion traits.

Some believe that humanity loves violence. That we get all excited when we watch violence.

When I went to film school to get my MFA in screenwriting and filmmaking, our teacher would not accept our screenplays unless they included violence and conflict in accordance with certain Hollywood rules and formulas for a motion picture screenplay. Of course, such rules could bring us a lot of violence in our movies, but we were told this is what people want.

What is this kind of story teaching us? That if we want to hurt someone, it is important to first demonize them, in other words, to fit them into our good-versus-evil story (us vs. them). That is why the first casualty of any war is the truth. And Solzhenitsyn was a genius in demonstrating this fact in many of his stories.

Today, many believe that when we are good, we try to fight evil. When we attack and destroy the evil outside us, we feel comfortable and secure inside because we sense our decency. That is why we lean toward war. We realize that wars can cut through the petty problems of daily life and unite us good guys, who are here against the bad guys, who are there. Of course, there is fear in that, but for many, it can be the norm, perhaps even exhilarating. Plus, it can clarify the meaning of life.

A friend, who was high up in the US Military, probably the second in command, once gave me a VIP Tour of the Pentagon. As we were having lunch, he said to me, "Angel, it costs a lot of money to support all this!" As I felt the pain in his eyes, I realized that it's not easy just to end the war machine and send everybody home! Especially since we've been living mostly in the Realm of Disunion and letting the Age of Disunion grow freely globally throughout the twentieth century!

Not taking the time to analyze the problem to see that with this approach, we're focusing on evil, where there is a tendency to think, say, and do bad stuff (evil, not good) to get rid of evil. In other words, we employ disunion attributes that promote the Realm of Disunion instead of union attributes that promote the Realm of Union. We forget that when we are in the Realm of Disunion, we cannot obtain the Divine Light and Love that can dissolve the Realm of Disunion for us.

In a passage from the Sutta Nipata, Ajita asks Buddha, "What is it that makes the world so hard to see?" Buddha replies, "It is ignorance and greed." Greed can force people to act. Ignorance can cause people to make wrong choices, leading them to use disunion rather than union attributes.

Hence, the key to Heaven's Door is to learn how to transform our greed into generosity, our ill will into love, and our ignorance into wisdom, thus converting every disunion attribute to a union one. That lets us stay close to God in His Realm of Union, which dissolves disunion and allows us to live in Heaven on Earth.

The bottom line is, "Where would you rather be, in Heaven or Hell?"

I believe this book shows us how to return to God and stay with Him in His Realm of Union, Heaven on Earth, for good. He is watching us, hoping that we will begin to listen to Him after years of separation and suffering.

For our atheist friends, believing in yourself and your ability to connect with everything is important as you seek to witness the Logos (the universal order) and continually support it through the balance of oneness and uniqueness. Before you know it, you find yourself in the Realm of Union, where God dwells, and truth resides. And, in His presence, you feel so loved, cherished, and safe that you no longer think about the past or the future. You are in the present moment, with no expectations or worries, so that you can witness the Divine Logos like never before.

At least, this is what I've tried to do ever since I received the Divine Message on January 12, 1997.

Here is the divine message:

Angel, tell your story. After yours, others will follow. Together, they will form a living document of thoughts, visions, and events, connecting humanity through a web of colors and waves.

Look inside yourself. Try to remember everything. Study the patterns in your life. In you, humanity resides in all its diversity.

See what has happened to you and how your life has been directed. You have always listened to me, and you will continue to do so. You strive to be in the Realm of Union.

The Realm of Disunion has lured many away from my realm, leaving a shortage of childlike wonder and qualities. You, however, have learned through your devotion to remain a child in the Realm of Union, even while experiencing the Realm of Disunion.

Children live in the Realm of Union, but it is difficult for them to communicate this to adults. They lack the tools to do so. In your case, it is different. You have experienced this realm as an adult and can now explain it to others.

You must write your story, including every special, spiritual, and miraculous event, with testimonies from people who witnessed them alongside you. Make it simple for everyone to understand.

Your story will resonate with many who are seeking me. People will sense my presence and pay attention, as you have always done. Slowly, they will enter my realm, the Realm of Union.

You may invite your friends to tell their stories. Every story and event will be unique. People may share these stories openly or confidentially on the TellRTale by posting them. Many TellRTales will collectively form a pattern through which humanity will be seen.

These TellRTales and other recommended tools will become an extension of humanity, helping everyone perceive patterns more clearly and feel comfortable sharing their story.

Gradually, people will appreciate diversity in themselves and others and understand their interconnectedness. This process will balance oneness and uniqueness, bringing humanity closer to me.

It's time for my children to connect with me directly, without filters, so their words can resonate in my spirit's vast, dark-blue chamber.

Over the next twenty-seven years, I repeatedly read this message about the Realm of Union versus the Realm of Disunion. Although intended for me, I believe this message applies to everyone.

The divine message comprises four parts, representing wholeness and completeness belonging to the Realm of Union, highlighted throughout my work.

The first time I tried to describe these two realms to a friend, I remember him saying, "Perfect." When I asked him what he meant, he responded, "Your example is nice and simple." That is how I described the Realm of Union and the Realm of Disunion.

In the Realm of Union, we surf the ocean of life. We see the waves rolling, but instead of being hit and bruised by them, we float on top, watching the flow in its beauty while feeling every motion, large and small. It is lovely to surf the divine waves.

Our children know how to surf. They do it every day. They live in the Realm of Union, enjoying the journey while most of us adults swim and waste our limited energy battling the waves.

When we swim in the ocean of life, waves of circumstances, large and small, roll around us, hitting us from all sides. By the end of our journey, we are exhausted from trying to stay afloat. We struggle to remain in control, but it is only an illusion. It is sad; not only do we not get to enjoy the ride, but by the time we reach the shore, we are so bruised that it is painful to relax and recall our journey. The Realm of Disunion is not a place you want to be.

When we surf, doubts and fears can make it hard to stay upright. The more we trust our surfboard and master its use, the easier it becomes. We take the time to stay in tune with the divine flow, just as it takes many months of practice to stay afloat and ride the ocean waves. Over time, we realize that trust and dedication are vital to becoming a surfer.

After surfing for a while, we gain more trust in God (and His natural ways, including His immense love for us) and our ability to flow with the divine waves. At that point, we no longer wish to return to arduous swimming, except during times of empathy, when we opt to swim with another person, mainly to share the experience. In this learning process, we can reach a point where we forget we are surfing and enjoy the ride.

And we are not alone in this. As smaller waves are unique to each of us, many feel the larger waves, depending on their intensity. We all need to practice surfing the divine waves, for nobody else can do it for us. Such knowledge can help us stay in tune with God and His wishes for us.

The key is recognizing our divine nature and its boundless potential. By aligning ourselves with God's plan, we unlock the power to achieve whatever we desire.

I must say, it took me a while to witness the Divine Logos after repeatedly chasing it and watching it perform, each time in a unique manner, teaching me more and more about God and His way. The first time I experienced it, I thought, *my Lord, so that's how we ought to see; how things truly are!*

At first, it was overwhelming. I didn't want to do anything else. I just wanted to stay with God and witness His Logos, the eternal, rather than the temporal world.

Then I remembered that I still had certain responsibilities to the temporal world and its inhabitants. I couldn't leave my beautiful children and grandchildren behind!

I began wondering about those who live in the temporal world, from which I now knew how to free myself! A world in desperate need of perceiving things, not as before, caged in the Realm of Disunion, but anew in the Realm of Union.

For the longest time, I witnessed the Divine Logos and then came back to be with others, again and again, until I finally decided to do whatever it may take through God and His guidance to merge the temporal world with the eternal world, which is the Divine Logos.

What I could barely see before, I was now equipped to witness all the time. My perception was not limited to what is biologically or socially useful, but what is intrinsically significant.

I've been so happy with my daily exposure to the glory and wonders of pure existence. Most people don't know about this state of existence. Those who experience it try to tell others about it, but very few people can believe it, relate to it, or perceive it.

I watched Shirley MacLaine the other day, talking about her life and other fantastic stuff in a 92Y interview with Leonard Lopate. So many good questions Leonard could have asked Shirley, but for whatever reason(s), he did not; perhaps he was not equipped or allowed to do it. It's difficult to get to the bottom of things when we live in the Age of Disunion with so many limitations.

It's always a pleasure to see Shirley and other courageous people among us who wish to elevate humanity's consciousness and unite people with both the expertise in spirituality and the drive to share their experiences with humanity. Another union person is Vladimir Pozner, who is truly an ambassador of love between the Russian and American collectives. Humanity needs such people to augment our collective caring and consciousness.

For the past two decades, I've explored more and more of God's universe and learned how to transform disunion into union through Divine guidance, gradually building the Kingdom of God right here on Earth, sure enough, around me. Hopefully, when the book comes out someday, I will try to get together with others to make it happen collectively.

A righteous man belonging to the Realm of Union does not have to stay in his room. He can go about his business without being fooled or manipulated by the Realm of Disunion.

When we can witness the Divine Logos, His Reality, through Him, what motives can we possibly have for the ego, greed, power, and or materialism?

We should do our best never to become addicted to the Realm of Disunion, make wars, or take more than our share. We must try to become partners with God, loving Him, yearning to be with Him, and seeking to please Him. Not to employ disunion attributes that may make Him leave!

Today, most of us have been conditioned to emphasize disunion attributes over union, thereby contributing to the Realm of Disunion. But this hopefully changes soon.

It's time to get together and bring the Divine Light, His pure energy, inside and around us. When an imbalance or drainage occurs, and a person is no longer filled with Divine Energy and Light, it is then that the Realm of Disunion can enter.

Some people try to calm themselves with empty sex with no mutual love, not realizing that the Realm of Disunion can drain people through love and sex. So, we have to be careful! Especially since the sexual act can be a great source of pure energy!

Those who enjoy promoting the Realm of Disunion have learned how to use love to destroy lives. They're the DRAGON women and men who have become addicts in conquering the opposite sex through disunion love rather than falling into the blob of love of the Realm of Union with them. Love is supposed to be an attribute of the Realm of Union, but it can become the greatest cause of our drainage when it is misused, generating disunion attributes. We must learn the tricks of the Realm of Disunion.

You should try to live your life this way because every human being is born here on Earth to experience this state of existence. **It is our *raison d'être*.**

Throughout history, many collectives have tried to experience this state of existence. The Jews dedicate at least one day a week to the Sabbath, a day set aside to feel the Divine Presence. Jews used to feel God's presence in the Holy Temple in Jerusalem. That's why they can't wait to build the temple again and experience Heaven on Earth through it. That's why they honor God's rules and try to abide by them.

They realize that God departs when we go against Him and His rules by employing disunion attributes, for He honors His gift of free will to us. After all, His presence alone can melt away all disunion. So, He leaves us to take care of the Realm of Disunion ourselves, unless we ask Him to handle it for us, as we solely employ union attributes in everything we do, including the transformation of disunion into union.

Naturally, I have tried to stay in the Realm of Union, where I can be full of energy as I follow God's will and remain in harmony with it, rather than go against it, and follow my own will or other people's wills that their desires may influence for money, power, greed, and/or other materialistic gains, no matter at what expense.

Of course, those who promote the Realm of Disunion and its attributes try to drain others rather than go to the source to obtain energy, thus spreading polluted energy. That is why most of us live on Earth today, spending most of our time feeling drained. It does not have to be this way. We can obtain pure energy from God through acts of oneness and uniqueness to increase our happy moments and feel good about ourselves and our lives.

The time has come to unite against the Realm of Disunion, our true enemy, and together build a Realm of Union structure on our planet, where people can help each other to lean toward union attributes and union stories, which can then make it easier for all of us to remain in the Realm of Union.

Too much darkness and chaos can make it easier for the Realm of Disunion and its people to bully everybody so that they can gain an upper hand to take from other things that do not belong to them for free or at a discount without compensating the owners and/or the creators of such things.

The disunion people, who are the global bullies, have become disunion addicts wishing to employ disunion attributes and techniques to get things done. They have learned how to communicate with each other in ways that can notify all disunion compradors and supporters without divulging the same information to the rest of us.

The broadcasters are supporters of the disunion structure, whether willingly or fearfully. Regardless, they get their directives from the disunion structure on what to say and what not to say, to give enough information to the public to know that the disunion structure is still in control, so watch out, but at the same time, let each other know what's happening regarding the plan of the disunion structure, in other words, the proactive history that has been active ever since the early nineteenth century.

We need to learn how to hear, see, and speak with the disunion supporters, always through the Almighty God, who solely employs union attributes and techniques. We need to decipher the many messages coming to us, whether from the Realm of Disunion or the

Realm of Union, and help each other stay above it all! It's time to stop the disunion structure from taking us on a destructive path. Our children and grandchildren deserve a better future.

For instance, the United States and its allies used to employ disunion tactics against many countries around the world, primarily to seize their valuable resources, such as the copper in Chile and the oil in Iran, under President Nixon, who seemed to lean toward imperialism. Then, a few decades ago, we saw this bullying come home to roost, where the United States is now applying such disunion procedures to its citizens.

After all, when the Realm of Disunion grows, it expands its territory to exploit more and more members of humanity. That is why I say the Realm of Disunion is our true enemy.

After all, the disunion people may prefer the Realm of Union, but since they don't know much about it, they stay in the Realm of Disunion. They don't want to go to a new territory; they are accustomed to the Realm of Disunion and how it works. They have become experts in making money through disunion means, so they want to continue doing what they do best. That is why we say money is the root of all evil.

But, when you think about it, money is just a tool that can be used to promote the Realm of Union or the Realm of Disunion. The key is to use it to empower the Realm of Union, which in turn can make the world a better place for all.

When we are filled with disunion stories, especially in our media, that does not mean we have not had any union people and/or events that have been successful. It just means that the Realm of Disunion has succeeded, so it can now prevent the union stories from being considered, told, and/or recorded.

In actuality, most lies are told to hide the Realm of Disunion's destructions and manipulations, to keep us from knowing the truth about our history and thus from knowing ourselves! As we build a union structure on our planet, we will be better supported, which will be great for all of us, including the elites.

When the Realm of Union begins to win over the Realm of Disunion, then history will be able to effortlessly capture the success stories of the Realm of Union heroes because it is then easier for the truth to come out, especially since the Realm of Union is God's realm with incredible powers, possessing every union attribute and technique to support us all.

Plus, our true stories make up our true humanity. It helps us find our true identity by allowing us to discover our uniqueness through our oneness, and our oneness through our uniqueness. A sort of balancing act that can aid us in becoming who we are, our Divine selves, our perfect selves, which can be closer to Jesus and in the image of God.

That is why we need to spread union stories to energize the Realm of Union, not the disunion stories that can drain humanity. Of course, stories can never drain God's creation unless people are influenced to do so. But before any drainage can cause permanent damage, it usually dissolves in the universe. So, it cannot last.

The key is to be careful not to spread darkness that can move us all toward the threshold that may be beyond repair. We must reassess our situation, both personally and communally, and question what is gained and what is lost, over and over again, to develop ideas that can benefit all by considering everyone and everything.

Those who are fragmented cannot see the whole, the union of things, so they cannot prioritize as a whole person. To prioritize correctly, we must become whole enough to see the whole, not just the parts.

A whole person always prefers the Realm of Union over the Realm of Disunion. Heaven rather than Hell!

Those who prefer Hell are people who have been so fragmented and damaged that they've forgotten their souls. This condition prevents a person from becoming his or her Divine Self, each self a part of God. When a soul is forgotten, it still exists and can witness its existence, but not through the person. There is a disconnection between the soul and its projection in this reality, which is the person, because there is no knowledge of how to activate this connection to reconnect with the soul through the Divine Self.

This volume, which you now hold, is here to show you that you can always reconnect with your soul because God created us to live in Heaven on Earth with Him. However, we cannot reach Heaven until we leave Hell. The reason for this is that we cannot be in Heaven and Hell at the same time.

This volume is all about the Divine Union Path. It consists of fifteen chapters, each of which takes us closer to our overall goal of reaching Heaven on Earth.

These fifteen chapters provide the foundation for the Divine Path, helping us better understand it.

Chapter 1, "Heaven vs. *Hell,"* describes these two realities as the accumulation of union versus disunion attributes. It explains why and how today's disunion structure tries to keep us all in bondage in the Realm of Disunion through confusion, lies, and deceptions, so that we may never reach the Realm of Union, which is Heaven on Earth.

Chapter 2, "To Unity vs. *Duality,"* discusses duality as a concept created and widely used by the disunion structure to confuse us and keep us away from unity, making it easier to keep us in the Realm of Disunion.

Chapter 3, "Eternal vs. *Temporal,"* explains these two modes of existence and how the many erroneous definitions of duality versus unity have kept us in the temporal rather than the eternal.

Chapter 4, "Whole vs. *Fragmented,"* discusses whole vs. fragmented people and how we may each reach wholeness.

Chapter 5, "God's Plan vs. *Man's Plan,"* compares these two plans and how to follow God's plan to align with Him and His Reality to reach the Realm of Union.

Chapter 6, "God's Way vs. *Man's Way*," compares these two ways and how to follow His way to align with God and His Reality to reach the Realm of Union, which is Heaven on Earth.

Chapter 7, "Union vs. *Disunion* Attributes," compares the attributes of union and disunion. It discusses the union and disunion structures and how each is built through the accumulation of union versus disunion attributes. It shows us how to align with God, who has tailored the Logos for each person and the collective to make it easier to distinguish between union and disunion.

Chapter 8, "Union vs. *Disunion* Thresholds," discusses the thresholds of union versus disunion and how to monitor them to strengthen the Realm of Union and dissolve the Realm of Disunion.

Chapter 9, "Building up Union vs. *Disunion*," discusses how a union or disunion structure is built. It explains how this buildup can result in a union or disunion state, and why it's best to build a union structure that supports us all.

Chapter 10, "The Eternal Light vs. *Darkness*," focuses on light versus darkness, with light emanating from the union state and darkness from the disunion state. It explains how Divine Light can lead us to spirituality, which can then help us better understand religiosity.

Chapter 11, "True vs. False Messiah," discusses our salvation, which will come through our transformation. It addresses the coming of the Messiah to take us to Heaven on Earth. It emphasizes the importance of honoring all messiah claimants and why such a union attitude may be necessary to move us toward the Realm of Union that is the Kingdom of God on Earth.

Chapter 12, "True Messianism," discusses the Messianic Age as a period of transformation in which humanity seeks redemption. It describes religion versus spirituality and why our world religions have become infected by the Realm of Disunion over the years.

The next chapter shows us how to stop living in hell so that we can reach heaven on Earth and stay there for good. The disunion realm is in italics.

HEAVEN VS. *HELL*

Heaven is the Realm of Union. Hell is the Realm of Disunion. These two realms are distinct realities that do not overlap. We can exist in either the Realm of Union or the Realm of Disunion.

Imagine two states of mind, where one state cages us in the Realm of Disunion with limited perception, seeing the parts but not the whole, and the other, in the Realm of Union, where we can see more and more of the whole, as we grow in our servitude and appreciation of the whole, toward an unlimited, infinite perception.

Humanity has been living in the Realm of Disunion for more than two millenniums even though the Realm of Union has been available to us. This volume tries to explain this concept in detail. In this chapter, I wish to provide a background.

THE FIRST STATE or REALITY is aligned with the Realm of Union. It is outside of this societal structure that we have built on our planet. This reality is right here, ready to embrace us if we just stop using disunion traits and instead learn to use union traits, allowing it to grow through us until one day it gains sufficient strength to become visible.

Of course, throughout history, we have had a few fortunate people who have lived in this realm, which our prophets and mystics have experienced. But overall, most people have lived in the Realm of Disunion rather than the Realm of Union.

THE SECOND STATE or REALITY is what we have come to know in our everyday experience. It is a set of disunified views that have firmly formed a linear time sequence of events, in which our perceptions are strictly limited to the boundaries of the present mingled with the past and the future, and our minds are separate and distinct from the universe around us. That is the structure that most of us are used to, a fragmented disunion structure, leaning toward the Realm of Disunion that has kept us in bondage for more than two millennia.

Later in this volume, the Chapter "God's Way vs. Man's Way" will explain this further.

The higher consciousness that belongs to the Realm of Union is immensely powerful and can slip in quietly to dominate our old, ordinary consciousness. However, the old structure shall persist, yet the new one shall prevail, for it is fueled by God and His Realm of Union, which is filled with His Light, His pure energy, and His Love, His full support. All we have to do is to wish it and embrace it, as we try to solely employ union attributes, always through God and His Realm of Union.

These two disjoint realities are available to everyone. We can either live in the Realm of Union, where we receive the Divine Light and Love from Him daily, be full of energy, and genuinely happy, living life to its fullest, or in the Realm of Disunion, where we are mostly drained and unhappy.

After all, the Realm of Union is where God dwells, and truth resides to set us free from the Realm of Disunion. There is no end to the infinite light and love that can fully support us all. But there is a requirement to be in this state of existence. We have to clean ourselves of all disunion attributes and instead solely employ union attributes.

Simply explained, we have to think, say, and do good things, as Zoroaster directed us to do.

We cannot use bad thoughts, words, and actions that lean toward the Realm of Disunion and then expect to be with God in the Realm of Union. It does not work that way!

Each religion has offered us a unique technique for reaching Heaven on Earth, the Realm of Union. Christianity through love, Islam through submission to the Divine Will, Judaism through work and mitzvoth, and Zoroastrianism through goodness and joy in life.

Those who live their lives in ways that contribute to the growth of the Realm of Disunion, whether they're victims of disunion or promoters of disunion (i.e., the non-union collective), can't help but absorb polluted energy from others, since they don't know how to obtain pure energy from the Source. After a while, they can become like vampires who get up each day and try to find new sources of polluted energy. So, regardless of whether they get drained or try to drain others, they end up in the Realm of Disunion rather than Union.

It's important to note that the Realm of Union is not the same as goodness; the Realm of Disunion is not the same as evil. That is why it took a long time and many volumes to explain these two realms in this book, exploring how they may be influencing different aspects of our lives, personally and collectively.

I believe God loves us so much that He is now guiding us, once more, to reach heaven by showing us how in this book, which I've been blessed to channel and hope to bring to you soon.

As you read this volume and the other volumes of this book, you will see the big picture and how to allow the unfolding of the Divine Plan for humanity. Who knows? You may even come up with new ways, not mentioned in this book, to take us closer to the Realm of Union!

The bottom line is that if we contribute to the Realm of Disunion, we cannot exist in the Realm of Union, where God dwells, and truth resides to set us free.

Those who are limited in perception are incapable of seeing the totality, all the way to the Almighty God. As a result, they are driven to benefit themselves, often promoting the benefit of the few, whereas those who can see the totality and feel a part of it, naturally work toward the benefit of all, including themselves, all the way to God. They try to serve God and His Realm of Union, all of which naturally pleases God, for it allows Him to be with us and manifest through us. I'm talking about the Divine Self of each person experiencing the Realm of Union and living life through the 'I Am' that is a part of the 'I Am Who I Am.'

Throughout history, we can see a continuing battle between those who can see and those who can't. This dichotomy has played out again and again, with those with limited perceptions coming into conflict with those who can see more of life. But today, humankind is destined to reach a new level of consciousness that will lead us to a better future for all, where we become enlightened to seek peace on Earth and less conflict.

In this new consciousness, we gradually learn how to rely on the Lord, as the Bearer of Burden, to take care of the Realm of Disunion for us, diligently working with Him to obtain the knowledge and wisdom of the Realm of Union and its many cool tools and techniques. After a while, through practice, we each stop getting drained by the Realm of Disunion and thus can keep most of our pure energy in our bodies. The more energy, the greater intuition, and the easier it is to reach the Realm of Union, where we are aligned with God and His universe. That is when the Realm of Disunion can no longer touch us!

Those already enlightened can live in the FIRST REALITY while simultaneously watching the SECOND REALITY. Thus, they can live in the Realm of Union, witnessing the Divine Logos and interacting with it daily, and at the same time, observe the Realm of Disunion and its continual abuses and the draining of everyone and everything in it. They get to see every person's struggle against the Realm of Disunion to reach the Realm of Union. Of course, the Realm of Disunion can no longer affect such people unless the damage is too large, influencing the collectives to which they may belong.

That is why we must promote union attributes daily to strengthen the Realm of Union so that it can gradually bring all union people together to rescue the victims and transform them into union people. It is then that the network of union people will become large and strong enough to create a union structure on the planet that can dissolve the current disunion structure.

Today, the disunion people are probably around five to ten percent of humanity. The rest are the victims, who are the majority, probably around eighty percent or so, and the union people, who are the minority, probably around five to ten percent of the population. However, this may be changing rapidly as the majority (the victims) become union members.

We, the union people, must not let the victims or the disunion people take us under so that we become victims as well. We must remember that the disunion people and the victims may be scared of His Light, His pure energy, and so may find different excuses to avoid it.

If you can raise awareness among such people and help them obtain the Light from the Source, that's great; if not, try to move on. That can be unpleasant when dealing with family members. However, if your heart directs you to let go, then you have to do it. Of course, after you've tried your best to remind such fearful people that it's possible to formulate their wishes in a union bundle, in other words, package them in a way where the forces of nature can just make things happen naturally for them toward the Realm of Union.

The best way to communicate with people is to always go through God to connect with them, whether they are union people, disunion people, or victims. Because when you connect through God with everything and everyone, you are in a state of awareness filled with the Divine Logos and its magical powers. You are no longer occupied with the regrets of the past and/or worries of the future, which can lower your level of awareness, connectedness, and communication with the Divine Logos.

It's best to let God do His work in moving us toward the Realm of Union without interfering with this natural process.

So, in effect, feeling fearful, angry, or sorry for one's or someone else's condition can involve the employment of disunion attributes that can hurt nature's flow. Why go against the natural way and try to run the show? Not too productive! Blessed are those who know when to stay out of God's way!

After all, through the Divine Logos, we can access the eternal world beyond this temporal three-dimensional reality. Why have we forgotten that we're in His image and thus capable of accessing the eternal as well as the temporal?

Moreover, remember that we're not the only collective in the universe that is in His image. Everything and everyone is pretty much in His image.

Let me explain this.

As God creates, He has an image of His creation, which is then manifested in His Logos, the Divine Reality. So, every entity in the universe is the manifestation of an image that is a part of God, including man. When we're told we're in the image of God, it means we're like an image of God. That means the Realm of Union is also a part of God and in His image, but not the Realm of Disunion.

The reason for this is that God did not create the Realm of Disunion. Man did this by going against God. That is why the Realm of Disunion lacks God and His Light. However, God has total dominion over the Realm of Disunion since His presence alone can dissolve all disunion. So, the Realm of Disunion exists solely in the darkness where there is no light of God, even though His light is infinite and in abundance in His Realm of Union.

The reason we haven't yet understood this concept is that humanity chose to be in the Realm of Disunion a long time ago, consistently promoting disunion attributes, and God allowed it until the end of the Age of Disunion, which is coming soon to usher in the Age of Transformation.

If you just sit quietly and imagine what it means to be in the image of God, you will come to see that any image belonging to God is a subset of the Master Image, the Master Set, which is the totality of God, where every image reflects a part of the Master Image.

A perfect mirror can reflect the sun and other objects so that we can see the natural form and color of all things, so that when we look into the mirror, we can see the sun itself. The same can be said about the way everything and everyone may speak to us of the glorious God.

The key is to go through God to see the rock with its strength and solidity, the tree with its magnificent beauty and leaves turning to distinct colors, the animal with its marvelous senses, instincts, and power of movement, and the human with its potential to become the Divine Self, in the image of God, and the Divine Logos in the flesh.

Most members of humanity, past or present, have not allowed themselves to be in the Divine image. However, humanity, as an integrated being, which is all of us together, our collective, has so far been close to the image of God. But this is changing rapidly as we become increasingly divided, losing the purity and order required. There is a threshold of polluted energy beyond which a collective could become too impure and chaotic to coexist in God's creation.

Today, the Realm of Disunion has grown so much that it is almost draining everyone. It's time for all of us to wake up and realize that we've been CHECKMATED, in other words, cornered with nowhere else to turn to but toward the Realm of Union where God dwells.

And God is ready to forgive whatever may have happened in the past, through Jesus the Lord, if we do our best to transition from the Realm of Disunion to the Realm of Union and are ready to help each other to go through this process.

Likewise, we need to forgive ourselves and each other because most of us didn't know any better. Even though we thought, we knew, I don't think, we did. There is evidence that our religious organizations may have been in darkness as well, even cooperating with the Realm of Disunion, not knowing that it would lead us all to our current situation.

We need to consider this issue and fully understand it. As we begin to conceive this concept, we come to understand that God's creation is always in His image and thus perfect. It is the Realm of Disunion that is the true enemy of humankind, always fragmenting everything and everyone to take away from this perfection, His perfection.

That is difficult to do for many who have convinced themselves that they're not worthy to be in the presence of God to witness His Logos, not realizing that God has the wish to be known and so He is ready to guide us to enter His ultimate Reality, the Divine Logos, which is made out of the same substance as His Light, His pure energy, through which every creature may reach Him no matter how cruel and or tormented the entity's past may be. All anybody ever needs is His pure energy that comes from union thoughts, words, and acts that always honor the balance of oneness and uniqueness!

Furthermore, since God wishes to be known, and we can get to know Him through His manifestations in His creation, then when we acknowledge, appreciate, enhance, and share our uniqueness, and let

24

others do the same, we empower the unfolding of the Divine manifestation through every person, entity, or event. This empowerment naturally enables us to feel Him and to stay with Him, thereby promoting the Realm of Union that brings everything and everyone closer to God and His Plan for us.

On the other hand, acknowledging, appreciating, enhancing, and sharing our oneness lets us see the world through the Divine Eye, which can make it easier to stay with Him on His path, customized and dedicated to each of us, leading us to the Realm of Union.

Also, our uniqueness and our oneness are connected and interdependent. We can determine our uniqueness solely through our oneness and our oneness solely through our uniqueness. Hence, this balance becomes super important in keeping us whole and in balance with Him and His creation. Otherwise, we stay limited in our oneness and/or uniqueness rather than reach our potential toward the Divine Infinite Path.

Can you imagine the possibility of reaching the ultimate oneness and uniqueness through God, yet going against it out of fear, doubt, and/or laziness?!

Why have we limited ourselves and our potential to operate beyond the space-time continuum to recall the many realities in which we exist, even interacting with the many versions of ourselves or others, whenever possible, always promoting the Realm of Union? Surely, the more we can experience through Him, the closer we can get to Him, and the wiser we can become. And, with true wisdom always comes the Realm of Union. Never Disunion!

We must learn to rely on God. The more people can do this, the greater the pure energy in the world and the easier it is to reach the Realm of Union.

As pure energy accumulates on the planet, more Divine Light becomes available to help people heal faster, making it easier to let go of our past baggage and be ready for the reunion.

People will begin going through Karma Crash Courses, realizing that every person belongs to a soul that can split into two projections, one as the true self, the Divine Self, and the other as the false self. They will also realize that God has an infinite degree of every union attribute that can help us reach the Realm of Union, Heaven on Earth, where we can each consciously unite with our Twin Partner, our Divine Self. It is then that one becomes active and the other dormant, until the inactive one dissolves due to a lack of the Holy Spirit.

In the end, the 'I Am' of each person or entity comes to experience the presence of 'I Am Who I Am,' who dwells in the Realm of Union.

We're all one, even though we're each unique. That is one of the miracles of God's creation. Those who can see this miracle acting every day in His Realm of Union, giving birth to new miracles, no two alike, yet all reflecting the image of God, are the luckiest people in the world!

Nothing can compare with this, for it is the ultimate achievement in life, our *raison d'être*.

When an individual reaches the highest state of spirituality, becoming perfect in His sacred image and aligned with God and His Logos, there is no direct connection to other living or non-living entities.

All connections are through God.

We live our lives aligned with our true selves, in other words, our Divine Selves that can be said to be our souls, each soul a part of God. Soon, all fears, sorrows, pains, and worldly sufferings disappear, allowing us to joyfully witness and feel the universe in the present moment as it is changing, in other words, the Divine Logos and its nature. Soon, we begin to learn how to interact with His Logos that can teach us everything we need to know, always according to the level of our servitude, on a NEED-TO-KNOW basis.

Today, we're at a point in humanity's spiritual development where we can explore whether we're in heaven or hell.

I mentioned earlier that I've been in heaven on Earth for a few years, and I'm sure others like me have achieved this state of higher spirituality. But overall, I believe we have been living in hell on a collective level, even though humanity has longed to live in the Realm of Union, largely because of the Age of Disunion. Overall, humanity is still within the threshold of existence, but this is changing rapidly.

Let us go deep and analyze the situation.

If we're in heaven personally, does that mean we are living in heaven on Earth with no trouble whatsoever? If so, then humanity has succeeded in its spiritual journey and already reached heaven on Earth, which is not the case, for we can look around and see that we're kept from reaching heaven on a collective level.

If we have reached heaven while others are still in hell, then the Realm of Disunion is still strong, not letting us live comfortably in heaven on Earth. Then, we must help our brothers and sisters reach heaven first on a personal level, and, as we come together, bring heaven to humanity on a collective level.

Are we in hell if we're not in heaven? If so, how did we get here, and what must we do now to reach heaven on a personal level, and then together on a collective level?

No doubt, God wants us to be in heaven, personally and collectively, so that He can be with us right here on Earth. That is why He has continually guided His messengers to rescue humanity throughout history, teaching us the way to heaven.

I'm sure, this time, we are going to get to our destination because this book in many volumes is here to provide us with a unique view of the world, where issues are examined and solutions are recommended, all according to union versus disunion attributes of life, which may be a better tool for understanding and resolving issues at this time in human history.

Those few who know how to live in the Realm of Union can obtain His Light (pure energy) and His love (God's support and guidance) and are truly fortunate. They are awake, witnessing Divine Reality, His logos, and interacting with it daily to obtain their Divine guidance, while the rest of us are asleep or confused, suffering in the hell of the Realm of Disunion.

The Realm of Disunion is here to drain everyone and everything. It employs whatever possible means to blind us so that it can separate us from the natural way. No one is safe. No matter what your nationality, wealth, race, religion, sex, age, education, or any other characteristic, you are susceptible.

The Divine Message, which I received on January 12, 1997, directed me to write *And God Said to Angel*, which became a series, each volume containing approximately 400 to 500 pages. I believe this book series is God's gift to humanity, helping us understand the Realm of Union versus the Realm of Disunion, so that we may stay with God in His Realm of Union for good.

I have included the Divine Message at the beginning of each volume of this book. At the end of this volume, the conclusion contains a guide summarizing the techniques of the Realm of Disunion and providing many examples of why we are in hell, on both personal and collective levels.

What's remarkable is that in the summer of 1996, I had just begun living a new life as a housewife with an atheist without any intention of someday writing this book about God. It was my time to relax after years of working as an encryption expert and an executive in the business world, and I must say, totally fed up with it.

I honestly believe that our Beloved Creator loves us all so very much that He has gradually brought the pieces of a puzzle to me, and often helped me to put them together, so that one day, I could see the total picture (the puzzle), and realize its importance, not just for me, but for all of us, as members of humanity.

Hopefully, soon, we will recognize the importance of this book in figuring out where we are, how we got here, and what we must now do to join the Realm of Union movement that is going to be built for humanity by humanity to benefit humanity, where we can come together and help each other enter Heaven, first on a personal level, and then, on a collective level, as we gain greater perception to move toward God's wish and plan for us to transition from the Realm of Disunion to the Realm of Union.

It seems to me that every time humanity is confused and in crisis, perhaps in need of guidance, a new projection of the Divine Presence comes, like a mirror, reflecting the problems of the time and providing solutions to resolve them.

That means God's projection becomes stronger, manifesting in various events, one of which may be His wish to guide us by assigning someone to deliver His message to humanity.

For example, right now, we may need an encryption expert, who is also a mathematician, an expert in pattern recognition, a computer scientist, a female who is used to giving tender loving care, and someone who knows a lot of cultures, languages, and religions, an Iranian full of love, etcetera, and so here I come fully trained and refined by God's holy universe to guide the masses.

God knows how many others may be here with similar backgrounds and missions. Believe me. I'm not the only one! There are many like me, driven toward the Realm of Union—people from different cultures and races around the world, whether white, black, red, yellow, or brown—wishing to promote the Realm of Union.

Simply put, God created us in His image so that He may manifest through us as we experience His logos. But His presence requires holiness, which we have failed to acquire, keeping us from reaching our overall purpose. So far, He has waited for us to reach the maturity required to become whole and holy in His presence. But this has not yet happened, delaying His dreams for us.

The summary I included in the conclusion of this volume is also here to let us know that it's not too late; we can still shape up and follow the recommended steps to reach heaven on Earth. But if we don't listen and continue on a path of ignorance and selfishness, benefiting ourselves and our loved ones at the expense of others (humanity's collective) and Mother Earth, we will not make it. For God's creation won't allow it!

Imagine a group of people (two or more) in a meeting trying to solve a problem. When every person is equipped and capable of moving toward the Realm of Union rather than Disunion, they can get closer to the Divine Mind that always carries the best solution to every problem. That allows the group to realize the potential of what is possible rather than remain in actuality, which may be mediocre and not belong to the Divine Reality, His Realm of Union.

Here, people's perceptions can truly matter. When perception is high, it is easier to see the totality that belongs to the Realm of Union. Otherwise, we are dealing with too many fragments, often not organized or organized improperly, preventing the overall picture from emerging and keeping us in the Realm of Disunion.

We've been in the Realm of Disunion for too long, gradually forming the Age of Disunion, an era of humanity's spiritual development, which is destined to end soon to let the Age of Transformation come and embrace us all.

The overall purpose of the Age of Transformation, which is a part of the Messianic Age, is to reach our maturity to become whole and holy. This way, we can live again in the Realm of Union, where God dwells, to experience His presence in His logos and learn to interact with it daily, so that we may live our lives through our Divine Selves, moving along our Divine Path.

Why not make it easier for Him to manifest through us? Not just for a moment but a lifetime.

The day we realize that we can get to heaven on Earth by satisfying His wish to be known and by doing what it takes to return to Him and get to know Him will probably be the most joyful day for humanity and for God regarding His creation of man. Then, our wish to be in heaven will merge with His wish to be known, making both wishes come true.

So far, we have obviously not cared much about God and His wishes, but from now on, we must begin to care and learn to live confidently with Him, obey Him, and consider what He may want from us!

We can no longer allow the Realm of Disunion to continue abusing His universe, His planet Earth, His humankind, and every person and collective, all genuinely loved by Him with no end. We must honor Him and His creation. If we don't, then we have no right to benefit from it. From the air we breathe, the water we drink, the warm sunshine, the bright moon, and everything else that He has given to us for free!

It's time to thank Him by acknowledging His awesome gift to us, which is truly infinite. The best way to do that is to start acting responsibly, as He has always instructed us to do, which most of us have ignored, primarily due to the Age of Disunion that grew as a result of a flawed global structure that leans toward the Realm of Disunion, primarily due to ignorance and selfishness.

But, truly, as shown in this volume, we may be sitting in a great position right now with the possibility of empowering the Realm of Union to dissolve the Realm of Disunion.

We must look deeper to perceive our potentialities as well as our actualities.

After all, God has helped us so far, and He will surely aid us in the future to reach our destination. He has guided every collective through His union messengers, doing their best to manage the Realm of Disunion as it grew and spread around the world, while maintaining the planet's stability. Of course, some collectives contributed to this effort more than others.

For example, the English collective, as the great strategists, managed the growth of the Realm of Disunion while keeping the planet's stability. The Jewish collective, as the chosen people of God, advised and guided the English and other collectives. The Persian collective, as the great transformers of disunion into union, provided its oil to fuel the industrial revolution and to fund the many projects involved in this effort, including the transformation of disunion into union whenever and wherever possible. The American collective, as the young and energetic cowboys with no fear, often tried to wing it all.

Others involved were the French collective, as the great engineers and maintainers of the equilibrium between union and disunion; the Russian collective, as the most passionate lovers of life; the Chinese collective, as the great innovators; the German collective, as the great builders; the Indian collective, as the great informers of spirituality; etcetera.

Every collective has contributed to humanity's growth during the Age of Disunion and should be recognized and celebrated to empower the Realm of Union. That is super important and entails a delicate process.

The key is to understand that in the late nineteenth century, when global managers realized the importance of oil for fueling the Industrial Revolution, they asked the Persians for their oil, and the Persians agreed to provide it as a Taarof (a gift) to humanity.

The Jews agreed to facilitate this effort because of their long relationship with the Persians and the Arabs in the region, and also to safeguard Jerusalem as the future seed of the Realm of Union's growth around the planet.

Looking back, the English, the Jews, the Persians, and the Americans did their best to work with other collectives to facilitate this effort, which has, fortunately, led us to an amazing point in humankind's history, where we may now be ready to transition from the Realm of Disunion to the Realm of Union.

No doubt, God has allowed for all that has transpired in the past, perhaps because it was the best option for humanity. But there is a catch to all this, and that is, we must come to recognize it as such. It is only then that we can empower it from a Realm of Union standpoint. Otherwise, we may go deeper into the Realm of Disunion, which we can no longer afford.

Of course, some people can always see all this negatively, which will surely draw humanity closer to the Realm of Disunion, perhaps contributing to the destruction of humanity and the planet. So, we must be very careful about how we view our past, present, and future. We must see things positively and realize that everything has happened pretty much according to the Divine Plan and, as such, should be acknowledged and appreciated rather than kept secret due to misunderstandings. We cannot continue living in shame and secrecy when, in reality, we've done our best to safeguard humanity and prepare every collective to transition from disunion to union.

Surely, we must take the union path that will lead us to a better future for humankind, and not the disunion path that will take us deeper and deeper into the Realm of Disunion. Please read the four volumes of *And God Said to Angel* for more information regarding this delicate transition.

Shame is an assault on the soul. Regardless of its origin, shame can go deep, reaching the inner core of a person's soul and the collective soul, which can then lead to anger and grief. When shame is mishandled for many years, people stop feeling it. They become like living machines with no heart! We must never let the Realm of Disunion take away our hearts. We must ask the Lord to hold us and protect us from shame, since He is here, ready to give us a hand.

Every human is in the image of God and a member of humanity, and as such, deserves to be treated respectfully, especially after all the sufferings we have endured over the years. We don't need to be validated by a bunch of filthy unrighteous people to know who we truly are! There is a universal order that validates us all! It is through this universal order and our servitude and love for the Father that we can ever hope to know who we truly are, personally and collectively.

Without this caring and sharing, a culture can surely decay and die!

The worship of money over everything else, including our humanity, is a disunion trait that prevents us from honoring one another and goes against God's will! That is why, when money drives us, we often end up promoting the benefits of the few rather than those of all, competing with each other to gain more, often at the expense of others or of the collective. Today, people are hurting each other just to make a buck!

In such a structure, bullies usually end up at the top, where they stop playing fair and often take more than their share. So, it's not a healthy environment for humanity. A horrible place to be, even for those who think they're benefiting from taking from others without giving much in return!

The question is: Why have we allowed ourselves to be ruled by such bullies and a disunion structure that continues to act this way, where we allow for such abuses and exploitations from top to bottom, and really, from the bottom to the top? Why don't we acknowledge such disunion behaviors, try to understand our cultural disparities, and find solutions that can take humanity to the Realm of Union?

The answer is: The disunion collective's power comes from the Realm of Disunion and its disunion attributes, such as deceiving and abusing others to better compete with and steal from them. They've learned how to compete and employ disunion tactics to do so, and so far, they think they've succeeded, unaware of anything else.

Such people don't know much about the Realm of Union. At the same time, they have no interest in taking the time to learn about it. It's just too risky for them to follow the benefit of all rather than the benefit of the few. So, they do their best to weaken the Realm of Union and its people, thereby strengthening the Realm of Disunion, which empowers them to do what they do.

Looking back and understanding the main theme of the Divine Plan, as detailed in *And God Said to Angel: Toward the Divine Plan and Heaven on Earth*, it is clear that all this aligned with the Divine Plan and thus was part of humanity's destiny to get us here to hopefully prepare us for our transition from the Realm of Disunion to the Realm of Union, for which we must all be thankful.

At the same time, we must recognize that the Divine Logos has been here all along for us to observe, witness, and interact with, so that we may learn from it and obtain its support, as every part of God's creation has been doing for billions of years. But due to the Age of Disunion, we have moved away from God's natural way, as seen in nature, where everything balances oneness and uniqueness toward greater harmony.

34

The Western establishment should try to comprehend the Persian culture and other similar cultures that honor the balance of oneness and uniqueness and learn to do the same, rather than continue abusing humanity and its awesome collectives.

We can't continue on this path of bullying others. We must begin to care for one another and God's Plan for humanity, especially since the Realm of Disunion has reached its peak. We must stop generating disunion attributes, for there is a threshold beyond which humanity can dissolve.

The Realm of Disunion is like spiritual pollution that tends to blind people to seeing and making the right decisions. As a result, humanity has become like an addict who has to be gradually cleansed of its addiction.

The money that we have used to support the disunion structure and its people has come from taking advantage of the assets and resources of different countries and collectives around the world, either directly or indirectly, sometimes unwillingly through various forms of exploitation, or willingly like in Iran where the oil was given to the Western establishment as a Taarof, a form of union giving, which has been misunderstood, and thus turned to disunion rather than the union that it is supposed to be.

All this has created too many imbalances that need to be addressed gently. Still, surely through union techniques, not disunion, especially since the Realm of Disunion has reached its peak. It can take us deeper into such ugliness and destruction, most of us would rather not experience.

We must understand that we had to go through the Age of Disunion because we had to see the many faces of evil and obtain the required technology and tools to use as an extension of humanity to transform every disunion into union, to dissolve the Realm of Disunion for good so that the Realm of Union could appear in all of its glory.

We must get together and help each other stop our disunion behaviors; forgive whatever has happened; transform every disunion into union, and realize that the situation is not as bad as it appears. We may be sitting in a miraculous space-time continuum, where we can soon transition from disunion to union by dissolving the disunion side of humanity and its structure to empower the union side, always through Divine guidance.

God has brought us His solution to open up the path to the Realm of Union for us. Let's run with it! Before you know it, you will have gained enough of His pure energy and witnessed enough of His Logos to gain the knowledge and strength to stay in the Realm of Union in His presence for good.

It is then that you come to see the balance of oneness and uniqueness in such a way that wholeness, the totality, and its parts are continually dancing together and holding on to each other, so that, within sameness, there is a difference and vice versa.

We all have an urge to transcend the self. Without self-transcendence, it's difficult to communicate with our souls. Thus, this is the principal appetite of every soul. Ideally, every person should be able to obtain guidance from his or her soul in some form of pure or applied religion to reach this spiritual state of being. We take part in rites; we listen to sermons; we repeat prayers; yet our thirst remains, for we don't know how to witness the Divine Logos and interact with it in a way that allows the Logos to become flesh in us, as Jesus tried to show us the way.

Every day, we tell stories, creating mental and verbal replicas of our inner and outer worlds, adding to their rhythms and shapes, going back and forth between the inside and the outside, and vice versa. We try to organize the order and complexity of the physical world so that we can abstract, assimilate, and reproduce it as we see it, sometimes multiplying its meanings in the minds of many.

Meaning is the fruit of the human mind, a signature of our understanding and interpretation. Dance, poetry, journaling, drawing, and rituals reiterate nature's patterns, the order of the cosmos, the waves, and the flying birds. We belong to God's universe and, as a species, possess its creative rhythms and patterns.

Those who are living in LAJAN (Shit in Farsi) are all stuck in it, smelling to high heaven, and unable to move freely. Some are wealthy, living in palaces, but are always busy protecting and growing their wealth, with no time for anything else. Some live modestly on a small boat but have the time to row and row gently down the stream of pure sparkling water, freely moving through the water of life and enjoying every moment of it.

Look around you. We're surrounded by filth; what we do often turns to filth and imbalances because we're in the darkness of Hell, not the light of Heaven.

Humanity has been living in shit for more than two millennia. We've been living in the Age of Disunion, promoting a disunion structure that, by its very nature, promotes the Realm of Disunion. Ever since Alexander the Great conquered the Persian Empire, we've been living in hell, competing and killing each other to get ahead to somewhere better, rather than cooperating and helping each other to live in heaven on Earth.

Today, we can see how the disunion people have gone to a level of disunion that no longer honors humanity. In other words, they consider themselves human beings, members of the human collective, yet they are dishonoring their collective by taking a knife and chopping off their arm or leg or cutting their eye or ear. They've gone insane, and they don't know it!

This attitude has slowly but surely fragmented everything and everyone over the years, including our worldviews. Most people don't know what's going on. They're confused. This state of confusion, accompanied by falsehood and secrecy, has allowed many corporations, governments, and other entities worldwide to take advantage of the situation and do whatever they want, benefiting the few at the expense of the many.

The perception of union is the key to comprehending the totality rather than the fragmented parts. Without this union mentality, these entities cannot possibly care for humanity.

As a result, those managing this disunion structure are unable to see the totality of things and are thus willing to harm people and deplete their energy, either directly or indirectly, to benefit the few. Not realizing that we're all humans, each a part of humanity that is a part of God.

The Persian poet, Saadi, declared that we are all parts of the same body.

In his poem "Bani Adam," meaning the "Children of Adam" that is inscribed on the United Nations building entrance, Saadi wrote:

> Adam's children are limbs of one body.
> We share a similar substance, one essence.
> If one member is hurt and afflicted with pain,
> Others should feel severe discomfort and strain.
> If you have no sympathy for people's sufferings,
> Then, should you be called a human being?

I'm sure you know the answer to that. We cannot call the person a human being! Humanity must take the proper actions to force such people, who have stopped being human beings, out of any kind of management and or leadership positions, where they can have access to humanity and its precious, valuable resources for weakening and or destroying humanity, including themselves!

Of course, there are people in every government, every collective, and every organization around the world who do not belong to the disunion collective. We need to learn how to recognize and unite such people to empower the Realm of Union to dissolve the Realm of Disunion. To achieve this goal, we must understand the Realm of Disunion and its techniques; however, we should never become entangled with it. Sometimes, it is difficult to do this when you're still a beginner. But God is here, as the Bearer of Burden, to help you. So, let Him handle it for you.

As you continue watching Him dissolve disunion for you, one after another, you come to understand how He operates: always employing union attributes, never disunion.

Over the past few decades, as the Age of Disunion grew and promoted the Realm of Disunion, evil spread worldwide through our many communication tools, electronics, computers, the internet, media, and other technologies.

It is now easier to confuse the hell out of everybody and make them get so overwhelmed with the Realm of Disunion that they go insane! In such an environment, there is no question that falsehood and secrecy reign everywhere. Not the truth and openness to get to heaven!

Most people prefer heaven, the Realm of Union, but with a structure that solely supports the Realm of Disunion, it is impossible to reach it collectively.

Believe me. The disunion people are very few and very weak. They're scared to death. Deep inside, they would rather not support the Realm of Disunion, but they don't know what else to do.

Of course, one can exclaim, "Why have the disunion people continued supporting the Realm of Disunion?" even though every person can decide to move toward the Realm of Union and do whatever it takes to get there on a personal level. But let's face it. Since the structure does not support it, it is not currently possible to reach the Realm of Union collectively. This shortcoming allows the Realm of Disunion to grow, making it increasingly difficult for every person to reach the Realm of Union and remain there. For those of us who are used to getting things done the disunion way, letting go can feel almost impossible!

Some people try to create a union atmosphere for themselves and their loved ones while collaborating with the Realm of Disunion, unaware that one cannot promote disunion while simultaneously remaining in the Realm of Union. It doesn't work that way!

And the reason for this is that God is the totality. God is the unconditional, infinite love and light. God is the truth and every other union attribute one may think of. There can be no disunion around God. So, we cannot promote the Realm of Disunion and expect to end up in His presence. We must do the opposite.

We must employ union attributes and promote the Realm of Union to become holy enough to be in the Divine Presence. Undoubtedly, whenever the Realm of Disunion wins over the Realm of Union, it's because we have not empowered the Realm of Union that is here to support us all. Instead, we have empowered the Realm of Disunion, which only supports disunion people and tactics to weaken the Realm of Union.

We've been kept ignorant and away from the truth because the truth always promotes the Realm of Union, and we are now living in a disunion structure on the planet that has become super strong, continually promoting the falsehood of the Realm of Disunion.

So, for those of us who have a longing for the Realm of Union, we should try to build a new union structure, side by side with our current disunion structure, through union attributes, such as the promotion of truth, love, and kindness, as we jointly work toward the Realm of Union.

If a person prefers the Realm of Disunion, then that would be unfortunate for him or her, and actually for all of us. However, the Realm of Union will eventually triumph, as the Age of Disunion is now ending and the Age of Transformation is soon to come, aiding us in our transition from disunion to union.

Our time is up! We've been checkmated!

Since the disunion people are in the minority, not in the majority, and we now know how to strengthen the Realm of Union to dissolve the Realm of Disunion, through God and His union attributes, our transition from disunion to union is going to happen because we're now on our way to reaching the Realm of Union.

But we must consider that the Realm of Disunion won't go away by itself. It will continue to project a united front, which, in essence, is its opposite, while recruiting and promoting compradors of the Realm of Disunion who are willing to confuse people to generate enough disunion attributes and polluted energy around the planet to delay this process. Such people often do what they do to be rewarded by the Realm of Disunion, its people, and its structure, not realizing that the Realm of Disunion is our true enemy and is driven to destroy us all sooner rather than later.

Let's analyze where we are, how we got here, and what we must now do to reach the Realm of Union, first personally and then collectively, to build a union structure on the planet that will support us all.

Of course, the Realm of Disunion will do its best to stop us from reaching the Realm of Union, as it has done in the past. But with enough awareness, perseverance, and unity with God and humanity, the Realm of Disunion should slowly dissolve, freeing us from its bondage and allowing us to enjoy the Realm of Union with the Almighty God permanently by our side.

It is then that the many disunion techniques, such as the promotion of duality and other disunion attributes that confuse us, and make it easier to manipulate us, shall no longer work on the masses, because we will finally come to understand everything for what it is.

The next chapter shows us how to move toward greater unity, not duality. It describes duality as a major disunion tool employed in the past to keep us from understanding the true meaning of the word, and thus the Realm of Union versus the Realm of Disunion. Duality is a disunion view belonging to the Realm of Disunion, so it is shown in italics.

Many other words have been defined inaccurately, whether intentionally or unintentionally, to confuse us and delay our journey to reach the Realm of Union. We need to set up a project soon to redefine all such words, this time accurately.

To Unity vs. *Duality*

S ince we've been living in a disunion structure for more than two millenniums, we have continued to empower duality rather than unity because the disunion structure always leans toward the Realm of Disunion, not Union. It tries to promote disunion attributes, not union, primarily to survive. That has created the Age of Disunion, which is now destined to end, allowing the Age of Transformation to unfold and bring us unity.

So, let's address the concept of duality and, if possible, simplify it so we can finally reach unity.

Duality splits our attention. It provides us with a limited disunion (disjoint) view of something rather than a union view. That's done to confuse us and keep us in the Realm of Disunion, where we can only see the parts rather than in the Realm of Union, where we can see the whole.

That's why the Realm of Disunion is always fragmenting everything and everyone to keep us from perceiving the whole.

The goal in life is to align with God's creation and plan that promotes wholeness, not Man's creation and plan that often goes against it. The creation of man is the only set in the universe that can belong to the Realm of Union or the Realm of Disunion, thereby causing duality. Everything else belongs to the Realm of Union, where there is unity, and within this unity, there is the balance of oneness and uniqueness and other union attributes that can always take us to the Realm of Union, where no disunion can exist.

Let me first discuss what we've been told about duality throughout history, then explain why our concept of duality has remained confusing and often inaccurate.

We're told to believe that every word, thought, and act exists in pairs, not alone. This partner is the exact opposite, where it is not possible to have one without the other, just as it is not possible to have one side of the coin without the other.

Thus, a person can have both attributes of A and not-A, plus whatever is in between, because in the universe, there are many examples of entities with both attributes of A and not-A. The world we live in is not black and white; there are many shades of grey.

We're told that when we form a concept, we inevitably form its opposite. For instance, in society, there are Christians and non-Christians, Jews and non-Jews, Chinese and non-Chinese, capitalists and communists, men and women, black and white people, and so on.

The universe is filled with pairs of opposites: darkness and light, night and day, morning and evening, land and sea, black and white, birth and death, growth and decay, creation and destruction, past and future, yin and yang, beauty and ugliness, solitude and companionship, excitement and depression, good and evil, up and down, left and right, wise and stupid, peace and war, life and death, east and west, north and south, etcetera. The list goes on and on.

We're told that identifying one side can help us understand the other by showing what the first one is not. We must understand both sides, the two extremes, and try to find the middle ground. It is only then that we can reach harmony. Thus, we must bring all opposites together in our consciousness to see the wholeness. It is through this wholeness that all conflict ceases to harm us, both personally and collectively, and that we heal.

Hence, a wonderful sense of wholeness can arise when we accept and embrace all opposites and reject none. In other words, when we look at both sides of every situation.

For instance, most of us are not entirely feminine or masculine; we have characteristics of both genders. So, any model that purports to be a true representation of the totality of existence must take these essential features of the universe into account.

We're told that there are self-contradictions in the universe, and so the model we build of the universe itself must be self-contradictory. For if self-contradictions are eliminated from the model, just because we feel uneasy about them, then we would not be able to see the universe as it truly is. Understanding unity versus duality is a mark of natural intelligence. Etcetera.

All this concludes that it is quite impossible to describe the sense of wholeness in words, so it is difficult to reach this state of unity where there is no duality. If it were easy, then we would have reached it long ago because this is what we all yearn for deep inside.

But this mentality, entangled with duality, is flawed and partially untrue.

For instance, we view the words "give" and "take" as opposites. We state that one cannot exist without the other. If someone is giving something, there must be someone taking it.

But this is not a good explanation. It cripples us to look deeper to better understand these two attributes.

Let me tell you a story.

Imagine I'm walking on a trail near my home every day. The trail passes through a park next to a lake, then crosses a stream and circles my house.

One day, as I try to jump over the stream, I get a glimpse of a little boy jumping over the stream and twisting his leg.

So, a few days later, I go to the hardware store and buy the lumber and other materials to build a bridge over this stream. I figure, why not make it easier for everybody who may be walking on this trail? It takes me a day to finish the bridge. Nobody sees me doing it, but I'm happy to do it as a contribution to the community.

A few years later, I have a son who has grown up and is now a little boy going to school. I notice that he loves to go walking on the trail every day. Then, I remember my vision of a little boy a few years back and am glad to have built the bridge that can now protect any passerby.

In life, when we give, it is possible to do so, just to promote the Realm of Union that is here to safeguard God's creation, not only in this three-dimensional reality but also in higher dimensions all the way to God, who can see everything. After a while, we realize that giving does not just please Him; it allows us to be with Him, where we can be free from all disunion attributes. After all, in the Divine presence, there is no place for the Realm of Disunion.

According to ancient Advaita-Vedanta non-duality philosophy, which originated from Persia, there is just One Spirit in the universe, and everything, living or inanimate, is an inseparable and indivisible part of this One Spirit. Anything but this oneness is an illusion caused by the mind and play of the senses, separating us from everything and everyone in the world.

However, with this oneness comes uniqueness, balancing the Divine universe, which is totally in the Realm of Union, where God is manifest in everything and everyone. When we see oneness, we can also see uniqueness and the balance between the two.

When we cannot see the oneness and the uniqueness as they continually balance each other, then we are not seeing the totality of something. We are only seeing the parts, not the whole, and its true nature, thus preventing us from understanding it fully.

Hence, unifying all opposites in our consciousness and seeing how they interact cannot necessarily heal us or our sick society unless we recognize the oneness and uniqueness in everything and everyone, and learn to balance the two. This truth applies to everything in the universe.

Pairs of opposites do not constitute the essence of our lives. If we experience joy, we won't eventually have to experience sorrow. If we are happy, we won't have to be unhappy for another. If there is a beginning, then it doesn't mean there must be an end. Yes, night follows day; and after the storm comes peace, etcetera, but everything in the universe must be analyzed according to the Realm of Union versus the Realm of Disunion, knowing that everything and everyone can exist in the Realm of Union but be fragmented in the Realm of Disunion, as different parts.

As we come to understand the Realm of Union and Disunion and how to differentiate between the two, our fate will no longer be doomed to force us to experience pairs of opposites, whether we like it or not. There is a way out of this vicious circle of cause and effect, action and reaction caused by our limitations. All pairs of opposites woven into our lives can dissolve when we come to understand these two realms and finally transition from the Realm of Disunion to the Realm of Union.

In the Realm of Union, we can feel our oneness and our uniqueness, each a part of God, continually balancing one another. We can enjoy bliss and peace of mind while still acting and functioning normally in our day-to-day lives. We can be active in the world yet maintain a state of inner detachment. We can be aware of our oneness with the One Spirit and aware that the One Spirit is wishing and waiting to act and manifest through everything: things, plants, trees, animals, and people.

That's the experience of non-duality (unity) in its highest form.

Ordinarily, the veil of thoughts and the five senses draw the mind outward to the external world and obscure awareness of the consciousness beyond the mind. Meditation brings peace to the mind and develops the ability to silence it, thus enabling us to experience this state of non-duality.

In this state of inner silence, we rise above the illusion of identification with the mind, thoughts, and ego. We get beyond the illusion of separateness. We realize our oneness with the One Spirit and His wish to manifest through us, bringing us our uniqueness. We experience a new consciousness that lets us see the world in a new way, where no one is around to shove us into a box, nail the lid down, and stick a label on the side saying, "scientist, artist, businessperson, politician, spiritual teacher, or whatever." In this world, we are completely free to be and do whatever it is in our innate nature to be or do. It is a world of total liberation. We become like children.

We regain our essence, which is a part of God.

We no longer blame anyone for our current tragic situation because we acknowledge that humanity as a collective decided to explore the Realm of Disunion a long time ago causing the gradual formation of the Age of Disunion and its duality, which we can no longer afford but we must let it unfold naturally to bring us to its end as we learn how to begin the Age of Transformation that is the Messianic Age filled with union attributes, including unity.

Paradoxically, it is only when we are free from the delusion that there is a need for duality to make our decisions properly that we will finally take full responsibility for our lives personally and collectively to recognize the necessity to redefine a lot of stuff that we have in our collective consciousness so that God's Reality can replace our distorted mentality. It is time to develop new definitions and/or arguments that are clear and accurate.

For example, we're told that as humans, we know what life is. It is what we do every day. But it is difficult to understand death, since it is a mystery and cannot be fully explained. However, we know that we must live before we can die, and so we cannot have one without the other.

We're told that peace and war lie at opposite ends of a continuum, each a reaction to a particular experience or situation. People can choose to be peaceful or create war. Both are reactive and can cause repercussions from the decision people make to choose one over the other, not realizing that we cannot have peace without war, and vice versa.

We're told that love and hate are close on the emotional spectrum. Under the duality continuum, they are on opposite sides. Love is a more pleasant positive emotion, whereas hate is perceived as a state of anger or loathing. Both are extreme reactions to someone or something. Indifference occurs when people find themselves caught between these two emotions. If you can define these two opposing forces, you can also find the middle ground of indifference.

We're told that if we follow spirituality, we can reach a state of harmony one day, where we begin to see the two sides as different perspectives rather than as right or wrong. When we stand at the center of the two extremes, we stop fearing death and accept the life we must lead. Thus, to define each, we must know the other. That will help us to understand both extremes and try to stay on the central path.

However, such explanations are incomplete, providing partial answers that are confusing and sometimes inaccurate.

Life and death don't necessarily have to go together. The Divine Love and Light can prolong life and even bring immortality, as I explain at the end of this volume.

Peace and war don't necessarily have to go together. We can become whole and, as whole people, learn to live through our Divine Selves rather than our egos, where war is never chosen over peace. The Divine Self is a part of God with total distaste of the Realm of Disunion and its attributes, and surely, with great powers of the Realm of Union to dissolve the Realm of Disunion.

The Chapter, *How to Rely on God*, in *And God Said to Angel: How to Transform Personally*, explains all this in detail.

Love and hate have positive and negative connotations. If we view love and hate as two different perspectives, then we will never reach contentment. We will continue to struggle to find the middle ground between these two when our lives are in turmoil.

We will always swing one way or the other because we will not truly understand these two attributes to realize: 1) the whole reason for our existence is to gradually align with the Divine way to become partners with God through our Divine Selves; 2) each Divine Self can easily witness the Divine Logos and interact with it properly to know the Divine will and plan for us at all time; 3) when we're our Divine Selves then we are filled with the Divine Love and Light (His pure energy) that continue to keep us in the Realm of Union where there is no disunion whatsoever; 4) being in the Realm of Union and sharing our experiences can help us to gradually know the Divine will and plan for us collectively, which means personal to collective salvation.

It is not possible to hate anybody or choose war over peace when we live our lives through God.

Bill Maher was talking about words, and he said, "Eight words are clear, and so they don't need to be redefined: hate, victim, hero, shame, violence, survivor, phobic, and white supremacist." So, here, let me briefly discuss these eight words and what each means to me, to show that Bill Maher is correct in making this statement. That is because these eight qualities, if misunderstood, can really screw up the human pool and harm us all, both personally and collectively.

So, it's best to take a stand and not rationalize when it comes to these eight attributes:

1. **Hate:** Love and hate are by-products of union versus disunion emotions. Love is a state of being. It is a blob of Divine Love. When we're filled with union attributes of appreciation, creativity, kindness, etc., we fall into it and feel its warmth caressing us. That's why we say, "Those two have fallen in love," because they have fallen in the blob of love. Hate is not the opposite of love. There is no blob of hate in the universe of God. Hate comes from different disunion attributes. So, hate can come from fear, jealousy, envy, and other lopsided emotions, all originating from the ego. The ego can only exist when we are separated from God, humanity, and other natural collectives. When we find the Divine Self within us and connect to everything and everyone through it, then there is no place for hate. Only love reigns. This word is simple to understand and uncalled for. There is no reason to hate anyone or anything, especially since this quality can damage the hater more than the hated. When we hate, we stop seeing whatever is related to our hatred zone. It limits our perception, which is not good for us. Imagine the whole universe created by God and managed by Him, and then the hater, who is also created by Him, hating a part of His creation, thus Him. What stupidity and truly simple to see, yet so many people are suffering from it!

2. **Hero:** This quality is about the courage to go beyond our comfort zone and boundaries to make a change that benefits not just ourselves but others. Becoming a hero requires compassion, a very deep feeling about something or someone, which means we're human beings with a strong connection to our humanity. That is a good thing, but there is a catch. A person can be a hero by making a change that benefits the Realm of Union or the Realm of Disunion. Also, a hero can sometimes be a false rather than a genuine one, like when people believe someone is a hero when he or she is not. For example, let's say someone goes to rob a house. While in the house, let's say, an explosion happens, and the thief ends up saving the owner's life. The thief tells everybody that he was passing by, saw the fire, went inside, and saw the owner in need of help, so he helped him. People accept his story and call him a hero. After a while of feeling so good about being a hero, he slowly learns to transform from a false hero into a real hero. I've seen this happen.

Another example is, let's say, the disunion structure selects a person to act as a whistle-blower against the establishment, and that person is in bed with them, serving the Realm of Disunion. People believe the story, not realizing the disunion trick, and begin following this person as a union soldier when he or she is a servant of the Realm of Disunion. After a while, this false hero feels so good about being a hero that he or she becomes a true hero. It is important to be able to differentiate between false and true heroes and between disunion and union heroes. In addition, since the false or disunion hero has a seed of compassion in him or her, which is a union attribute, it can always grow and transform the person to become a true hero of the Realm of Union. Thus, we must always allow for this transformation and try to help the person become a true hero. So, regardless, it's a good thing to be a hero.

3. **Victim:** Those who become victims end up getting drained by the Realm of Disunion, never union. Union people know how not to get drained by the Realm of Disunion, and the Realm of Disunion seldom drains its people, who are compradors of the Realm of Disunion promoting disunion attributes and techniques. So, it is

easy to figure out whether someone is a victim or a disunion person. Anyone can learn not to be victimized by the Realm of Disunion. The key is to learn to rely on God and to know the tricks of the Realm of Disunion, so that such techniques and attributes do not affect our lives. In other words, we can stop being victims. And, if we ever become a victim, we can transform the situation to stop it from victimizing us. Some people tell everyone they have become victims and so copy the negativity and broadcast it everywhere, which is not a good thing to do. It's best to dissolve the situation and turn it into a union event rather than a disunion one.

4. **Shame:** This is a horrible emotion that the Realm of Disunion and its compradors can project onto a person, group, or collective to prevent people from reaching the Realm of Union. I've seen this happen a lot with children getting attacked by adults who lack pure energy, and so they go after children to fill up with energy. Every human being must stop this quality of shame whenever and wherever it is encountered, because the effects of shame can affect not only those who have been shamed but also the collectives they may belong to, which is, naturally, humanity. The reason this is important is that it can negatively influence our overall threshold, as I will explain in the Chapter, *Union vs. Disunion Threshold*. So, again, this is a simple quality that everyone should know NOT TO DO, yet so many people act stupidly and do it!

5. **Phobic:** When a person has a strong irrational fear of something that is not real, then he or she is phobic. Such a fear is a sickness that must be dealt with and healed ASAP. Otherwise, it can cripple the person mentally, physically, emotionally, and spiritually because such emotions can replicate throughout a person's life. It can limit him or her, and even take the person near insanity. When you think about it, such emotions can be easily dissolved if handled properly. True and clear explanations can help resolve this matter.

6. **Violence:** When we use physical force or power, whether threatened or actual, against another person, group, collective, or even ourselves, that can result in injury or death or psychological harm, then surely, we should not allow it to happen. What is so

difficult about this to understand? That is a simple word that every human being should comprehend. Otherwise, the person has lost his or her humanity and is a broken entity in need of full repair.

7. **Survivor:** When a person has learned to cope well with life's difficulties and has consequently survived disunion attacks, we call that person a survivor. There is nothing complicated about this word or someone who happens to be a survivor. We must truly appreciate the survivors in our global society, because they're like lamps bringing light to the darkness of the current disunion structure around the planet due to the Age of Disunion.

8. **White Supremacist:** A person who believes that white people constitute a superior race and should therefore dominate society is called a white supremacist. Can you imagine the level of stupidity of such a belief?! First, when a person thinks their collective is above others, they can abuse others to stay in power. Any feeling of supremacy is insane and a demonstration of the inadequacy of the person, again, in need of rehabilitation.

The choices we make in life today determine the path we will be on in the future, whether toward the Realm of Union or the Realm of Disunion.

The opposite of duality is oneness and uniqueness in balance, where there is a sense of collaboration among all parts of the whole, caring for and sharing to optimize the functionality and well-being of all the parts and the whole being collaborated upon.

We tell each other that there are two sides to a human being, one preferring evil over good and the other good over evil, but then we create so much fear over this that we disable ourselves from exploring any further.

The Realm of Disunion is filled with lies, deceptions, secrecy, and other disunion attributes, often requiring falsehood and or other awful qualities; otherwise, people may get to see the truth, which can then threaten the Realm of Disunion.

It's like a bird having two wings, where one wing on its own is useless for flight, but both wings together make the flight.

When we shine white light through a prism, it splits into the colors of the rainbow, and vice versa. By understanding the inherent order and simple perfection that lie amidst the apparent chaos and contradiction of the two opposing dualities, it may become easier to see the reality manifesting.

If you learn how to do this, you will become like a ballet dancer holding on to the ONE (the oneness) and the MANY (the uniqueness) while keeping the ultimate balance as you dance away to the universal symphony of God and His Realm of Union. This exercise lets you get to know yourself as the holder and the promoter of the ONE, which is the whole manifesting in MANY, while keeping track of both sides.

That means: As two things come together, each unique with certain qualities, including each entity's energy, it becomes clear to you that the union of the two things has a separate existence and energy that may be less, the same, or more than the actual summation of the two. When you hold on to the whole, care for it, and nourish it, you're promoting the Realm of Union, whereas ignoring and draining the whole is a disunion act belonging to the Realm of Disunion.

Hence, promoting the union always takes you to the Realm of Union, where you're traveling on the Divine Path of Infinity. That is where the Holy Spirit resides, allowing you to live continually in Truth, according to the Spiritual Formula. As you live this way, day after day, you become your true essence that is whole and can see wholeness in everything and everyone, even though the person or the collective may still be struggling to find the Divine Path to Infinity and learn how to walk on it to remain in the Realm of Union.

I just saw a TikTok video of Alan Watts talking about yin-yang and duality. As he pointed to the symbol of yin yang in a circle showing the dark and white fishes together, he explained:

But what happens if the white fish succeeds in eating up the dark fish? The white fish would disappear as well as the dark one because the white one is only there in relation to the dark one. So, then, if these two fish were to wake up, which is called awakening in Buddhism, they would realize that they're one. In other words, they go together; they're inseparable. The disorder is necessary for the manifestation of order, just as you must have a black background to show up a light figure. And when one sees that, a profound transformation takes place in one's attitude to the world. That is to say, instead of looking upon life as a contest, it becomes a dance. It becomes a game. One doesn't withdraw from it; one doesn't stop living. One goes into the game so that these revolving fish stop trying to eat each other and start dancing and having the biggest fun in the world.

As I researched this symbol, I found that in Daoist Philosophy, dark and light, female and male, and yin and yang are represented as yin (the black side) and yang (the white side). On this white side, yin is characterized as slow, soft, yielding, cold, wet, and passive, and associated with water, earth, the moon, femininity, shadows/darkness, destruction, and nighttime. In contrast, yang is characterized as fast, solid, focused, hot/warm, dry, and active, and is associated with fire, sky/air, the sun, positivity, masculinity, glowing/light, creativity, and daytime.

This video was very interesting. I knew about it, but I had never seen it before. And, when I saw it, I wasn't looking for it. It just appeared, as usual, to make me think about it, so that I may address it in this section of the book. So, let me explain it to hopefully clear up the many misconceptions that may have come from such a view, confusing us and keeping us in duality.

Today, we have been given knowledge of the Realm of Union versus the Realm of Disunion, allowing us to analyze everything and everyone in terms of these two realms. Surely, we must be thankful for this knowledge and try to understand it and learn how to use it.

Women are used to giving tender loving care and telling stories. As a result, they are closer to the Realm of Union. In contrast, men are accustomed to dealing with disunion attributes and trying to make ends meet, thus leaning toward the Realm of Disunion. Of course, this is not general, but it does exist, nonetheless.

The Realm of Union is filled with union attributes, including the Divine Light and Love, thus positivity, creativity, and warmth, whereas the Realm of Disunion is filled with disunion attributes, including lack of light, causing darkness that can bring more fragmentations and negativity, all leading to greater destruction. Thus, this whole categorization is flawed. And it is interesting how women are often affiliated with destruction rather than construction; one is a property of the Realm of Disunion, and the other belongs to the Realm of Union.

Looking at all this, it is evident that we have not properly defined duality for humanity, confusing everyone and keeping humankind in the Realm of Disunion, whether intentionally or unintentionally.

So, let us study all this and try to go deeper.

In the next chapter, I talk about eternal versus temporal existence. Children experience the eternal, but they're gradually taken out of it by adults and by the current disunion structure, which exists mostly in the temporal, even though we're all equipped to exist in the eternal while witnessing both the eternal and the temporal realms.

When we reach the eternal as adults, then we experience the Realm of Union, where we get to see the true relationship between the dark and the light sides. We come to recognize that every person and collective has an inherent ability to exist in the Realm of Union, where we are no longer driven to destroy any person or collective, for we recognize the potentiality of every part acting as a manifestation of the whole, all the way to God. Instead, we long to build toward balance and order, not toward disorder.

Hence, the disorder is not a necessary condition for the manifestation of order. Any disorder prevents God from manifesting Himself through the part, keeping us in the Realm of Disunion rather than the Realm of Union.

Life should never become a dance or a game in which both order and disorder coexist. Such a view will surely keep us in duality and prevent us from experiencing the Realm of Union, where it is possible to truly dance with the universal symphony that is the balance of oneness and uniqueness, thus true unity.

If children were allowed to stay in the Realm of Union rather than being forced to leave it for the Realm of Disunion, they would not be gradually conditioned to accept this flawed duality and not follow the universal order. They would remain their true selves and act through their Divine Selves, each Divine Self allowing for the manifestation of God, thus enabling uniqueness and oneness in total balance, which means the Realm of Union and its many miracles, daily showing us the glory of God.

Man is a finite being with the potential of perceiving the infinite. He is not free from various conditions, whether union or disunion, but rather free to take a stand on whatever conditions might confront him. Man can detach himself from even the worst conditions through union attributes. When we each open to a new dimension, we rise above our personal and collective levels and move toward the dimension that best serves our unique purposes in life and aligns with the Divine Plan for us.

Speaking of higher rather than lower dimensions does not imply a value judgment. A "higher" dimension just means a more inclusive and encompassing dimension.

Every human being can rise above him or herself to judge and evaluate his or her deeds in moral and ethical terms. Because of this self-transcendent quality of human existence, being human can be defined as someone much more than itself, in other words, its actuality. That means the potentiality can be humongous if only allowed to unfold naturally.

Zoroastrianism is the religion of free will, where each man can choose between the Truth and the Lie, leading to the true religion revealed to us by the prophet.

The outward symbol of Truth is fire, in which Good is symbolized by light and evil by the lack of light, which is darkness; thus, the destruction of evil and the sole sovereignty of good can only mean that the material world is transformed into pure light.

It is the union of all separate wills with the will of God, each person remaining himself or herself, each soul glad to be in the glory that is peculiarly his or hers, while making his or her individual contribution to the perfect whole, a contribution that none but he or she can make and without which the whole would be less than perfect. Here is the Realm of Union where the spirit and the matter are fused, and the fusion implies no confusion of identity.

That is an infinite existence in which finite time merges into infinite time. God, Himself, becomes all that exists. We are united with His will, thus free of evil and death, where we can participate in His absolute goodness and bliss, each person according to his or her capacity and level of servitude to satisfy our Divine mission.

As we reach balance, we will not only be perfectly at peace but also filled with the light and the love of God.

Zoroastrians drank HAOMA, called "the drink of immortality," and saw that the Joys of heaven cannot be compared with the joys of the earth, for one is infinite and the other finite. This world is finite, transient, and subject to diminution. In contrast, the eternal life that is endless light is neither transient nor subject to diminution. That treasury of eternal benefit is indestructible, thus all joy with no pain.

According to Zoroastrianism, the three phases of the history of the cosmos are 1) the creation, 2) the progress of religion, and 3) the final rehabilitation.

We each play a part in the Divine Story that we can barely understand at this time because we can only survey it in fragments. Consequently, we figure our decisions about what to do with our brief lives can have no basis outside ourselves. But then, in this sense, we are ungrounded, especially since every claim about the world relies on assumptions, and each layer of assumptions relies on further layers, with two limitations to this approach.

The first limitation is that our methods of exploration are suited to parts of nature rather than nature as a whole. The second limitation is that our assumptions are based on historically provincial views of how nature works rather than on how nature operates.

The world has a history, extending backward and forward in time, beyond the present universe. When we come to understand this history much better than we do now, we will still be confined to play a tiny part in it, but at least we will better understand how to empower the best possible past to arrive at the best possible present from which we may move to the best possible future for humanity, as I explain in other volumes of this book.

The Realm of Union message is here to let us comprehend that nothing is for keeps and that everything turns into everything else. As Anaximander said, "All things originate from one another, and vanish into one another, according to necessity, under the dominion of time."

The major religions of the world, Judaism, Christianity, and Islam, have each told us that our Father made both the world and humankind; that He did so out of an abundance of His creative and life-giving love; and that He formed us in His image with a plan to make it come true, someday in the future, at the end time of disunion. In other words, our salvation is to transition from the Realm of Disunion to the Realm of Union.

In the implementation of His plan, He even brought us Jesus and directed us to reach eternal life through him and to participate in a community of the faithful who stand by Jesus and are willing to live in harmony with God and His creation, and with one another. That is what the symbol of the cross means. The love between the Father and each person, and the love of each person for another.

We must try to create a meaningful order within a cosmos too complex for us to grasp at this time. We may never come to understand the cosmos and the reasons for our existence, other than figure out those fragments of necessity and chance that scientific inquiries suggest to us. And it seems that the growth of scientific knowledge will not alter these limitations unless we gain greater spirituality and higher consciousness.

Perhaps, if we learn to restrain our hatreds and wars that have caged us and limited us, we may be able to establish the Divine Presence on Earth, aiding us in dissolving the Realm of Disunion and achieving eternal life. At the end of this volume, in the last chapter, I talk about immortality versus mortality.

The bottom line is that we can overcome the world through God the Almighty, or we can struggle in the world as limited human beings.

For more than twenty-five hundred years, we have struggled in the Age of Disunion, but now that the Age of Disunion is ending and the Age of Transformation is starting, the time has come to transform both society and the self, hopefully rewarding us with incomparable beauty and balance, which means a greater share of the Divine attributes, thus more godlike, in other words, in His image.

In other volumes of this book, I discuss the Divine Path to Infinity and how to find it so that we can travel on it, always toward the Realm of Union. It is through this path of infinity that we can finally triumph over evil, which is death and, beyond death, the diminishment of being. We can either succeed or fail in getting rescued from what seems to be our condition. The key is to reunite with God and each other.

In our struggle toward unity, we must remember the following:

1. **Our reality is real.** It is a three-dimensional reality that is a part of a bigger reality. This larger reality has many projections, some of which exist in parallel to it. Seers can see more than one reality, sometimes seeing themselves in different parallel realities. I sometimes can access different realities through the Dream World. Viewing ourselves through time before we were born in other lives is also possible. The Chapter, *Dream World as a Tool,* shows us how to remember our past lives and other lives in different realities.

The Dream World can be an excellent tool for witnessing the Logos across different dimensions and realities. Please remember that every person can become a seer through contemplation, meditation, and practice of higher spirituality and consciousness.

2. **Our time is real.** Time is not an illusion, as the more radical versions of the metaphysic of the overcoming of the world represent it to be, nor as many of our established ideas about causation and the laws of nature imply. Time often touches certain aspects of reality, even though it holds sway over everything; nothing is exempt from its influence. However, as a person moves from temporal to eternal time, the perception expands to include more and more of the universe, depending on the level of servitude and the reason for being here, always toward the satisfaction of the Divine Plan. It is possible to reach a state of existence where we can experience both the temporal and the eternal, witnessing and interacting with both, so that we may see everyone and everything as they struggle to conquer the temporal for the eternal. With this ability, of course, comes compassion and empathy, feeling for others as we would for ourselves, wishing to help them succeed in their struggles. That is where the balance of oneness and uniqueness becomes a crucial component of a greater perception.

3. **The new can replace the old.** Many people are afraid to let go of the old to experience the new. But any change toward the Realm of Union is a blessing and should be allowed to unfold naturally. There is no reason for fear of any other disunion attribute. We must learn to maintain a positive outlook and not let negative qualities dominate our psyche. That is a process that can take time, but with enough dedication and perseverance, I assure you that anyone can reach higher levels of spirituality and consciousness to overcome any struggle. We're often told that it is not simple to achieve this or that, but truly, this is the biggest lie of the Realm of Disunion, trying to keep us from reaching the Realm of Union. Every moment can bring us a unique blessing. The key is to shed our disunion attributes and acquire new union attributes that empower Divine Reality to interact with us and bring us new goodies. God knows

better than anyone, even yourself, what is best for you. Please trust Him and let Him take you to His Path of Infinity.

4. **History is open from the past to the present to the future.** We tend to think the past is gone and that there's nothing we can do about it. But this is not the case. It is possible to empower those elements of our past that belong to the Realm of Union so that we may come to a union present from which we may move to an optimal union future for us, whether personally or collectively. *And God Said to Angel: Toward the Divine Plan and Heaven on Earth* shows us how to do this. It is called reality engineering. Hence, the openness of history means that the course of history can change and that we have the power to change it and rewrite it in accordance with the Realm of Union. That is great news for all of us who tend to regret the past but do not know what to do about it. When you think about it, HOPE can be one of the best union attributes in reality engineering. So, please do not let anyone take your hope away. Rely on God and let Him take you to the Realm of Union.

5. **The true self is the Divine Self with unfathomable depth.** Always try to see the positive in everything and everyone, including yourself. To go through your struggles in life and succeed requires a lot of pure energy, so try to obtain it solely through God and His Realm of Union. Don't let anyone drain your energy. The more energy you have in your body and your surroundings, the stronger your intuition becomes and your ability to figure out what's best to do. Don't ever use disunion techniques to get things done. Only union techniques and attributes can keep you close to God and His love and support. Don't let anything or anyone reduce your self-power to social standing. Don't pursue an established social division and hierarchy plan, all prepared for you by the Realm of Disunion and its people. Don't ever become a victim, and if you do happen to be victimized, remember that God has a role for you, through your Divine Self, which is a part of God. Let Him manifest His wishes in you. Believe me. Sooner than later, He will act out His plan for you, through your Divine Self with immeasurable qualities

and powers, so that you may better serve Him. He loves you and needs you. Always remember that.

6. **The ordinary can become the most glorious.** "I shall pour out my spirit onto all flesh." So speaks God in the Hebrew Bible. The reason for this statement is that He wants you to know that people may appear ordinary because of their limited views of the temporal versus the eternal, but every man and woman has a divine spark in him or her. We are each a dwelling of the Holy Spirit. The key is to learn how to let the Divine Spirit flow through us. We should never belittle or drain anyone. We should let every person become their Divine Self, in the image of God. We can all ascend as long as we have faith in Him and feel His love and grace to help everyone.

Man has not fully comprehended life's struggles due to a lack of understanding of the Realm of Union versus the Realm of Disunion.

So, now that we've been given this knowledge of the union versus disunion, we need to get together and analyze our struggles to better understand them. We must share our struggles and properly categorize every face of evil using our tools. We must learn to measure things by union and disunion, but all this must be done to bring us closer to the Realm of Union, never to Disunion.

Remember that the freer a society becomes, the stronger every person and collective becomes, and the weaker the power of the dead over the living.

In such a society, since we honor the Realm of Union and the potentiality of every person and collective to walk on the Divine Path of Infinity, then the differences that we create matter more than the ones we inherit and remember. They matter more because they give us a chance to better understand the Realm of Union versus Disunion and how to move toward the Realm of Union, never Disunion.

We care about who we are and what we become, always appreciating and honoring people's different tastes and preferences. We explore the broad range of humanity's practical, moral, and spiritual interests. We cooperate because we love God and His love for every member of humanity and for His creation.

We get up each day and just take the next step we can see, and then the next one after that until we get there. And the closer we get to our destination, the clearer the path will become. But that does not mean there is an end to our exploration. Remember that the Divine Path is infinite with no end, thus no boredom or sameness or any other disunion attribute. Instead, we're going to be surrounded by God's miracles and His glory, continually receiving insights and creating new ways of union to see things, even seeing the same thing with greater clarity within layers of spirituality.

As time passes, we learn to enhance our vibrations and attract more and more qualities of Jesus, our other prophets, and mystics. The key is to set our minds, bodies, intuitions, emotions, and senses to be ready for this incredible state of manifestation.

The true essence of every person is aligned with his or her soul, or Divine Self, for it belongs to God and His spark. The Messiah comes to show every person how to become their essence and to progress without taking others down. We learn that we don't need to go away from our essence, but rather our disunion ways, so that we can create, share, cooperate, and collaborate to benefit all, rather than continually compete to keep everything for ourselves and our family, thus benefiting the few.

In Buddhist cultures, both good and evil are perceived as an antagonistic duality that itself must be overcome through achieving emptiness in the sense of recognition of good and evil being two opposing principles (not a reality) where we empty the duality and achieve oneness with the Divine Logos, as we each achieve uniqueness, through the Divine Self, which is a unique manifestation of God.

In God's creation, there is no drainage, only the transformation of one mode of existence into another. It is solely man who can bring about drainage through thoughts, words, and acts that drain people. A system where we are either the disunion people draining others or the victims getting drained by others. The union people have learned how to stay outside of this system. They recognize the system as the battle between the Realm of Disunion and the Realm of Union and try not to get involved.

Both the disunion people and the victims are in the cage of duality, seldom able to see unity, while the union people can see unity as they continue to observe the struggles of duality. We must join the union people and let them teach us how to take this approach in life.

The Bible says that if we know how to do good and don't do it, or if we know something to be wrong but we do it anyway, then we're committing a sin, for we're knowingly harming someone or something, even though God has directed us against such behaviors. So, when we commit disunion, we are going against God and His Laws and commandments.

I believe we often go against God because we can't see the totality. It is hard to figure out what to do when we see only fragments of the whole. That's why the Realm of Disunion is always fragmenting everything and everyone. It doesn't want us to see the whole.

When duality is gone, you can see that life happens through you, not to you. This concept is super important to grasp, so please take the time to understand it and practice it until you can feel it in your bones.

When you understand and believe this concept, you naturally let go of your desire to control things. Instead, you learn how to listen to God and continually follow Him and His will that is aligned with the natural way of the Realm of Union.

In short, you let life flow through you.

At first, it may not be easy, but over time, I assure you, you will learn how to do it.

Living life this way helps you to recognize that whatever promotes disunion, you must stop doing it. However, sometimes you may talk of disunion, wishing to resolve it so you can move toward union; surely, that should be okay.

64

Some people reach a state of higher consciousness but cannot talk to others about it because no one can understand them, like Michael Jackson. He was so creative and full of pure energy that he could see things others could not see. Unfortunately, in the end, the disunion people hurt him terribly, and most victims were too blind to see the Truth. The union people could see it and tried to tell others about it, but they were in the minority.

The bottom line is that the ego often gets in the way because it doesn't want to go away. But you've got to let your Divine Self replace your ego. Your Divine Self is your soul that is a part of God, so you will be relying on God and His guidance to live your daily life through your Divine Self that is here and has been here all along to take you to the Realm of Union, never Disunion.

As you practice this approach, you come to realize that it's best to be empty of all fears, desires, expectations, and/or any other disunion attributes that may come from your ego to hinder your ability to follow God's daily instructions for you.

All artists are lucky people, for they must go through this process to create, and so they learn to go through their Divine Selves, which can then help them move closer and closer to the Realm of Union. That is why the Realm of Disunion often tries to drain and/or damage our artists to keep them from accessing the Realm of Union and its creativity.

It's amazing how the Realm of Disunion has developed so many techniques to keep humanity away from the Realm of Union.

But all those who know better should do their best to go to the Realm of Union and stay there, if possible. I'm talking about living in NOW and learning how to get to it. Sure, it takes practice, but it is doable and super important.

All union people should do this every day, then unite as a collective to help the victims of the Realm of Disunion do the same. Before you know it, the network of union people will grow and become so large, more than eighty percent of humanity, to affect the current disunion structure on the planet. That's the only way to reach heaven on Earth collectively.

It's amazing how little our holy books tell us about heaven! They do to some extent, but never clearly. Don't you ever wonder what heaven is like or why?

Some people describe heaven as a place where we can have whatever we want. Some see it as a place where true freedom reigns. But then, they can't define freedom, how to achieve it, or what to do to bring it about.

Freedom means to be free to live in God's Kingdom because it is only in the Divine Kingdom that a person can live freely.

Look around you. Everything is free, even God's Light and Love, each infinite with no end.

Every day, we can get up and obtain His pure energy and His love and support to let us live God's Story, which is every person's true story to spread union, not disunion, to plant the union seed, not disunion, to build a union cell with our family, extended families, and friends, to connect all union cells, and build a union network to melt away the disunion structure slowly.

The key is to see everything positively rather than negatively so that we can transform disunion into union. That is a requirement of our time, where we help each other recognize that we're all sitting in a miraculous space-time continuum that is here to take us to our transition from the Realm of Disunion to the Realm of Union.

The Age of Disunion has kept us from living freely, but this era is now ending. The Age of Transformation is coming to help us return to God. Turning away from God can no longer be an option. Turning to Him is the only path, bringing blessings beyond compare.

Remember what I said earlier about being an atheist and living in the Realm of Union, where God dwells, and truth resides to set us free. So, whether you believe in God or not believe in Him, you will end up with Him if you just follow the Realm of Union and its many blessings, one of which is the process of alignment with the Logos that always leads to God.

I love watching the birds fly from one tree to another, never thinking, never planning, just playing, and constantly being filled with Divine Energy. In Elie Wiesel's play The Trial of God, the character Yankel asks, "Do birds fly only when they have somewhere to go?" and the answer is, "They fly because they love freedom and the blue sky."

It's great to live like birds, to move in accord with one's essence, and to allow the Divine Spirit to flow through us and manifest in and around us, always remembering that the Divine Spirit brings us Divine Energy.

Like other living and non-living entities in the universe, birds can't help being the best that they can be! Why can't we be the best that we can be? Why do we go away from our essence, sometimes thinking, saying, and/or acting against the universal divine force that is continually trying to keep balance and harmony? Why not strive for harmony and wholeness in all that we do? Why control things to go our way rather than the universal way? True artisanship understands that no one thing exists apart from another.

Everything is interconnected. So, it is crucial not to see only the parts but also the whole. The key is to learn to transform disunion attributes and events into union attributes and events while keeping oneness and uniqueness in balance. This process can help reduce pain and confusion, allowing us to see the wholeness of everything and everyone. It is then that we begin to see the different fragments that make up the whole and how to bring them together so they can function properly.

Everyone can do this and must try to do so to become whole again. Wholeness allows us to see the wholeness of time and space, which then takes us to the eternal rather than the temporal existence.

The next chapter discusses eternal versus temporal existence, and the chapter after that shows how to undergo a process of integration to reach wholeness. The temporal existence is a limited realm belonging to the Realm of Disunion, so I show it in italics.

ETERNAL VS. *TEMPORAL*

T hose who are in the Realm of Union are living in the eternal, while the rest of us are living in the temporal. These two modes of existence differ greatly. In the eternal, we have God with us, helping us at every turn, whereas in the temporal, we're mostly alone, wondering what to do next and how to do it.

This chapter shows us how to live in the eternal, not the temporal, and some of the differences between the two.

THE ETERNAL TRUTH

The one eternal TRUTH deals with our need to be saved so that we may stand with God in TRUTH, both personally and collectively. The reason for this is to stand in real time with God rather than the made-up time of man.

Newton saw time as the measure of change and also recognized the possibility of true time, absolute time, passing by independent of things and their changes.

The question is: which of the two conceptual schemes is more efficient for understanding the world?

The entire evolution of science suggests that the best language for thinking about the world is that of change, not of permanence, not of being, but of becoming.

We look at speed as a property of an object with respect to another object, thus a relative quantity. We measure distances using the speed of light. However, the universe can have a stillness from which we may measure our speeds. The stillness could be the speed of light, depending on how we look at it and decide to measure it.

There is nothing unnatural in imagining that the universe has "special" settings according to our views of it.

The flow of time is not a characteristic of the universe, like the rotation of the heavens; it is due to the particular perspective that we have from our corner of it.

When we do science, we want to describe the world as objectively as possible. We aspire to objectivity, to a shared point of view about which it is possible to agree. That is a great tool and can be very useful. However, we should be concerned with what we may lose by ignoring the point of view from which we observe. We must not forget that our experience of the world comes from within. Every glance that we cast toward the world is made from a particular perspective.

Words like "here," "now," "this," "that," "tonight," and many others assume different meanings depending on who says them and the circumstances in which they are said.

The world that we have been given is the world seen from within it, not from without. Many things we see in the world can be understood only if we take perspective into account.

The history of the world can only be an effect of our perspectives, an effect of our particular point of view.

We try to imagine eternity, but we don't know how to describe or define it accurately, or to determine whether we share similar visions. When someone gets a glance at eternity and tries to describe it, most of us can't relate to it because we haven't experienced it.

Eternity is where God stands outside time, seeing the entirety of His creation in its full presence alive. As we get closer to God, we begin to sense what it's like to be with Him and live with Him in eternity, a timeless, lasting forever with no beginning nor end, creating infinite possibilities and realities.

Eternity pulls all life into a single point, and as it gets smaller and smaller, it becomes more visible, where we can finally see it and experience it in its totality, which is the Realm of Union where God dwells, and Truth resides to set us free.

Most of us have no idea how to live in the eternal NOW, the still point between the past and future; however, we are familiar with the temporal existence in which we spend most of our lives regretting the past and/or worrying about the future.

God has told us, "I am the Alpha and the Omega, the one who is and who was and who is to come."

Those of us who can comprehend this statement, and its powers, do our best to stand in eternity since it is in this state of existence where God and His Realm of Union can be best manifested. I'm talking about the many manifestations of God, whether in the past, the present, or the future, throughout eternity. That means whatever exists has existed, and will exist. Everything that could be!

To be continually aligned with this level of consciousness, where the information we receive and process is understood according to our pure awareness, transcending the many limitations currently imposed upon man; where all-knowing comes to us allowing us to simultaneously experience all aspects of life, handling and practicing as much as we can manage, like hearing local and distant sounds at the same time, all notes of the universal symphony, and witnessing the Divine Logos in all of its glory; until this whole process becomes second nature, done subconsciously and effortlessly, even when we're sleep.

Imagine seeing a picture where everything is clearly shown, but it's so long and layered that it may take us many lifetimes to take it in.

Over time, through practice, we move from one layer to another until, at last, we're in the Divine presence. No need to go back in time and remember, for there is no time, so nothing ever fades away, and nothing is lost. We're at the end of a journey in which we've been searching for God and longing deeply to be with Him, only to realize that not even one instant of eternity has passed or even existed.

We are in a miraculous existence, ready to learn from it, knowing that it will never end, for it is infinite.

Living in eternity means we're always in Now, in the Realm of Union. But human perception capacity normally requires time to assimilate things as they occur in sequence. Our memories retain impressions of everything we have ever known, but we cannot access this knowing except for when we're under hypnosis or having dreams and recollections until we're in pure awareness, where "all of our beings," whether a projection of our soul in this or other dimensions, frequencies, or realities, hold together in identity as an entity. It is a world in which there is only one knower of the entire reality and nothing else.

Everything belonging to you is together as one (a part of your soul). Everything belonging to another is together as one (a part of another soul). Then, all souls together lead to the ONE God. That's why the balance of oneness and uniqueness is so crucial and continually emphasized throughout this book.

Thoreau knew all this very well, for he lived it, noting people's inability to be with God in the present moment and visibly see His truth, yet believing that the absolute truth is remote: "In the outskirts of the system, behind the farthest star, before Adam, after the last man." But all times and places "are now and here."

Faulkner observed it, saying, "There is a sense in which the past is not gone; it is not even past. Effects linger on. If a thing is actualized, made real, rather than merely possible, it remains imprinted in reality."

Emerson said that eventually all the events of our private histories will soar and sing, "Take on the endless life of the archetypal forms." Then, our memories will become God's memory.

In our dreams, we sometimes see our lost ones again, but only in passing, and often imperfectly. God's memory is perfect and spans the past, present, and future, holding everything in the brilliant light of knowing where everything is eternal.

The great mystics of the world describe eternity as ecstatic love, the apocalyptic embrace of God and Man, where God is love, and whoever remains in love remains in God and God through the person.

Deep down, the mystics knew about this aspect of man's potentiality long ago. That is why the Jewish mystics have longed to study and practice the Torah, which teaches us how to get close to God with a love that burns like fire.

The mystical task is to take a journey into the interior of the self and rescue that love that is infinite and a part of God, through which we may love unconditionally our Creator and His awesome Realm of Union universe, and at the same time, reach a certain level of wholeness and holiness that is required for the Divine presence so that we may continually obtain His guidance on how to witness His Logos and comprehend His will.

The soul is infinite and intangible, yet it can, in some ways, inhabit finite, tangible bodies. Certainly, this is a paradox, but one with which we live, and must come to understand its significance.

Over and over again, God has sent us His messengers, who have told us that, even though God, the Soul of the world, is infinite and inconceivable, His wish is to be known by inhabiting the world that is physical and limited at this time, as perceived by man.

The key is to expand our perception from the limited temporal existence toward the unlimited eternal one where God dwells.

I assure you that all this is feasible, but solely through God and His Realm of Union. That is why we must always try, inwardly, to move ever closer to the root of the soul while we fathom the infinite who gives life to the world.

It is not simply that the soul in its relation to the body is like God in His relation to the world, but that every godly soul is a part of God. At the highest spiritual level, man does more than relate to God. He contains part of God's reality. That is why witnessing the Divine Logos is essential and a raison d'être for every individual who wishes to become whole and live in a universe that is also whole eternally.

"But God," Maimonides said, as one of the principles of the Jewish faith, "is ONE and indivisible." Then, how can each of the many souls be a part of something that cannot be split into parts?

The truth is that, at the deepest level, the entire community of humankind, especially the Jewish souls, is a single unity, standing in relation to one another as do the limbs of the body, in other words, the many parts but a single entity.

The Torah says, "You shall love your neighbor as yourself," a statement Jesus repeated. For most people, this is undoubtedly easier said than done. But then there are cases where love flows easily and naturally, such as the love of a parent for a child.

When you're loving through your Divine Self, you're interfacing with and loving another person because you realize that he or she is you, and that his or her Divine Self and your Divine Self belong to God. Through this loving that is unconditional and infinite, thus eternal, you allow the other individual to become his or her Divine Self with the same essence as your Divine Self that comes from God.

If you could attain this level of love, that love would flow unforced and without limits, gradually helping you expand your perception from the temporal to the eternal. That is what the mystics do, and after a while, they become better and better at it, moving from lower to higher levels of spirituality until they become one with God, where they reach the balance of oneness and uniqueness that dominates God's Kingdom.

At such a level of spirituality, even though we may think of human beings as bodies, each certainly separate and distinct, we can still relate to them at the level of the soul that is a part of God, always remembering to keep the balance of oneness and uniqueness that can aid us to remain in the Realm of Union.

Hence, the task of the mystic and, in truth, the task of Judaism as a whole is to move from body to soul, from reactions prompted by ordinary physical stimuli to those wholly spiritual in character and motivation.

The result is a profound emphasis on the love of every Jew and, through it, every human being, an emphasis that flows not simply from an emotion of benevolence but from a new way of viewing our identity and that of our fellowmen, always through God the Almighty, and never directly.

It means we enter the Blob of Love or fall into it, that is the Realm of Union where God dwells and nothing else can exist but Him. Everything is Hashem, and Hashem is in every person. We are with Him and can feel Him through His manifestations in everything and everyone. So, in effect, we love everything and everyone through Him, including ourselves, for nothing else remains but Him.

That is the true definition of love.

It is then that we can truly love every individual because he or she is a part of God, and every fragment of infinity is infinite. Similarly, we love every collective or community because, at the level of the soul, there are no divisions that set person against person, creating ultimate loneliness.

Surely, these are revolutionary ideas, and certainly, they are implicit in the Torah, the Bible, the Quran, and other holy books. But it takes a special mind to uncover them. That is why we must do whatever it takes to expand our perception from the temporal to the eternal through witnessing the Divine Logos and obtaining Divine guidance. Nothing else is as effective.

The two aspects of God, His Oneness and His uniqueness, and the balance between the two govern everything in His Realm of Union universe, where an individual cannot harm himself without harming the whole of humankind, and an individual cannot be content with self-perfection while ignoring the fate of the community.

Let me give an example.

When you're in the eternal rather than temporal, you are with people's Divine Selves, for they feel comfortable enough with you to come out and interact with you. You can witness and interact with all entities of the universe because you are interfacing with them through your soul, which is your Divine Self and a part of God.

But what is so interesting is that you can, at the same time, see people's egos and temporal identities interacting with each other. You can see the many conflicts that go on between people's egos and their Divine Selves, where the ego tries to dominate the Divine Self and the Divine Self tries to free itself from the ego, a continual battle due to shame, expectation, and other disunion matters. You can see all this, but you are filled with compassion through the infinite love of God, wishing to help those who are ready to let go of the ego.

Can you imagine being privy to all this and the incredible insights that you can gain from it daily?!

It's time for us to understand that we each play an intrinsic role in the life of the eternal, its overall process and interaction, even though at this time, we may not discern the process or our place in it; whether great or small, we must do what we can to satisfy the soul that is a part of the Most Holy manifesting throughout the Divine Logos. Let us take the time to perceive it in ourselves, in our fellowmen, and in everything else in this awesome universe of God.

In eternity, all meaning is perpetually present. All we need to do is step back and see as much of the whole pattern of events as possible, with each part interacting with the others, rather than merely seeing certain events by themselves. In other words, a union view, not a fragmented one.

Today, we can follow God, walk on the Divine Path of Infinity, and live fulfilled lives in heaven with no limitations, yet we follow each other, mostly living in hell, caged in a temporal existence with many limitations. Even though deep down, we suspect that we are "eternal beings" living as human beings, we are thus capable of living in heaven rather than in hell.

Heaven is the divine reality that has been activated, recognized, and maintained in our lives. It is the collective manifestations of God in everything and everyone throughout eternity, through which we may experience God's presence and His wish to be known.

Solomon wrote, "God has made everything beautiful in its time. He has also set eternity in the hearts of men, yet they cannot fathom what God has done from beginning to end."

Some may wish to ignore all this and immerse themselves in temporary pursuits, rationalizing, "Maybe if I don't think about it, I will forget it or wish it away."

How terrible if we were to miss it and remain in the desert of our impoverishment, suffering in the Realm of Disunion, with no way to reach the Realm of Union.

How great if we were to recognize His signs and go through our transition to the Realm of Union, where we may experience the Divine presence bringing us the deepest joy of life possible.

The mystic, living in the moment, is always open to what is in the process of becoming. A new quality of the divine consciousness that can be established both inside and outside of one's true self in life.

This new consciousness needs to be lived if it is to take root and flourish. Mystics have always stood at the forefront of consciousness because they are not attached to the past or the future and can witness the form and fragrance of the present NOW, where God dwells.

Yet many mystics are reluctant to live among us so that we can see them and learn from them. They are often reclusive and introverted, looking inward towards the Source. They cannot stand our collective activity that is often in the Realm of Disunion, smelling super hellish with attributes of disunion, like the benefit of the few rather than the benefit of all.

The mystics would rather live their truth inwardly in the solitude of their devotion, where the power of the disunion structure cannot reach.

To establish a mystical consciousness within the collective is a dream that belongs to the lovers of God, who know that the path to God is not about self-improvement or a ten-step program to God. Instead, it's about the intensity and passion of their own hearts, where they can't help but long, in despair, to get closer to God and experience His presence.

And they know how easily this possibility can get corrupted, and how subtle the ways the ego can fabricate an image of the path and make it look like the path. Yet their natural inclination is to remain silent, to withdraw within their devotion. No one can be converted to love. It is too free to be packaged, too potent to be forced. But the need of the time is pressing.

The Age of Transformation is coming and needs our participation as the collective of humanity!

For centuries, His lovers have held the secrets of divine love within their hearts, shared only with initiates. But this knowledge needs to be made public, the song of His oneness to be heard. If the music of divine love is not played in the marketplace, life will lose its meaning, and the collective despair of the soul will be too terrible to imagine.

Look around you and see the many signs of this already happening. Everywhere, there are indications of our forgetfulness, sadness, and wretchedness of a world that has forgotten its pledge to remember God.

Without recognizing and understanding God's signs, we cannot find our way back to Him. But who is here to discover His signs and then translate them for us?

There are so few spiritual brokers around. Those who are willing to show us the sacred path to the Beloved with no strings attached. The signs are all around us, but we don't know how to read them. Our attention is so caught up with money and how to get more of it that we don't know where to look or how to see things.

We need a new quality of consciousness to recognize and read the signs of God. Without His lovers acting as Helpers and Comforters of man, this new consciousness may remain dormant and not get established in the collective.

His lovers must now work together to assist humanity. To give us what we need, what the soul of the world is crying for.

What does it mean to work together? It means consciously recognizing a purpose beyond every individual or collective path. Humanity has forgotten its place in the wholeness of life.

We've been so busy thinking about material well-being that we have forgotten about God and the fact that He is here to provide for us. It's time to remember Him, to no longer abuse Him, and never to abandon Him again.

His lovers know the wonder of grace, the miracle of transformation through which He wishes to reveal Himself within every heart. While the path can be walked in solitude, its meaning needs to be shared.

It's time to create a collective affirmation of the ways of love and of a consciousness that can recognize His hidden face. We must come together and wake humanity and its many members to recognize the signs of God showing us how to transition from the Realm of Disunion to Union, and we must be ready to embrace such a spiritual journey.

It is only then that humanity can learn to read God's signs and come to know who we truly are, as we see His face reflected in His world, in each of us, as we become our Divine Selves. It is for the mystic to make this new quality of consciousness accessible to humanity, and for each of us to be willing to learn the truth about God and what He has done to provide us with peace in our hearts to experience eternal joy in paradise on Earth through our Divine Selves.

It is then that we will be able to feel, for the first time, the heart of the mystic, allowing us to see the Truth as it is revealed to us moment by moment.

Surely, this is the crucial need of our time.

Do we need to continue living in the Age of Disunion, forming this collective misery, this alienation from our divine nature? Or can we look to a future born from the Age of Transformation, the eternal present, in which the one we truly love is no longer a hidden secret but known and honored as the sacred substance of everyday life?

No doubt, we all long to recapture this eternal present, this completeness of our essential nature. It's time to dance again to God's universal symphony, to feel the presence of the ONE, which is the eternal substance of our self, the oneness to which we all belong through each of our uniqueness.

Indeed, this is the balance of oneness and uniqueness that governs every part of God's creation.

The light is all around us. What we long for has already been given if we would only recognize it. The signs of God are alive and are calling us by our real name.

Those, who are driven to live in the Realm of Union where God dwells, must take the time and effort to analyze and properly understand the general implications of what it truly means to love our fellowmen, to be concerned with the welfare of others, to refuse to tolerate isolationism, and to sanction attitudes that can lead to the dismissal of any individual as unworthy.

Also, what it truly means to love ourselves, care for our needs, and be the best that we can be, living fulfilled lives, where we're able to satisfy our dreams as we follow the Realm of Union, never Disunion.

Love can be expressed in many ways. Some are better at talking in words, and some in action. We need to recognize both and the many other forms of love.

These are all complex issues that have to be studied, understood, and practiced; otherwise, we can miss out and give up, not seeing that every complex issue can be made simple, and when this is done, it can be better understood and practiced. So, it takes time and effort, but it's surely worth the trouble, because it helps us become whole and holy to be in the presence of God, who is the holiest of holy.

Before I continue, I must emphasize that every person is responsible for monitoring and evaluating his or her condition and well-being and no one else. We have no right to evaluate or judge anybody but ourselves because we're not responsible for anyone else unless we are a minor's parent. We must always protect our children and help them to remain whole, not fragmented, holy, not unholy.

I have noticed that whenever holiness or righteousness is mentioned, most people are overwhelmed, asking, "How should one measure such qualities?" or "Who is going to decide whether an act is unholy or unrighteous?" That is exactly why we need to learn the Realm of Union versus the Realm of Disunion, and how to differentiate between the two, while comprehending the holy books that show us how to maintain our holiness so we can be righteous beings.

Furthermore, to be holy or righteous and to remain so is not an easy task. It needs lots of practice unless we understand mysticism and its practical applications, which cannot be comprehended solely through Judaism, Christianity, Islam, or any other religion with a limited perspective.

We must try to move toward greater spirituality and perception, always toward infinity, so that all limited views of agonizing to make moral choices that reside in the Realm of Disunion and temporal existence are slowly transformed from disunion into union to take us to eternal existence that is the Realm of Union.

Eternity stands outside of time. It is changeless, yet still, it is the sum of all things. That means we can see everything together, integrated as a whole, with a single metric that represents the union of the parts. I explain this quality of the universe throughout this book, where the metric of the union is the summation of the metrics of the parts. Time, on the other hand, is pretty much an aspect of our three-dimensional perception imposed on the flux of experience, where we can see things, either in disjoint sequences, maybe with meaningful patterns, but not together as a whole, or together as a whole in a union form of the parts.

For example, every life may contain its share of joy and pain, but suffering can be bearable if we find it meaningful and accept it as part of human spiritual development and maturity.

God is "I Am Who I Am," which indicates His time is a perpetual Now. Boethius calls it "Eternal Life," in which the full web of meaning is always present to Him, as well as to every Divine Self, through higher perception and spirituality.

Let me explain this further through an example.

Two weeks ago, I was attending our Torah Study when one of the ladies managing our synagogue's library showed us a book titled "Basic Judaism" by Milton Steinberg and two copies of another book titled "Night" by Elie Wiesel, saying, "These are extra copies, anyone interested?" A young woman took one, and I took the other two.

First, I read "Night" about the Holocaust and cried my heart out. Then I started reading "Basic Judaism" and soon realized how incredible it was, so I began taking notes and summarizing it. I must say, a great book, published in 1947, the year I was born.

In the next few pages, I am going to insert into my text the summary I made of this great book, of course, in my own words and as I understood it.

Long ago, as long ago as a full two thousand years, when Judaism was old enough to have a defined character, several attempts were made to catch that character in some brief formula.

Hillel, a Palestinian sage, said, "That which is hurtful to thee do not do to thy neighbor. That is the whole doctrine. The rest is commentary. Now go forth and learn."

Rabbi Akiba said, "Thou shalt love thy neighbor as thyself." Simeon indicated that the love of man is the awareness of his kinship with the deity.

Rabbi Simlai taught, "Six hundred and thirteen commandments were imparted to Moses — three hundred and sixty-five of which were prohibitions, answering to the number of the days of the year, and two hundred and forty-eight positive precepts, corresponding to the number of members in the human body.

Then came David and reduced them to eleven. Then came Isaiah and reduced them to six. Then came Micah and reduced them to three. Then came Isaiah once more and reduced them to two. Then came Amos and reduced them to one, "Seek ye Me, and live." Then came the Prophet Habakkuk, confirming the one who said, "The righteous shall live by his faith."

In brief, Judaism is about God and man: man seeks God to know Him, love Him, revere Him, and do His will, while loving his fellowmen through Him with righteousness and mercy.

But then, Judaism is not the only religion setting the love of God and man as its key motif. Christianity and Mohammedanism, born from Judaism, rest on the same foundation and reach the same pinnacle. However, Judaism is quite distinct from these other two faiths because the Jews are expected to "go forth and learn," as Hillel declared long ago.

In form, the Torah is a narrative describing the events from the creation of the world to the death of Moses, as the origins of the nations of the Earth, the beginnings of the people of Israel, the lives of the Patriarchs, the enslavement and deliverance of the Jews in Egypt, and the revelations of God's will which came to them in the wilderness of Sinai.

But the Torah is much more than a narrative. It is a guide for Jews to study as they seek to live their lives through God to best fulfill their covenant with Him. All synagogues have one feature in common. They possess, enshrine, and make accessible at least one copy of the Torah, which means, in Hebrew, "to guide" or "to teach," so it simply stands for "guidance" or "teaching."

In Farsi, the word "To rah" means "your path," and "Too rah" means "on your journey."

That means: Toward your unique path, which is the Divine manifestation in you through your Divine Self. It emphasizes a moment in the space-time continuum that has never existed and never will. The only way to be in this moment is through Hashem, the Almighty God.

That is why we say, "The Living Torah."

Because the Torah is a living document, it can speak to us differently in each unique moment.

That is significant for it indicates that in Judaism, we're expected to live our lives through God, as we search for the truth through Him, following His will and His scroll, the Torah, and, if necessary, every Jew may question things to find his or her answers, which may change over time, whereas in the other two religions, the truth has mostly been set with very little need for more wondering and or questioning, which doesn't make any sense considering we are still on our journey, not knowing much about the end, like what, when, where, and who is going to be, etcetera.

The tradition holds that man's redemption, and the world of man, can be affected by every man making the world a better place for all.

Touch Judaism where you may, and you will come upon this kind of expectation of the ultimate deliverance and vindication, the concept of the Kingdom, the dream of a perfected world peopled by regenerated men. After the Jewish God's faith and ethics, the concept of the Kingdom ranks as Israel's most precious gift to humanity.

Some may wish to remind us that this concept of the Kingdom was first envisioned by Zoroaster, the Prophet of Zoroastrianism, and communicated to the Jews by the Persians during their stay in the Persian Empire and afterward, during the Second Temple period.

But what is so important here is that the Jews didn't forget about it. They realized its importance for God and humanity and tried their best to include it and carry it with their other insights and teachings over the years, so that now, after Cyrus and his Persian Empire are long gone, we can still talk about the Kingdom.

Furthermore, the Jews have continued to explore and investigate this concept of the Kingdom over the years, to better understand it, expand on it, and finally allow for it to become the confidence that for Israel and humankind, a better time lies ahead than has ever been before, where there is the TRIPLE HOPE: 1) the hope for every individual soul, 2) the hope for the collective of Israel, and 3) the hope for the society of humankind — to return to God someday in the future.

No doubt, this continual effort of the Jews to talk and wonder about the Kingdom spread globally, and there is no surprise to find the concept of the Kingdom throughout Christendom — in Augustine's City of God, Hegel's Philosophy of History, or Tennyson's allusion to "one far-off divine event." And also, in the writings of many Muslim Shiite Sufis over the years.

Another aspect of Judaism inherited from Zoroastrianism is monotheism. Even though Zoroaster was the first prophet of God, declaring Him to be the one and only, what's crucial here is that the Jews understood this and could clearly explain it, without ambiguity, which contributed to the spread of monotheism around the world.

This concept of monotheism, where Judaism clearly explains to all that God is one, has had a deep impact on humanity, where we have been so busy proving everything else to be false that we have often gone overboard and missed the boat that can take us to integration, and instead have remained divided for centuries. Let's look at this more closely.

From the start, Judaism emphasized, "God is one, and not many." This statement was made mainly because Paganism was considered a religion worshipping many gods, causing confusion, and the Jews had to intervene to make it right. But if we look at it more closely, we will see that the Pagans worshipped the many manifestations of God in nature.

Then, Judaism emphasized, "God is one, not two." This statement was made mainly because Zoroastrianism was sometimes seen as a religion with two gods, one standing for goodness and the other standing for evil, continually competing with each other. Again, this brought confusion, and the Jews had to intervene to make it right.

Judaism's repudiation of Zoroastrianism occurred over time, but if we look more closely, we will see that Zoroastrians believed in only one God but in two forces, good and evil.

Then, Judaism emphasized, "God is one, not three." This statement was made mainly because of Christianity's Trinity believing in the Father, the Son, and the Holy Spirit, but if we look at it more closely, we will see that the Trinity is not three aspects of God. It is one God indivisible. It is the dynamic of love that spills over to the whole cosmos.

God the Father generates God the Son as His idea of Himself. God the Son is eternally and equally God. The Holy Spirit is generated as the Father's Love for the Son and the Son's Love for the Father. Then, God creates the world out of nothing other than Himself.

Humans can distinguish between good and evil and thus freely choose between the two. So, our alienation from God is our choice, not God's, and therefore God has not the slightest obligation to save us from the consequences of our choice. However, God has mercy, so his eternal plan is to save us from the consequences of our folly. And that is why God the Son became human in the person of Jesus to restore the imbalance that humans had created.

Here, God is allowing everyone to reach redemption at the end time of disunion, when He will bring us back into harmony from alienation. This redemption from evil powers represents the first stage in the process by which the Israelites will be enabled to live in God's presence, which feels like heaven.

Then, Judaism emphasized, "God is one, not none." This statement was made mainly because Atheism insists that God does not exist and that He is only a human conception. Judaism affirms that God's existence is independent of man and that He is not only actual and real but the most actual actuality and most real reality of all.

But then, as I explain in detail in one of the volumes of this book, in the Chapter "Believe in His Promise," when we reach the Realm of Union, we are with God, for this is where He dwells.

All this division, as part of the Realm of Disunion, naturally cast a shadow over the Light of God, prompting the question: "If God exists, then why don't we have a better world?"

Over the years, many tried to provide answers through theories that seek to account for evil: 1) in moral terms, 2) in metaphysical terms, 3) as something temporary destined to be transcended and retrieved in the end, and finally, 4) as a hard question to answer, an enigma known to God alone.

But, Judaism stood firm throughout this long-term division, seeing God as the Creator of all things, the Lawgiver, the Guide to History, the Helper and Liberator of men and their societies, and the Savior of souls, and saying, "Though He slays me, yet will I trust in Him."

Some Jews believe the Torah to be God-revealed, thus true throughout. They are the strict traditionalists who refuse to move even in the slightest degree from their ancestors' faith, morality, and practices.

But then, there are other Jews, the modernists, who see the need for Judaism to be adapted to modern ideas and circumstances.

However, these two groups have remained united over the years, for they realize they must follow the Divine will to fulfill their Divine mission; thus, they are more in common, perhaps their viewpoints making up not two versions of the Torah but variants of one.

That is why to modernists, even though they see the Torah as a composite of documents done by different authors and sewn into unity by some unknown editor(s) where some portions of it may not be factual, the truth and goodness that can be found in the Torah, according to the space-time continuum, make it meaningful, especially since it contains the original text with many insights and commentaries that grew over the years.

When you think about it, this empowerment of the Jewish people's togetherness has helped them fulfill their Divine mission to manage the growth of disunion while maintaining the stability of the planet.

That's why, looking back, it is clear to both groups that Judaism, together with the Torah, was complete and perfect at Sinai. The prophets, sages, and rabbis neither altered its essence nor added to its substance. They run it through fresh, timely applications in which Judaism persists as one and the same from Moses to our day.

Also, it appears that the rivalry of scholars may have increased wisdom, hoping to better understand Judaism as the faith that has embraced the following:

1. **The Election** through which the Jews became the central figure in the drama of human salvation. Of course, some have wondered, "Why the Jews?" One answer that has been given is that the Jews may have accepted being the central figure, not so much out of heroism but their desire to please the Almighty.

2. **The Covenant** between God and the Jews, where God chose the Jews to assist in His plan for human salvation, and the Jews, in turn, accepted to do whatever it may take to satisfy His will, which has, of course, entailed hardships and obligations. Consequently, they've been referred to as a holy nation of priests who pledged to serve God, even if they were to suffer for it, as stated, "All that the Lord hath spoken will we do and obey."

3. **The Mission** can be simply summarized in a few words: the deliverance of humankind. However, most people, even the Jews themselves, have not been able to explain what this mission entails clearly. The reason for this is that this mission of God's chosen people extends beyond this three-dimensional space-time where we all live. As in life, it is only at the end of it all that we can look back and see the reason for everything. However, this volume of the book seeks to clarify certain matters, as much as is possible at this time, so that we may better understand what it means to be the chosen people of God.

4. **The Justification** for the election of the Jews, the covenant between God and the Jews, and the mission of the chosen people can hopefully be determined and explained in full someday in the future as part of the redemption of the whole human family. What is

clear is that, so far, His chosen people have been dispersed and persecuted while overall trying their best to satisfy the Divine will. But thank God, we're told that the future will be very different from the past. The Jews will be reassembled in their ancient land, where they will be able to enjoy peace and security proportionate to the bitterness and length of their exile.

Today, the election lives on; the covenant is in force; the mission goes forward; and the justification awaits the predestined time when the Jewish religion, so long mocked at and scoffed, will be universally recognized as the true faith, and the City of Jerusalem will be elected as the city where the Temple will be rebuilt to stand as the House of God and the House of Prayer for all nations.

But with this comes the necessity for Israel to learn to be the best and truest servant of God, while patiently waiting for the Messianic Age to unfold, so that we all may see the sacredness of the Land of Israel and its rightful place in the vision of the future, fulfilling Jerusalem's Divine destiny.

The traditionalist believes in all this, and if we were to ask the modernist, "But where is God's hand in aiding this whole process?" he or she will most likely respond, "Where is He not?" God is the power behind all human aspirations, driving men toward the good, the true, and the beautiful. So, though the traditionalists and modernists differ over the Torah, they both revere it and study it for guidance as they try to surmount their disagreements to meet their shared purpose.

Moses Maimonides wrote, "The foundation of all foundations, the pillar supporting all wisdom, is the recognition of the reality of God." Indeed, this belief is so fundamental to Judaism that the Torah takes it for granted. Hence, there is no need for proof; only a declaration, as in the opening lines of Genesis: "In the beginning, God created the heaven and the earth."

However, at the same time, Maimonides saw the need for the Messiah to come someday to help humanity recognize the reality of God. That became a part of the 13 Principles of Judaism.

Man has to stop projecting his erroneous perceptions and views on God. Such incomplete ideas have spread the culture of illusion or silence at the top and the culture of confusion and fear at the bottom of our global society. None of this is God's doing. God never promotes the Realm of Disunion. It is we humans who can't help but spread the Realm of Disunion in and around us, affecting everyone negatively.

Today, the boundaries between God and the souls are shifting, where the "Unreachable" will soon be nearer than breath, than a heartbeat. Let us rejoice and be thankful! Let us become our Divine Selves, living naturally in God's eternity and continually witnessing the Divine Logos.

Every person and every collective deserve to transform from disunion into union, for God loves us all equally and unconditionally, wishing to be known by each one of us. There is no reason to be scared of God and His infinite quality.

Why not awaken to His awesome reality?

Why not just relax and be who you truly are, a whole person, a part of the Almighty, who dwells in the Realm of Union, the Heaven you've been waiting for? Since it can help you to see the wholeness of everything and everyone.

The next chapter shows us how to go through a process of integration to reach wholeness. Since any type of fragmentation is a disunion quality belonging to the Realm of Disunion, I show it in italics.

WHOLE VS. *FRAGMENTED*

Those who are whole can naturally see the whole, whereas a fragmented person cannot. This wholeness is the potentiality of a person or entity. Every whole person is naturally in the Realm of Union and filled with the Divine Light.

For years, we've succeeded in empowering the Realm of Disunion, which has fragmented everyone and everything, creating hell everywhere on our planet, often fooling ourselves and/or others, rationalizing our negative tendencies, and, in the process, adding to our lies. Falsehood has blinded us to who we are and where we are going.

The darkness is a perfect place for the Realm of Disunion to promote disunion attributes. That's why the Realm of Disunion always promotes darkness that can only exist when the Divine Spirit is lacking.

We must learn how to employ union attributes, not disunion. We must learn this art and learn to honor it personally and collectively, especially now that we know the Realm of Union versus Disunion and how to differentiate between the two.

Let me give a few examples of fragmentation on both personal and collective levels.

Imagine a simple project that can be learned in a week and performed in ten hours a month to maintain a business system on an ongoing basis. The owner of the business where this project must be done is not tech-savvy, so he has no idea how difficult it is to build and maintain this system, and he has no time, ability, or interest in finding out. So, he hires a technical person and lets him create and manage such a system.

The technical person is not a kind union individual. He is a selfish, disunion person who decides to take advantage of the situation and build a team that would do everything for him. So, he hires a few people:

one to handle data entry, another to interface with various providers and order products as needed, and a third to build weekly reports.

This technical person could have taken a few hours a month to do all this himself. Still, now three employees are reporting to him as the manager. In comparison, he can just relax and oversee three employees with a project that can grow to give him more responsibilities in the future, as long as he can keep up with the scam through fragmentation of everything and everyone, so that the three employees and the owner don't get too close to each other to figure out what's going on.

The planet is currently filled with such projects, but no one has the awareness and courage to do anything about it. Waste is everywhere. Waste of time, money, and other resources. We're living in a global society infested with such disunion tactics, where most things operate on scams! From top to bottom, this is the case, and fragmentation is one of the best ways to keep the scam going strong year after year.

It has gotten so bad in the healthcare business that most doctors have forgotten how to look at their patients holistically and heal them. The fragmentation has gone so broad and so deep that it can sometimes take hours and days to figure things out, and they don't have the time to care and or attend to one patient as necessary when they must handle many, too many, making things truly unmanageable. Such fragmentations can be seen in every field.

Now, let me give an example of fragmentation at the collective level.

In the early twentieth century, the English had to make a deal with Iran to take its oil for almost nothing. To achieve this goal, the British decided to fragment Iran and other countries in the Middle East to weaken the people of this region so that it would then be easier for the British and their allies to take the oil from this part of the world, especially from Iran, for years to come.

91

The Western establishment created a story to convince the Shah of Iran to give away the oil, not realizing that the Iranian people were already eager to help and contribute to humanity's need for oil.

The Iranians gave their oil as a Taarof (a special gift) to the Western world to benefit humanity. However, the Western establishment didn't understand this aspect of the Iranian culture, so they tried to do whatever possible to keep on taking the oil by first starving the people of Iran, killing half of the population, and then pressuring the country to keep on giving its oil and resources.

And God Said to Angel: Toward the Divine Plan and Heaven on Earth explains all this further and proposes the Divine Solution on how to view our past and transform disunion into union, including this unfortunate aspect of our global structure.

At the time, the British, like most nations around the planet, were driven by competition, so when they decided to restructure the Ottoman Empire with the help of the French (probably because of Rothschild), at the end of WWI (1918 to 1922), they created new nations, like Turkey, Saudi Arabia, Lebanon, Syria, Iraq, Jordan, and Palestine, not to ease their inhabitants' transition to self-rule, as it was stated under the mandate of the League of Nations (later United Nations), but to separate its inhabitants so that they would forget that, once upon a time, they used to be one nation, one people.

Furthermore, this restructuring of the land was carried out too quickly, with the borders of the Middle East drawn with no regard for the interests and backgrounds of the people who inhabited it, and without time to consider the future outcomes of the Great Plan. All this naturally strengthened the Realm of Disunion on the planet, causing the last one hundred years to become a century of bloodshed.

But then, this restructuring of the land and the use of oil enabled the global managers to remain at the top of our global pyramid of disunion and to continue managing the planet's stability during the Great Plan's development and growth, advancing humanity and its tools and technologies.

Our history books omit to tell us the truth about the Middle East, especially Iran, because we are not supposed to know what happened to its oil.

In fact, over the past 150 years, it appears that most events have been orchestrated according to a proactive history designed to facilitate the use of oil by global managers, while remaining hidden from the public.

The term "Middle East" was coined by Europeans in the early twentieth century as part of their effort to control oil in the region.

It has been said that, around the Caspian Sea, the oil was so plentiful that it was bubbling out of the ground! The map of the oil in the Middle East shows its oil scattered in the region, with its largest deposits in the southwest of Persia and the Caspian Sea (both areas belonging to Persia at the time), and then in Saudi Arabia, and to a lesser degree in Iraq, Kuwait, the United Arab Emirates, Libya, and Qatar.

The other countries in this region were not oil-rich or oil-producing. The oil-dry or somewhat dry nations were Oman, Egypt, Yemen, Syria, Turkey, Bahrain, Afghanistan, Israel, Palestine, Jordan, Lebanon, and Cyprus.

The tiny Gulf states of Kuwait, Bahrain, Qatar, and the United Arab Emirates were considered of little consequence, convenient ports on the way to India, populated by a smattering of pearl divers and camel drivers. So, these little kingdoms were left to local emirs who later became among the world's richest men when oil was discovered.

My father's cousins married a few of these emirs, so I do have a few mixed Persian and Arab cousins living in that part of the world.

These global managers are very smart. They realize that the Age of Disunion is ending and that the Age of Transformation is approaching, ushering humanity from the Realm of Disunion to the Realm of Union. They know this transition will bring our wholeness, so they're looking forward to it. But, as a collective, they feel they must keep up the facade.

93

Today, we have too many fragmentations to reach our Divine Selves. But, as we get rid of our fragmentations and approach our wholeness, we will slowly get to know our Divine Selves. Jesus became his Divine Self when he became the Word, the Logos, in the flesh. And he directed us to do the same through the Holy Spirit. So, every person can do this on a personal level.

But most of us have not yet achieved this wholeness because the Realm of Disunion has kept us away from it.

We must help each other transition from fragmentation to wholeness, for at the end of it all, humanity will be able to achieve wholeness, not just on a personal level but also on a collective level.

As we approach this wholeness, we will notice that, in general, there is no such condition where one feels good and bad at the same time. That, at any moment in time, one either feels good and energized living in the Realm of Union or caught up in the Realm of Disunion, feeling bad and often drained.

Some may not agree, stating that it's possible to feel good and bad simultaneously, but such feelings can result from the duality that comes from being fragmented, mixed up, confused, and emotionally troubled. Not a condition of a whole person!

Let me explain.

God has mercy, so He has given every person the ability to feel what is right and what is wrong through the conscience, connected to the soul and to the Divine Reality and order. When the conscience is strong and in balance with God and His way, then it is easier to make decisions. But when the conscience stops working properly, it can be difficult to decide, because the brain may direct us to do one thing while the heart wants something else. This conflict between the brain and the heart can screw up a person's life as well as a collective's life.

The brain is here to prioritize what the heart feels.

For instance, a couple may drift apart and wonder what to do about their marriage and their beautiful children. If they don't have their priorities set correctly (e.g., they may forget to consider the impact of the divorce upon their children's lives from childhood to adulthood and even later), then their brains may direct them to go ahead with the divorce, whereas their hearts may feel the impact of such a path on their poor kids and object.

The reason for the objection may be the heart's connection to the soul and to God's Reality, quietly directing the heart toward the Realm of Union rather than Disunion. But, if the heart gets weakened over time and can no longer feel, then the heart may agree with the brain that there is no path left but divorce. That's why it's important to figure out our priorities since this step can help the brain in the decision-making process, just in case the heart has been weakened.

In addition, it helps to stand in the Realm of Union, where it is possible to witness the Divine Logos, His reality, to figure out His plan for us as individuals and also as collectives. This ability makes it easier for us to move toward the Divine Plan, which always leads us to the Realm of Union and the union structure.

My friend Jeff asked me to describe the structure of the Realm of Union, so let me briefly outline it before I go any further.

In the business world, we say, "He or she negotiated himself or herself out!" or "Let's have a win-win situation." That refers to someone becoming so blind as not to see the total picture, the interests of all. They may, instead, only see their interests, in other words, the interests of the few. Such a tendency may become a weakness in negotiation and cause a deal to fall through the cracks (because of it), even if the deal's success would have benefited all. Sometimes, we say, "Would you rather have ninety percent of one million or ten percent of one billion?"

But here, we are talking about something much more precious than money. We're talking about living life fully in the Realm of Union. Believe me, nothing can compare to this awesome existence.

The elites are mostly smart people, even though in some ways, naive. They have tried to control everybody so that they could remain at the top and continue controlling the masses, not realizing the incredible price of keeping everybody in bondage, including themselves. How can one replace this precious Realm of Union existence with anything else? Nothing can come close, especially not money.

To keep humanity under control takes a lot of work. First and foremost, knowledge must be controlled to keep everybody ignorant, for if they were to wake up, they would know that the whole structure stands on the sand and is made up of a bunch of lies and myths rather than a great foundation of the Realm of Union that is aligned with the universal balance of oneness and uniqueness.

Consequently, the control of knowledge can affect every facet of our global society. In addition to the modification of our history, other areas to suffer are our education, our media and entertainment, our music, our food, our health, our work environment, our family unit, people's relationships, and even love, the holiest of them all.

The solution to this control problem is to establish a new union structure alongside our current disunion structure, which leans toward the Realm of Union, so that we can support everybody. But the elites are afraid to support such a path because they are unsure where it will lead us. So, they must depend on the ruling class and their compradors, who are often entangled with the Realm of Disunion and too blinded by disunion attributes to know what to do. It's no one's fault, for this is the nature of it all!

The current global disunion structure has been managed by various governments, corporations, and representatives that have emerged over time. We elected individuals to serve humanity, but instead, they've been busy serving themselves and other rulers of the structure. These global managers don't realize, at a conscious level, that everyone is getting drained, including themselves.

It is a pyramid where the few at the top rule the many at the bottom. Such a structure naturally lends itself to disunion. That is why it has been allowed to grow over the years, because humanity had to experience the Age of Disunion and the many faces of evil. Now that we have learned about the Realm of Disunion and its abuses, it is time to move away from such a dysfunctional structure.

God recommends a different structure. An upside-down pyramid system in which "we the people" can develop and manage a union structure. This approach is the opposite of what we have today, where a few global managers are running the current disunion structure.

However, we're told not to destroy what we've got today, but instead build a new structure of the Realm of Union to co-exist with the present structure of the Realm of Disunion, where the new structure will be humanity-based, and decisions will not be made by leaders who tell us what to do, but by humanity together as one unit working together with leaders who are eager to serve rather than to rule.

Here, it is important to emphasize that we are not supposed to restructure the current structure. We are asked to build a new, holistic structure alongside the existing one.

As the new structure grows, the old one gradually vanishes. It's like having ten hospitals in our city, all nourishing the Realm of Disunion, then building one hospital that promotes a more holistic Realm of Union way. Since this new hospital is holistic, it would grow in popularity as people prefer to go there. Gradually, new similar hospitals would be built using the same holistic structure, and this would continue until the city was filled with them. All the unhealthy hospitals would come to the healthy ones to learn how to improve, or they would disappear because no one would want to go to them.

As you read this part of the book, you see that it is a type of structure that is concerned with stakeholders or members. So, it is not through governance by a committee to benefit a few, but decision-making by the collectives of humanity to benefit all its members.

As an example of how we make decisions in such a structure, compare a situation in which the father or mother is the boss, commanding everyone in the family on what to do and how to do it. With God's new structure, everyone, including the children, is brought into the decision-making process. In God's realm, everyone needs to be heard. The governing structure is mass-oriented: no one gets paid for serving it, and no one gains power from it.

In God's realm, when people serve God, they are not looking for power, recognition, or money. They serve because they wish to remain in the Realm of Union with Him. They act by whatever the Divine Wills, and they always remain subservient to this cause. And God knows each of us well, so He asks us to do what we can do best. People live strictly for God and the Realm of Union. As they set aside their made-up individual identities to find their true selves and serve the Divine and humanity, each becomes their Divine Self, always a true servant of the Realm of Union. They gradually become children of humanity. And in return, God takes care of His children, who are His Realm of Union people.

Each of us belongs to a few collectives. I may be a Persian, an American, a woman, a mother, a mathematician, an encryption expert, a filmmaker, or any other label, but as a person, I'm a minuscule part of humanity. There is no way I or anyone else, no matter how knowledgeable or wise, can decide on a structure for humanity's wellness! A holistic, open structure for the Realm of Union can evolve only in an environment where we are all included and supported by the Realm of Union, where humanity can get to know its members and gradually become united. And this book shows us how to do that.

I've tried my best to describe the Divine Plan proposed for humanity to consider, but this is just a foundation upon which all of us can build a new, holistic, open structure as members of humanity to serve humanity. I'm sure I'm not the only person working on this plan. There are probably many other Realm of Union individuals on the planet right now contributing simultaneously to this plan, some by themselves, some in groups, often not knowing the plan or one another. Hopefully, this will change in the future. We will get to know the Divine Guides and Helpers as our activists, our teachers, our energy and TLC givers, and our leaders, who are here to serve the Realm of Union – if not by face or name, surely by functionality!

Remember that when the Realm of Union rules, society tends to support all people. In the Realm of Disunion, no one is fully supported. Disunion people are usually rewarded as long as they're needed and can benefit the disunion structure. However, this can change, so there is no security unless there is enough money to get out of trouble if necessary. Union people are never supported and always isolated. Thus, today, the Realm of Union people don't have the strong network that is presently available to the Realm of Disunion people. But this will change as the Realm of Union grows.

So, we must get together and rapidly build our Realm of Union network, not to compete with the Realm of Disunion people—because that would be a Realm of Disunion attribute—but to get to know each other so that we can properly support one another. That way, we won't feel isolated and even left alone with no support. Knowing each other and depending on one another will be essential to bringing a Realm of Union structure. The Realm of Union network would have many advantages over the Realm of Disunion network. For one thing, they would be helping each other for the benefit of all rather than cutting each other's throats to get ahead. Surely, there is power in that.

Even though the current structure of global communication allows everyone on the planet to share stories, ideas, and insights, it often takes money, power, and status to be heard. It should not have to be this way. We need to hear each other. I believe it is more appropriate to say that we must listen to one another because we are one family. And, right now, this precious family of ours, which includes each of us, is in big trouble, for it is continually being drained of its energy by the Realm of Disunion. It needs to be healed.

The only path to recovery is to involve as many people as possible, because together we are humanity. If we want to get out of this mess we are in right now, we must become one. I am sure we all agree that we have lost our balance of oneness and uniqueness. This equilibrium of our connectivity and our functionality is essential. Without it, we continue to become weaker as a family, making each of us susceptible to the Realm of Disunion.

Over the years, the kingdom of evil has grown, fragmenting and hurting more and more people, and it is soon reaching its peak. Many are stressed out, feeling pain, anger, fear, loneliness, hopelessness, and horror while continuing to hunger for the Realm of Union. Throughout history, we have longed for the day when humanity can be free of evil and one with the Creator. I strongly feel that today may be the day when our planet and our generation will finally be allowed to rid ourselves of evil and live in the Realm of Union, where we all belong. That is an exciting time for all of us! We must change our course before the Realm of Disunion can destroy us all.

I try to tell people that God is here, and that He wants humanity to know it. But this cannot happen if we are in the Realm of Disunion. If we were to truly wish for the Realm of Union and move toward it, then an interesting era would start, where it would be easier to obtain the support of God and His agents, facilitating our journey. In the past, when prophets came, we didn't have the technology that we have today. In a Realm of Union atmosphere, with today's media, if God were to communicate to us through a messenger, helper, or guide, everyone would be able to hear. Experts could ask about issues that humanity has always wanted to know. It wouldn't be the helpers or guides talking, but God speaking through them.

I believe this book is unique in presenting God's proposed system and its three subsystems, each of which can possess miraculous powers. It's a system that, over time, can accumulate many layers of functionality, never stopping to grow if monitored and kept in the Realm of Union. Because of its innate properties, which will grow as well, this system will finally take us out of the darkness and into the light forever.

The three subsystems are:

- **The TellRTale Archives** – This subsystem gathers, organizes, and archives people's journals and stories into collections of living documents and collectives, gradually correlating them in different forms of space and time. That naturally makes humanity's true history available and visible to us on an ongoing basis. I've been told that it is going to become a living document—an open system to add to confidentially. Today's history is often false and incomplete, preventing humanity from seeing itself. Every collective must know its past, present, and potential future, where it fits in the overall scheme of things. We need to understand ourselves, our collectives, and the universe to which we all belong. It's like putting a puzzle together. The humanity puzzle. Our true purpose in life and destiny. Our place in the universe. And through this connectivity and clarity, hopefully, we can join the universe rather than stand separated as we are today. Journaling and archiving our journals and stories can help us see our higher dimensions and gradual transition from the Realm of Disunion to the Realm of Union. This transformation is our Divine Destiny. And TellRTale is going to help us do that.

- **The Humanity Temples** – This subsystem gathers, organizes, and archives people's opinions regarding different issues. It starts with 20 issues and grows to whatever humanity desires as individuals and collectives. These issues can be discussed anywhere people gather to talk and record their conversations—at a person's home, work, school, place of worship, etc. It doesn't matter how many people are involved; it could be just one person, with their opinions recorded in any form possible. The Humanity Temple is our collective home, belonging to every person. That will naturally grow to include people's votes on different issues, always balancing our oneness and uniqueness. As time passes, the many faces of evil are exposed and gradually weakened until the Realm of Disunion is dissolved, and the Realm of Union stands strong, supporting all.

- **The Divine Fountains** – This subsystem is the money engine funding the entire system and ensuring all projects are cared for, properly grown, and not duplicated. Under this subsystem, Helping Hands International funds various projects globally, all under the Divine Fountains. Another component is the Divine Incubator, which provides the appropriate support to all the projects and organizations under the Divine Fountains. So that all overhead expenses are shared and optimized among the different companies and organizations under the Divine Fountains. These start-up companies are like babies, cared for to grow into adults who can take care of themselves. All adult (or mature) companies are grateful and give a percentage of their profits to the Divine Fountains to be distributed again. This cycle goes on and on, creating many organizations and growing indefinitely.

Plus, these three subsystems include many projects described in *And God Said to Angel: How to Transform Collectively*, in the Chapter "The Divine Projects." Every person or collective can add to this list of projects and should do so, as long as the project belongs to the Realm of Union.

For example, the TellRTale can be used to tell and share our tales as we measure different aspects of our personal and collective lives. Such metrics can help us gauge the levels of our energy, our spirituality, and the well-being of a person, a collective, a unit, an event, an entity, a culture, a story, etc., as well as various totalities for all to see.

Today, we're all getting used to cell phones and how to use different apps and software on them, so getting people involved in this measurement process should be easy. After a while, we may even share how far we are from heaven or hell and try to help each other get closer to heaven.

As we share our stories and measure our progress, we begin to see the many faces of evil and how to turn disunion into union, gradually dissolving the fragmentation that flows from the top to the bottom and again back to the top. The elites will naturally play a role in this, either to expedite it or delay it. We must help them do the right thing to empower the Realm of Union, thereby enabling humanity's healing and growth. After all, the elites are also members of humanity.

The key is for all of us to follow the Realm of Union. That's it.

Any way we can make this happen is okay as long as it follows the Realm of Union principles. It's time to explore all the ways. We need to tell each other about the path we choose, and how it may be working for us. We share our experiences as we travel on a path, so that we all get to learn about the many paths chosen and whether we would be interested in experiencing them, if we so desire, to find the one that best suits us. Over time, such spiritual journeys can help humanity discover new ways to dissolve the Realm of Disunion through God and Truth.

We must be allowed to experiment as we follow the Realm of Union. How can we address His plan, implement it, and see the results unless we permit it? How can we know whether a seed is from the Realm of Union or Disunion? Only by planting it, watching it grow, and evaluating its fruits. Only time can tell!

Other questions are: How did we end up here? In this nightmarish existence! Why has God allowed it? Why have we gone along with it? Why can't we talk about it to find a way out? And what can we do to reach the Realm of Union, where God dwells, and Truth resides, to set us free?

Today, we have a global community that is all about making money, and nothing else seems to matter. The greater the imbalances throughout the structure, the easier it is for the few to weaken the many to make money from them and the disunion structure.

Capitalism has grown to the point of devouring humanity while, all along, promising everyone the possibility of getting rich someday and joining the smart and fortunate few who have reached the top of the pyramid.

All this has allowed consumerism to spread throughout our global society replacing many of our past Realm of Union values with Realm of Disunion ones, mainly with one objective in mind, to make enough money or to take away enough resources from humanity to support the disunion structure that the elites and their compradors have built to remain in power at the top of the pyramid to continue ruling the many to benefit the few.

Together, we have convinced almost everyone that the highest priority in life is the accumulation of material wealth. GOLD has won over GOD, the Almighty! Today, most people's energy is directed down such a path! We are ready to do whatever it takes to get the Gold.

Without God, there is a tendency to feed the egos and pockets of those who manage our pyramid structure to satisfy the establishment's goals that promote the Realm of Disunion, not Union.

In the Realm of Union, God and His creation must always come before anything else, thus at the top of our priorities. And then somewhere below, we may leave a place for Gold! Not the other way around as it is today, where the Age of Disunion has grown to promote the Realm of Disunion, increasingly to benefit the few at the expense of the many.

The Spirit of Aloha, which allows us to care for one another and our collectives, seems to have vanished, leaving us all vulnerable to more abuses and exploitations.

For centuries, humanity has depended on the kings for their material needs and the priests for their spiritual needs, simply because the king says you need me to manage your material side, and the priest says you need me to manage your spiritual side, and people go along with it.

At the turn of the century, the elites realized that, with the Industrial Revolution, it was possible to produce, through machinery, a bounty of products for everyone to benefit from and, in the process, make a lot of money themselves. So, they sold capitalism as a solution to free us from the bondage of the Realm of Disunion.

Capitalism became a means to escape both the kings and the priests, and to pursue material production in which everyone would benefit from the goodies and the success of the free market.

Of course, the elites joined in, realizing that it would be the best way to satisfy everyone, minimizing conflicts among diverse groups of people who would be happy as consumers, while the elites would continue making even more money than before by expanding their capital in the capitalist system.

Over time, capitalism grew like any religion, with capitalists becoming the evangelists who told a great story that everybody accepted. A capitalist story. An illusion that humanity's desires would be met through technology, the free market, and the consumption of products. And that the previous exploitations would cease to exist, as there would be no limitations.

The capitalists and the aristocracy knew better. They were aware that capitalism had its limits and could grow solely through the gradual exploitation of the masses, but they kept the illusion alive, for they felt it was the best structure at the time, and maybe so, considering the benefit of the few always mattered more to the elites than the benefit of all.

The elites have been fearful of communism for years, always seeing it as an end to capitalism and its power. So, they came up with a great plan to let communism develop in different countries through proactive history rather than naturally, and it worked like a charm. That way, they could monitor it and manage it themselves until they could end it at the right time, while saying to everyone, "Look. It didn't work out, so don't try to do it again!"

Of course, such tactics have weakened us, perhaps preventing humanity from exploring different forms of governance and social structures, but looking back, it appears that the path we took kept us safe and, in a way, prepared us for our transition from disunion to union someday in the future. In the meantime, the elites remained at the top, managing the planet's stability.

Here are some rationales for such a path:

1. It brought us to the greater Realm of Disunion so that we could now see the many faces of evil.

2. It enabled the growth of our technologies and tools, potentially serving as an extension of humanity to help us move toward our transition from the Realm of Disunion to the Realm of Union.

3. It drove us to a point of no return, where we're now checkmated and forced to use our tools to explore our present situation and, hopefully, bring in a new structure for the Realm of Union that would truly benefit all.

Today, it's clear that our future success will highly depend on our understanding of the Realm of Union versus the Realm of Disunion and our desire to come together to strengthen the Realm of Union so that the Divine purpose for us will blossom and give us the fruits of the Realm of Union to dissolve the Realm of Disunion.

There is no way out of this miserable and chaotic situation unless we begin to feel and serve humanity and the Divine Plan to make the world a better place for all, not just a few.

And God Said to Angel: How to Transform Collectively describes the projects God proposed to help us achieve this goal.

No doubt, most people are tired of getting drained all the time. They want it to stop, but they don't know how to get there. Some Christians have learned to attain personal salvation through Christ and are now waiting for his return to show us how to attain collective salvation. Some Muslims know how to follow the Divine will, and so they try to do it to reach God. And some have stopped believing in God altogether.

Over the years, we have built many stories and myths to provide humanity with the best and greatest explanation for our existence, some stronger than others and some falling apart. We must explore these stories to gain a broader view of humanity's spiritual journey and to understand our past, present, and future, toward a better understanding of humanity, God, and His will for us.

We're at the peak of the Realm of Disunion because we have promoted disunion attributes over the years, strengthening it and leading it to grow into the Age of Disunion.

We soon have to make a choice: either welcome the Realm of Union or continue to decay in the Realm of Disunion until we die. I hope we become disgusted with the Realm of Disunion and its horrible attributes, and do whatever we can to serve the Realm of Union and its awesome attributes, so that it can grow strong enough in and around us to get rid of the Realm of Disunion. Indeed, this may have been God's plan all along.

And God Said to Angel: Toward the Divine Plan and Heaven on Earth shows us how to move toward the Divine Plan that is here to help us transition from the Realm of Disunion to the Realm of Union. As you read it, please remember that I may know a few things about history and how the Realm of Disunion may have succeeded so far, but nobody can know the Divine Plan. Only God knows! That is why I call this volume *Toward the Divine Plan*, rather than the Divine Plan.

Let's explore this continual employment of disunion over union attributes, even though most of us prefer the Realm of Union. This mentality, almost an addiction, has continued to keep us all in bondage due to ignorance, blindness, and laziness. This volume, you now hold, is here to help us free ourselves from this addiction to transition us from the Realm of Disunion to the Realm of Union.

The disunion people are incapable of seeing God in themselves and others. They don't believe in Him, so they concentrate on sharpening the weapon of the words in the Bible. They use these words to manipulate us. To keep us all so busy, to see what is happening in and around us. They make us focus on heaven and hell, but they misunderstand both. They add to the fantasy while they distract us from seeing everything for ourselves. We are fed the wrong story to prevent us from reaching the true story that could lead us to higher spirituality and consciousness.

There is something good in every person and collective. We must find this goodness and stress it rather than empower the ego or the negation of the negative.

Simon Sinek has a video on the power of the human mind that says, "The human brain cannot comprehend the negative. If you tell someone, 'Don't think of an elephant,' that's the first thing they think about.' Skiers know this. They don't think of trees when going down a wooded mountain covered with snow. They try to think of the path and follow the path."

The same is true here. It's best to think of the Realm of Union as we follow the Realm of Union path.

Mankind is destroying its gifts, including Mother Earth and humanity, by concentrating on the negatives rather than the positives. All over the world, there are unique attributes in each person and in the collective. We should treasure such gifts, not destroy them. Ego development pulls us away from this important goal. The ego takes us to the parts rather than the whole; in other words, it doesn't let us see the totality.

In Western societies, the ego is valued, so when one says 'no ego,' everybody wonders, 'How can we allow that?' So, we must emphasize that the ego is a construction that draws people away from the potential of humankind. We don't have to point to the negative aspects of the ego. Instead, we must show that anything that takes us away from humanity's potential is not good.

We've been told that communism is this homogenous acceptance of the communal life as a picture of poverty and non-creativity, but forgetting to mention or acknowledge the fact that communism was set up purposefully, through proactive history, with the idea that there is no God, to take us away from Him and His Realm of Union. True communism can be achieved solely through God. Not the way man has defined it. Such wrongful definitions have occurred everywhere to keep us all in the Realm of Disunion.

Surely, this is a massive fraud. But it's not unique. There are so many like this spread throughout our global structure.

Today, society is consumed with who did what to whom, with endless chatter about the latest exploitations. Our overall energy is getting wasted on matters that don't seem to matter because we've been abandoned and kept away from the Logos. From Divine Reality, which has the power to heal everybody.

The disunion people can't help but deceive us about what the past has been and what the future can bring because we're on a path of falsehood. But people are fed up with lies and savoring the anger they feel over deception and fraud.

What would people do? If the kid comes and says, "The king has no clothes on!" Would people kill the king or laugh at the king?

The Realm of Disunion is generating so many disunion attributes, such as anger and hatred, around the globe, continually contributing to the Age of Disunion and further spiritual pollution, that most people have lost their senses and intuitions. They cannot think straight and see that the disunion structure is weak; the disunion people are weak; everything that belongs to the Realm of Disunion is weak, and can easily dissolve and vanish, especially when we learn the best way to rely on God, as the Bearer of Burden.

That's why the disunion structure has to create new ways to screw humanity continually. New scams. New frauds.

Although fundamentally, we have to come to recognize: 1) there is a cost in all this, and 2) we all have to share this cost!

Given our current crisis, I believe it is now an opportune time for all of us to recognize our connectivity and collectivity, and to stand for the union that can dissolve disunion.

It's time to learn to say the following:

1. If you believe humanity is doomed, then let me be.
2. I am not going to just sit around and enjoy the ride.
3. Screw your logic if it is going to blind us to kill us all.
4. Get lost, and let us go our own way and live our lives.
5. Go away and let us live our lives in beauty and peace.
6. If you happen to be the enemy, go away and let me be.
7. Come with us if you believe in love and similar qualities.

Some elites and their compradors don't trust the masses. They have a low opinion of them. They believe the masses are not worthy of a better life. In bad times, when things get complicated, and they don't know what to do, they get very paranoid and do whatever it takes to control the masses.

For instance, they try to keep sensitive information hidden from the public; they confuse the public; they pressure the public financially, emotionally, and mentally; they go into isolation, and make plans to benefit the elites without any consideration for the rest of humankind, the non-elites; etcetera.

Sometimes it can get extremely dangerous because the elites have to rely on their advisors and compradors, who don't care about the elites or humanity as a whole. They have become blinded by selfishness and competition to get to the top faster than their brothers and sisters. This tendency has handicapped these gatekeepers to the point where they cannot possibly figure out the best solution for humanity!

One option that they have considered in the past is to build a colony in space, kill off ninety percent of humanity, and then return to Earth when time has passed long enough for everything to go back to normal. Not realizing that such a scenario is oxymoronic, because GOD DEPARTS when there is disunion, especially this massive one. So, things are not going to go back to normal. And, without God, there can be no Realm of Union!

You may ask, "What about Atheists? Are they going to reach the Realm of Union?"

The answer is that atheists may say they don't believe in God, but if they are aligned with the Realm of Union, then they are aligned with God and naturally close to Him.

I feel fortunate to have had a great childhood. My family lived close to nature, where we could continually draw on pure energy. Every summer, we used to stay at our farm near the mountains in central Iran, and the rest of the time, in the Shah's castle in Tehran. I was allowed to go anywhere I wanted. At the farm, I would get on my bicycle and just go up and down the desert hills until late at night. I am sure I still carry some of that calm desert energy with me.

Back then, people felt more connected to each other, to nature, and to God. They lived a more simple, stress-free life. They were able to relax and express themselves, perhaps having more quality time with their family. The media had not become as aggressive and polluted as it is today. There were some worries, but not as many as we are currently experiencing. Most people felt more secure and less afraid. This sense of security led them to believe they had control over things.

It is ironic. As our lives became more complex, our feelings of insecurity increased, and we felt less in control, so we were too scared to relax and just let things unfold according to the Divine Plan. Before, when we believed that we were in control, we could relax more and, in a way, let go of ourselves. That helped us a lot because too much control tends to block the flow of the Divine Spirit and, by extension, Divine Energy.

Humans are unique in wanting to control things, generating negative energy that has accumulated over time, fragmenting our perception, perhaps causing the mess we are in right now, where the Realm of Disunion has grown stronger every day, draining all of us. And our drainage, in turn, has negatively affected other elements of God's creation.

We don't seem to care much about depleting the animal kingdom and the nature around us. We bring our toxins to God's nature. We want to control everything for our selfish purposes. That cannot go on forever. God's creation will not allow too many imbalances.

Many want to know, "Are the elites and their advisors too blind to see that they're hurting themselves by hurting others?!" They feel the elites shouldn't do this to the non-elites, presently the majority of humanity! They should be kinder, not to drain so many others without any consideration for God and His wish for humanity to live comfortably.

But then, the elites don't know what else to do right now, since the Realm of Disunion has reached its peak and is almost unmanageable.

There is no question that the elites have also suffered, like everybody else. *And God Said to Angel: Toward the Divine Plan and Heaven on Earth* explains all this in detail, showing us that the elites have probably done their best to survive and keep the planet stable enough to manage the Realm of Disunion's growth. I'm sure many people may have a hard time grasping and accepting this about the elites, but it is possible that some elites and global managers have safeguarded us to keep us alive, and we need to thank them for what they've done.

It's not easy to manage a planet of seven billion people while destined to go through the Age of Disunion!

We should be proud of every achievement that we have made and rejoice in reaching a point in humanity's history where we're now approaching the end of the Age of Disunion and the start of the Age of Transformation, where the world is destined to finally end its cruelty and no longer stand for such a humongous gap between the rich and the poor. And, when I say this, I'm not referring to material wealth. I'm talking about spiritual wealth! The Realm of Union requires it, and most elites could truly benefit from it.

There is no question in my mind that we can all unite to bring balance between these two collectives, the elites and the non-elites, while keeping both in the Realm of Union.

The elites must transform all their emotions and attributes into a unified whole. They must figure out their true purposes in life that always belong to the Realm of Union, and through such determinations, truly feel worthy to live with God. Otherwise, they may have no strength to live in harmony with Him and His humanity.

The elites, the English, the Jews, and a few other collectives, who have been instrumental in managing our planet, are afraid to let go. They want to keep their control. They fear that a disunion person may come and seize power from all of us. Such fears have replicated throughout the global structure, keeping us all in the Realm of Disunion! We should get rid of our fears and other disunion emotions that can take us to the Realm of Disunion. We should learn how to rely on God the Almighty, who is here waiting to help us transition from the Realm of Disunion to the Realm of Union.

The key is to love God and His creation and try to feel His love for us. In his book War and Peace, Tolstoy describes everything so beautifully, saying, "The most difficult thing, but an essential one, is the love of life, to love it even while one suffers because life is all, life is God, and to love life means to love God."

With his quote, Tolstoy is reminding us that the best way to handle all of the sufferings of the Age of Disunion is to love life and through it, get the adequate pure energy to strengthen ourselves and our abilities to witness the Divine Logos through our Divine Selves that can allow us to live fulfilled lives in the present moment that is NOW, the Realm of Union.

It's time to get together and teach each other how to live in NOW. If we were to learn how to live in the present moment continually and not allow anyone to bother us, to keep us from being in NOW, then we would exist in the Realm of Union where God dwells, and the Truth resides, allowing us to witness the Divine Logos, and continually learn from it, so that we may no longer suffer.

We mainly suffer because of our own and/or others' disunion attributes and/or desires. But we can also suffer because we don't know how to differentiate between the Realm of Union and the Realm of Disunion.

It is time for man to gain greater perception and awareness to see that life has a purpose. That each of us has a purpose. Our purpose is to elevate the world from materialism to spiritualism. With spirituality comes a greater knowledge of God as a cosmic designer.

The understanding that we're each a musical note, together making a Divine symphony. That God placed us here to do our parts to repair the world and bring a shift in consciousness.

The next chapter explains why we must always strive to follow God's Plan for us, personally and collectively.

GOD'S PLAN VS. MAN'S PLAN

I t is so marvelous to watch the Divine Plan unfold, especially in times of crisis. In our holy books, we're told that humanity once upon a time chose the disunion path and that God, honoring our free will, allowed it to happen, and the Realm of Disunion grew. But then there is a limit to disunion.

So, God planned to let us experience the Realm of Disunion and learn from it until our time is up, at which point humanity is given a choice to progress toward redemption.

If this is true, then there is hope, because God loves us all unconditionally and is merciful. If He allowed the Realm of Disunion to grow, then He must have a solution to dissolve it. But this must happen according to God's schedule and plan.

Rabbi Heschel, the leading Jewish theologian of the twentieth century, explained that there are three ways in which we humans respond to creation. The first way is to enjoy it; the second way is to exploit it; and the third way is to accept it with awe, which is the beginning of wisdom.

Heschel stood in the Selma Civil Rights march with Martin Luther King, Jr. He later wrote, "When I marched in Selma, my feet were praying."

As I look back, I feel the joy of having had Rabbi Heschel and Martin Luther King among us, and I am sad about what happened to Reverend King! But the future looks very bright to me, for the Age of Disunion is destined to end soon, making way for the Age of Transformation to begin.

Below, I'm going to explain this briefly and why it is so relevant to our study of history.

One could say, "We're going through a gradual spiritual development that is a part of our Divine destiny, both personally and collectively."

So, our human story (our history) may be following these stages of spirituality, plus one more.

Today, it seems to me that we may have already gone through two phases, and in the future, we may be destined to go through two more, together, four major phases of spiritual development:

Phase One: Wishing Union Fearing Disunion (WUFD)
Phase Two: The Age of Disunion (AD)
Phase Three: The Age of Transformation (AT)
Phase Four: The Age of Union (AU)

In the first phase, we tried to enjoy the Realm of Union while worrying about the Realm of Disunion interfering with our enjoyment, continually monitoring and fearing disunion.

In the second phase, we bravely and cautiously experienced the Realm of Disunion, letting it grow so we could get to know it and learn from it while maintaining our stability.

The first phase ended, and the second phase started when Alexander the Great conquered Persia.

The reasons for the second phase are a) to let the Realm of Disunion grow for humanity to see the many faces of evil so that we may later reduce it, even eradicate its overall influence upon us; b) to let the Industrial Revolution and the Information Age to grow to obtain the necessary technology and tools to later use as an extension of humanity to accomplish (a).

In the second phase, we had to use oil to run the machines, so the planet's managers and their advisors decided to use oil in the Middle East for this purpose and convert it into cash to fund the many projects and activities required to maintain the planet's stability.

We may now be at the end of the second phase and entering the third phase. In the third phase, we begin to see the glory of God and His Realm of Union with awe, which will be the beginning of wisdom for humanity, preparing it for the Messianic Age, which can be said to be a subset of the Age of Transformation.

In the Messianic Age, we seek to align with God and His Messiah, who sometimes appears during this era to help us transition from the Realm of Disunion to Union.

In the fourth phase, we enter the Realm of Union and remain there because, by then, we have learned how to differentiate between the two realms of union and disunion and how to rely on God to handle the Realm of Disunion for us so that we may live with Him in the Realm of Union.

In the first phase, we had less mastery and awareness of the Realm of Disunion, whereas in the fourth phase, we will have already conquered it through God.

In the third phase, every collective is fated to help usher in the Messianic Age in the area best suited to it, and as they all come together to dissolve the Realm of Disunion, humanity will, through Divine guidance, slowly enter the Realm of Union.

So, we must learn to come together and craft a version of the past that can move humanity toward the Realm of Union.

That is going to be a unique process in which we first acknowledge that every collective has suffered over the last century due to the Realm of Disunion's presence and exponential growth, and that not every member of the collective necessarily possesses the attributes of a collective.

Then, we begin to genuinely appreciate the work each collective has done to bring us closer to the Realm of Union and to empower such efforts, so that there is greater trust in our diversity and in our unity, coming into balance.

For example, the fact that the Jewish collective has been instrumental in accomplishing the second phase (the Age of Disunion) with the help of the English, and the Persians doing their best to apply union tactics to transform disunion into union, continually, and so on.

There is no question that the Jewish collective has taken the role of the top emissary of God on the planet, strongly feeling that they've been

God's Chosen People. That does not necessarily imply divine favoritism, but a calling, perhaps a contract.

A contract, where the Jews follow God's moral laws (Realm of Union, not Disunion); where they keep on managing the stability of the planet while withstanding the Realm of Disunion fierceness growing; where they endure any environment, whether hot or cold, in plenty or scarcity, in hope or despair, adapting to whatever may come, always serving the Divine mission toward His Realm of Union path; and where they carry the Divine Plan on their shoulders amid sufferings.

Overall, the Jews have done their best to care for God and humanity, knowing and hoping that someday they will be able to return to their home and live there in peace. That is what their prophets told them; one of whom even predicted the birth of Cyrus 150 years earlier as the Messiah and King of Kings, who would be God's true servant, helping the Jews return home to Israel and rebuild their Temple.

Everything that had been predicted came true when Cyrus came, and not only did he do exactly what God had asked of him during his lifetime, but also after his death. The Persians, who love God and His Realm of Union, including His true servant, Cyrus, did everything in their power to serve God's Chosen People so that they may better serve their mission from God.

Looking back, we can see all this clearly by studying those events in history that God has driven and thus are essential to this aspect of our human identity, in other words, the Divine Plan for humanity and the Jewish mission to make it happen, starting from the time of Cyrus the Great until today.

The best way to see this is to shrink all the years and look for interesting patterns, as detailed in *And God Said to Angel: Toward the Divine Plan and Heaven on Earth.*

We know that God made a covenant with Abraham, saying, "To your descendants, I give this land from the river of Egypt to the great river, the Euphrates." Religiously and culturally, this area became the

Promised Land, destined to play a key role in the fulfilment of God's Jewish mission to help humanity reach redemption in the end time.

We know that Cyrus the Great was anointed by the Lord and given the power to build one of the most powerful empires on the planet, where the balance of oneness and uniqueness was honored, allowing the Realm of Union to reign. That he was directed to liberate the Jews and help them return to their homeland and reconstruct their Temple, the House of God. That he was so great, yet humble – a unique quality of a true leader chosen by God to serve Him and humanity. And that today, even after 2,550 years, his life, his abilities as a leader, and his method of governance, as described in Cyrus' Cylinder and Cyropaedia, are examined by many.

We know that the Persian King, Cyrus the Great, obeyed God's wishes when he rescued the Jews in 539 B.C. and brought them to Persia, where they stayed for a while, because during Xerxes I (who reigned from 486 B.C. to 465 B.C.), they were still in Persia, Esther being the Persian Queen, as stated in the Bible. And, before he died, he wrote a decree instructing his descendants to accomplish all that God had commanded of him.

We know that another Persian King, Darius (a descendant of Cyrus), reigned from 423 B.C. to 405 B.C., where he tried to follow Cyrus' decree by approving, funding, and assisting the Jews' return to their homeland and the reconstruction of the Second Temple, which was completed in 350 B.C., and by returning to Jerusalem the Jews' worthy assets, which were stolen from them by the Babylonians. So, if these dates are accurate, the Jews were in Persia for about 189 years. But then, at the time, that whole area, including Jerusalem, was part of the Persian Empire, so naturally, they would be in Persia, maybe even Persians themselves, as I will soon explain.

We know that Alexander the Great was trained by his mother, father, and teacher, Aristotle, to learn all he could about Cyrus the Great and his method of governance that honored the Realm of Union. Yet, Alexander was groomed, while growing up, to conquer the Persian Empire someday in the future, not through construction but through the destruction that planted the seed of the Realm of Disunion on the planet, growing to this day.

We know that Aristotle, as Alexander's mentor from childhood, taught him to be a philosopher seeking the truth, yet when Alexander found the truth in the Realm of Union, in Persia of all places, and personally transformed from disunion into union before he died, the Greeks, including Aristotle, despised him for it, perhaps even poisoned him to die.

We know that pre-Islamic Zoroastrian literature accuses Alexander of destroying Zoroastrianism by burning their temples and sacred texts. No doubt, Alexander destroyed and burned all that belonged to the Realm of Union for most of his life because this was his function on the planet Earth − to plant the seed of the Realm of Disunion.

We know that in Islamic Iran, a more positive portrayal of Alexander is provided, mainly to empower the union side of Alexander that emerged at the end of his life, but also to acknowledge Alexander's mission within the overall Divine Plan. That is what the Persians do; they try to transform disunion into union. So, when they see that Alexander was trying to transform, then they naturally acknowledge it to give it energy.

We know that Firdausi's Shahnameh ("The Book of Kings") includes Alexander in a line of legitimate Iranian shahs, a mythical figure who explored the far reaches of the world in search of the Fountain of Youth. Later, Persian writers associate Alexander with philosophy, portraying him at a symposium with figures such as Socrates, Plato, and Aristotle, in search of immortality. These three philosophers shaped Western thoughts and beliefs. Here, "Fountain of Youth" or "immortality" may be the Divine Pure Energy explained in this volume.

We know that after Alexander's death, his generals continued to spread the Realm of Disunion throughout the land, and the Western world followed Greek teachings that mostly promoted it.

We know that the Persians were the only world power that liberated and protected the Jews, while all others, including the Egyptians, Assyrians, Babylonians, Romans, and later Germans and Russians, discriminated against them, persecuted them, or sought to eliminate them. Without Cyrus' intervention, the Jewish Collective and Judaism, as we know them today, would not exist.

We know that the Jews and the Persians lived together in harmony in the Persian Empire for over two centuries; that Queen Esther of Persia courageously saved her people through Divine guidance; and that God is always ready to guide us to win over the Realm of Disunion no matter how distant and or uninvolved He may seem to us at the time; all of which we learned, directly or indirectly, from the Esther Story; yet, the Book of Esther is the only story in the Bible, which was not found in the Dead Sea Scroll, and the only book in the Bible where there is no mention of God.

We know that Aristotle called the Jews "the Kalani people from India," but the Kalani tribe existed in southern Persia and, like the Parses, was Persian.

From all this, it is evident that before Alexander conquered Persia, the Realm of Union reigned in the Persian Empire because Cyrus the Great, the King of Kings, knew how to govern the many kingdoms of the Persian Empire holistically through the balance of oneness and uniqueness, as it has been documented in many books about the Persian Empire.

Let's face it. The Cyrus Story is a rare event where: 1) the prophet Isaiah predicted Cyrus' birth and life over a century earlier referring to him as Jehovah's shepherd who will facilitate the Divine plan; 2) God asked Cyrus to do something special for Him – to save His people – and Cyrus listened and completed the task, even after his death; 3) Cyrus is the greatest ruler of all time, the King of the Four Corners of the World, who has everything, yet he is so humble and a true servant of God and humanity; and 4) God's people, who are the Jews, agreed to go to the Persian Empire, and stay there for a while until they returned to their homeland.

Looking back, even though it must have been exceedingly difficult for the Jews to go through all this, as usual, they stayed strong and overcame the hardship of living among the Persians until God's plan for them was met.

Not that the Persians were unkind toward the Jews, but it's always difficult to live with another collective away from your own home, something the Jews were forced to do repeatedly for years! But thank God they stayed in Persia, for otherwise, we wouldn't have the Story of Esther.

Both the Esther Story and the Cyrus Story are so filled with holiness that it's mind-boggling!

We need to understand the significance and eternal qualities of these two stories to better grasp the Jews and their mission from God to serve Him and humanity, and the role the Persians played in making all this come true.

Yet, in the past forty years or so, we've seen the erasure of Persia gradually growing, where it has become extremely difficult to figure out the truth about the Jews, the Persians, and their true relationship. No doubt, our history books have been tampered with, creating many false stories to benefit the few who are in power, primarily to erase humanity's identity.

There is now a tendency to minimize this Persian-Jewish togetherness of the past, even though it has great power and holiness behind it, certainly belonging to the Realm of Union more than any other event in human history. The reason for this is to weaken the Realm of Union and its people, not realizing that such acts can harm humanity to which we all belong!

All these events of God instructing Cyrus and Cyrus listening and following His instructions, and then helping Esther to become the Queen of Persia and later save her people, are unique and miraculous.

Indeed, these are the most extraordinary acts of God in international history!

It's better and healthier for all of us to acknowledge such HOLY EVENTS and ask ourselves, "What are the driving forces behind such erasure?" We must be careful in the way we view our history. We need to empower the union events of the past (the holy times, the miraculous times) and not turn them into disunion events. Why are we doing this to ourselves?

Our survival as a species is at stake here.

In *And God Said to Angel: Toward the Divine Plan and Heaven on Earth*, I show how Cyrus tried to follow God's way in governing the Persian Empire by keeping the balance of oneness and uniqueness and that this is the best form of governance through Satrapies, who are trained to follow and empower the Realm of Union, not Disunion.

But all this had to change because it was not yet time for humanity to live in the Realm of Union for good. As a collective, humanity had to experience the Age of Disunion until the end of the Age of Disunion to 1) develop a better understanding of evil and its many faces and 2) build a better set of tools to employ as an extension of man to finally put an end to evil.

No doubt, God allowed this path for us because He honored humanity's wish to experience the Realm of Disunion, so that we may better understand the evil side of life, often caused by free will and a lack of wisdom to manage it effectively.

The bottom line is that humanity was destined to truly comprehend the Realm of Disunion, just as teenagers try to do before reaching puberty, and God, like a loving parent, allowed it while monitoring the naive child to remain within the boundary, by sending His prophets whenever necessary to guide humanity until the end time of disunion.

That's why God directed Cyrus the Great to rescue the Jews and prepare them to better serve their Divine mission, and Cyrus bravely made it all happen, not just during his lifetime but afterward, for which he became the Divine Messiah.

Some people have misunderstood the Jews and their Divine purpose, thus resenting them over the years, as I explain in *And God Said to*

Angel: Toward the Divine Plan and Heaven on Earth. That is unfortunate since it has caused a lot of pain for the Jews and humanity.

But, looking back, it's interesting how the Divine force has safeguarded them to accomplish their mission from God and repeatedly outlive their persecutors, who have been many, like the Egyptians, the Babylonians, and the Romans, in the old time, and later, the inquisitors, the Nazis, and the Russians, massacring millions.

Ann Frank made an interesting point that may clarify all this. She said, "The Jews have something of noteworthy value to give to the world, and that is precisely why the world has resented and persecuted the Jews throughout history."

Ann was right. That is true not only for the Jews but for any other collective wishing to serve God and His Kingdom, especially if such a collective knows what to do and can do it.

Below, I wish to summarize the noteworthy value for the Jews and the Persians.

God chose the Jews: 1) to teach humanity the Laws of Moses, and the Ten Commandments, to stay holy; 2) to manage the growth of the Realm of Disunion and its sensitive threshold on the planet; 3) to help humanity see the many faces of evil; 4) to contribute to the technology needed as an extension of humanity to reduce the effects of evil on the planet; 5) to facilitate humanity's future transition from disunion to union; 6) to keep the Sabbath and safeguard the WORD of God; 7) to usher in the Messianic Age that is going to start from Jerusalem.

God chose the Persians: 1) to save the Jewish people from Babylon's King, Nebuchadnezzar II; 2) to protect the Jewish people and help them return to their homeland; 3) to fund and assist in the reconstruction of the second temple, God's House, in Jerusalem; 4) to return all Jewish assets to the Jewish temple in Jerusalem; 5) to prepare the Jewish people for their mission from God stated above; 6) to give their valuable oil and other assets as Taarof (gift) to benefit humanity; 7) to transform disunion into union whenever wherever possible.

So far, the Jews and the Persians have done their best, even though achieving all this has been difficult. Of course, many collectives have contributed to this effort.

It is important to note that as the Age of Disunion ends and the Age of Transformation begins, it will get easier for the Jews to satisfy their assignment from God and to bring holiness to themselves, so they can then help the Gentiles do the same. The reason for this is that the Jews have learned over the years how to keep the Sabbath, which can now help them let holiness unfold naturally from Jerusalem to the rest of the planet.

Some may argue that the Jews have gradually become less holy throughout the years, but we must consider the fact that it's been very difficult for the Jewish collective to continue managing the stability of the planet during the Age of Disunion, and at the same time know exactly what to do to accomplish their Divine mission. I mean, think about it, it's not that easy to do all this!

The Persians also suffered throughout this whole period. That's why they have become great transformers of disunion into union.

Fortunately, these two collectives have succeeded so far because we're all here and almost ready to put an end to the Age of Disunion. The key is to unite and help each other realize that every task mentioned above can be instrumental in bringing the Light of God to humanity and the planet, thereby improving the delicate threshold. For instance, in conforming to the Laws of Moses, a Jew not only extends his own life but also that of his collective, always standing on God's side.

Of course, the Jews, like everybody else on the planet, have made mistakes over the years. Surely, in the last century, it has been difficult for them to promote the establishment of Israel and, at the same time, the welfare of the Palestinians, often winging their progress while praying for the best and waiting for Divine guidance, which some feel has not yet come, causing many Jews to become atheists.

But truly, it is now vital for these two collectives to remember their mutual calling that began long ago.

We need to help them remember it and try to facilitate it because the Age of Transformation is coming, and these two collectives, the Persians and the Jews, are destined to assist humankind in the Messianic Age.

Every collective must come forward and act in sync with the Divine Plan now that we know about the Realm of Union versus the Realm of Disunion and the Divine Plan for humanity.

After all, it always helps to understand the different collectives' purposes in life and to empower the union side while minimizing the disunion side.

For instance, it appears that the British, as great strategists, were destined to work with the Jews, as their advisors, and the Americans, the Russians, the French, and a few other European countries, as their partners, to structure the Middle East in a way where it would be possible to get the Iranian oil.

The Jews agreed to facilitate this effort because, by doing so, they could manage the Age of Disunion and maintain the planet's stability as part of their Divine mission. They had to safeguard Jerusalem as the future seed of the Realm of Union's growth around the planet. Their long relationship with the Persians and the Arabs proved instrumental, as the Western world knew little about the people of this region. In return, the British agreed to let the Jews return home and facilitate the employment and monitoring of Iranian oil during the twentieth century.

No doubt, the Iranian oil had to be employed by the global managers: 1) to fuel the growth of the Industrial Revolution; 2) to fund the many projects of the Great Plan as part of proactive history; 3) to rapidly build the infrastructure of Israel; all of which the global elites wanted for they knew the importance of the Middle East oil in facilitating their goals and plans in the twentieth century.

The Shah of Iran was eager to help, so he gathered with his prime minister and ministers, many of whom were Iranian Bahá'ís, to aid this effort. During the time of the Shah, until 1979, Israel and the Shah worked together to optimize the employment of Iranian oil, even building an underground pipeline from Iran to Israel for the transport of oil. But after the Shah left in 1979, Israel gradually became the manager of this crucial black gold for the Western world.

I learned about this pipeline during my 2009 visit to Iran. Then, a year or two later, I read The King of Oil published at the end of 2010 by Daniel Ammann, a Swiss reporter, who talks about the secret lives of Marc Rich, briefly mentioning this pipeline and then telling us that Rich, a member of the Jewish collective, was able to get his foot in the door of the global oil trade and make a fortune dealing in oil with the Shah and Khomeini.

I also learned from Ammann that up to 90 percent of Israel's oil imports came from Iran.

Whoa! I couldn't believe it. Right there, in front of me, a sizable chunk of the Great Plan (GP as part of proactive history) was exposed! I wondered, "Why?" Then, I reread the first paragraph of the book, which is a fantastic start and explanation:

> "Oil. Black gold. The world's most controversial resource has created the mighty dynasties of the Rockefellers and the Gettys. It has tempted dictators such as Saddam Hussein into acts of aggression and brought down emperors such as the Shah of Iran. Even today, countries are prepared to go to war to secure access to this strategically significant resource. Without oil, there would not be an airplane in the sky or a car on the road. Without oil, hospitals would cease to operate, and shopping centers would remain empty. Our modern economy is unthinkable without oil. Oil is the world's most important source of energy. We live in the Age of Oil. We are "hydrocarbon man," whose very survival would be impossible without oil."

This paragraph from Ammann's book demonstrates why global managers had to do everything in their power to protect Middle Eastern oil, not just for their own benefit but also to advance humanity's desire to progress in the twentieth century.

In addition, Ammann's book detailing the story of Marc Rich confirms that Iran, the only non-Arab country in the Middle East, secretly supplied Israel with black gold since the middle of the 1950s.

The money produced from the Iranian oil is so massive that most parties involved became super wealthy, including some mullahs in Iran. Some agents of the intelligence community took a few million dollars for themselves, and nobody noticed!

Every time we heard about the Turkish police confiscating a truck coming from Iran with billions of dollars of cash and or gold, Iranians got busy talking about it quietly among themselves for a few weeks and then forgetting about it.

Unfortunately, some oil takers, like the US intelligence community, became addicted to this ongoing flow of easy money. This money allowed them to fund their black projects without anyone's approval! To this end, they even learned how to become the biggest drug dealers in the world.

What's interesting is that US politicians have been aware of all these global activities for many years. Most people who have any power in this global disunion structure know about the Iranian oil fiasco and the CIA's close ties with the mafia, including dealing drugs and prostitution, human and sex trafficking, on a global scale, while extorting many people at the top to keep quiet about such things.

I saw a documentary a few years ago that showed the Clintons' involvement in such disunion activities within the intelligence community, from which they gained greater power and money!

What I'm trying to say is that, unfortunately, most people at the top have been infected by the Realm of Disunion. The political machine and the intelligence community often work sporadically to keep everything confidential so that the masses won't get to see the Truth and get up in protest to cause a volcano! Of course, such an effort has brought pain, suffering, and death to many people around the world. However, this is not the fault of any person or group. It is the way the Realm of Disunion silences people.

In life, it's often easier and faster to follow the Realm of Disunion to get things done and what we want. But such rewards for disunion are destructive and cannot last. Today, most people are busy trying to get something from someone else with no acknowledgment or obligation in return. Imagine four billion people living their lives this way, generating disunion attributes everywhere, every day, all adding to the polluted energy of our planet. Surely, this is too much darkness for humanity and our mother Earth to stand!

It doesn't have to be this way. Not all people working at the top of the pyramid, whether in the intelligence community or other organizations that manage our global disunion structure, are driven by disunion attributes. We need to change our ways, especially now that the Age of Transformation is coming!

One may ask, "Why did we force the Shah out of Iran? Why couldn't we just let Him continue since he had cooperated fully with the Great Plan?" His son, Prince Reza, could have replaced his father to continue serving the GP agendas. But you see, such a scenario would have empowered the Iranian people, who were advancing rapidly toward becoming a major power in the Middle East, a path that may not have been desirable to the Western establishment and its members.

Considering the Persians' expertise in transforming disunion into union, their desire to choose the Realm of Union path, and their ownership of the Black Gold, thus the unlimited amount of money to fund whatever was necessary for growth, all three bundled together may have been too much power in the hands of one collective!

Plus, such a path would have disrupted the growth of the Realm of Disunion before the end time and also taken away the power from the Jews, both of which may not be aligned with the Divine Plan! I know it may be hard for us to comprehend all this right now, but I assure you that someday we will come to understand that everything in the universe must work together toward the accomplishment of the Divine Plan that always considers the benefit of all, not the few!

That is an important rule of the Realm of Union: to have faith and trust in God and His plan for us! A rule both the Jews and the Persians learned to follow over the years! That's why the Persians cooperated. Even the Shah kept his silence. It appears that everyone involved in the Great Plan has kept quiet, some honoring the Divine Will, and some just going along on the ride!

Israel benefited from the Iranian oil, which continued to fund the country's infrastructure and other needs, and the Persians and many other collectives tried to facilitate this process because they realized:

> **Without the Jews, Israel, and Jerusalem, there can be no Messianic Age! And, without the Messianic Age, humanity cannot reach redemption, which is true freedom from the Realm of Disunion!**

It's crucial to see the whole picture and evaluate everything in light of the Realm of Union. The Persians have done whatever they could to save humanity and spiritually transform people and events from disunion into union throughout history. Cyrus the Great was the first Zionist to try to satisfy the Divine Plan for humanity.

The Persians are so proud of this spiritual development in human history and also so in love with God and His Realm of Union that they've been willing to endure humiliation, abuse, and even erasure of their precious Persia by the Western world, knowing all along that such acts are caused by the Realm of Disunion wishing to hide the Truth, but that God is always in charge bringing His Realm of Union at the end of it all.

The Persians know many of the secrets detailed in this book. They know that the Divine Plan has allowed the Realm of Disunion to exist and grow to accommodate humanity's wish to take the Realm of Disunion path. And that there has been a Divine Promise set a long time ago that humanity will be redeemed someday in the future. That's why the Persians kept their patience. And, hopefully, that day will soon come.

Everywhere on the planet, we can find different collectives of humanity trying to be good and act kindly, but not their governments and institutions, primarily due to the nature of the beast. As a result, we can now see the many unrighteous and divisive acts that have accrued over the development of a proactive history that continues to this day. All done to facilitate the taking of the Iranian oil in secrecy with no need to acknowledge or properly reimburse the Iranian people, but then, we must understand that the Iranians gave away their oil as a TAAROF because they felt it had to be done to facilitate the Divine Plan in making the world a better place for all.

The Persians have always leaned toward Taarof, which is the benefit of all rather than the benefit of the few. This quality has been ingrained in the Persian culture for a few millenniums, ever since the time of the Persian Empire, when the Realm of Union reigned. Understanding this quality helps us to identify with the Persians and to realize how important Taarof can be in keeping a culture alive and healthy.

Let me explain this awesome attribute of Taarof.

The term "Taarof" encompasses a range of social behaviors; from a person getting up and politely giving his or her seat to someone else; opening a door for another person; offering to pay for another person's meal; helping a senior out of respect for the elderly; or being kind enough to help others and promote their interests; to a group trying to be civilized not to drain others and or take from them without proper compensation, always wishing to contribute to the collective.

Taarof also governs hospitality, in which the host tries to make everything as comfortable as possible for each guest, offering whatever the guest wants.

Today, Iranian shopkeepers may first refuse to quote a price for an item, suggesting that it may not be good enough for the buyer, trying to be respectful and kind, as the buyer insists on paying, usually three times, before the shopkeeper finally quotes a price, at which time, the negotiation begins. It is quite common for an Iranian worker (even outside of Iran) to work unpaid for a week or two before the issue of wages is finally raised.

According to D. M. Rejali, "For the feudal elite, the ornamentation of speech symbolizes prestige. With the advent of capitalism and its scientific paradigm, communication became more precise, and the formality of Taarof became a hindrance in the pursuit of rapid capital accumulation." That is true because money has become the most important criterion for living a good life!

This worship of money over everything else, including our humanity, is a disunion trait that prevents us from honoring one another and goes against God's will! That's why, when we are driven by money, we often end up promoting the benefits of the few rather than the benefits of all, competing to gain more, often at the expense of others. Today, people are hurting each other just to make a buck!

In such a structure, bullies usually end up at the top, where they stop playing fair and often take more than their share. So, it's not a healthy environment for humanity. A horrible place to be, even for those who think they're benefiting from taking from others without giving them much in return!

Here is a true story of Taarof.

During the last five years of the Shah's government, a few thousand Americans went to Iran as consultants to help the country become computerized. Naturally, as a computer scientist, I also got involved in 1974, until the Iranian Revolution in 1979. That's where I met my Irish-American husband. We had an American friend who had come there with his wife and children. I liked the family a lot, so we spent a lot of time together. We all worked for Computer Sciences Corporation (CSC), one of the biggest US companies in Iran at the time.

One day, this American friend told me, "Angel, something strange happened. Our Iranian neighbor invited us to dinner at their home. When we got there, we told them how much we liked their carpet, and they gave it to us as a gift to take back to the US. Expensive carpet! So, we accepted, and they had their servants carry the carpet to our home. Then, a few weeks later, they came over to our house and asked us to help their son enroll in a college near our home in the US and to watch over him from time to time. We didn't know what to say. So, we took their carpet back."

I laughed and said, "They gave you a gift, making their private property communal as if you were a family, and later, they asked you to help their son because you were now a family!"

So, Taarof can be a process of becoming a family that can grow for all to share happily.

I went online a few years ago and looked up CSC's website, and to my amazement, there was no mention of any contract with Iran, even though they had been there for over 5 years, making millions of dollars! Maybe billions! I told a CSC executive, who has been a friend of mine for years. He said, "Didn't you notice?" I said, "Notice what?" He said, "They were all spooks arranging for the change of government." In other words, they were there to get the Shah out and Khomeini in!

I once heard a top Pentagon official exclaim, "Why should Camel Jockeys in the Middle East own the bulk of a crucial global resource, Black Gold, which is so needed by everybody else!"

At the time, I was surprised and didn't know what to say, but later, I thought, what if the Iranian culture and its Realm of Union spirit of sharing to benefit all have generated so much pure energy in the area over the years that it has influenced Mother Earth to provide plenty of everything, including the oil?

That said, Taarof is a demonstration of love and caring for others as you would want them to love and care for you. Both the Torah and the New Testament directed us, "To love and care for others as we would want them to love and care for us." Jesus tried to show us how important this attribute can be in helping us reach personal salvation.

That's why the Persians love Taarof! They love to please God. It's in their blood. It truly pleases them to share, as a gift, what belongs to them, especially when they learn that someone else can benefit from the gift.

In turn, the recipient of the gift must extend similar generosity to others in need! Hence, with this gift comes the responsibility to expand the circle of love and caring to benefit all, and to inform every person and or entity benefitting from the gift that it's a gift from the Persians wishing to promote the Realm of Union, not Disunion!

Without this sharing, a culture can surely decay and die!

Not properly understanding the meaning of Taarof, a strong cultural attribute in Iran but less so in the Western world, has brought us a lot of unnecessary misery in the last century, as I explain in *And God Said to Angel: Toward the Divine Plan and Heaven on Earth*.

The Western world, especially Christians, should understand the meaning of Taarof and how to apply it properly to maintain universal balance. Unfortunately, the Western establishment has instead moved away from this Spirit of Aloha, continually taking other countries' precious resources to benefit the few rather than the whole of humanity, thereby surely polluting the spiritual realm that is here to provide plenty to every collective of humanity.

Taarof is just one of many Persian social traits misunderstood by the Western world. We've seen many Westerners, including the elites, visit Iran and then come back and report to everybody that the Iranians are so nice and hospitable, but unfortunately not understand the totality of why they're this way and what it all means.

The Westerners are too blinded by self-interest and money to see the true nature of the Iranian people and culture. The Iranians are kind and hospitable to each other and foreigners because they want everybody to feel comfortable enough to let their Divine Selves (their souls) come out and greet them, rather than their egos.

Meeting God in every person means a lot to the Persian collective! And, when I say Persians, I mean all people who are descendants of the Persian collective. Not just the people of Iran. The Persians are like Sufis, who love God and want to see His manifestations in everyone and everything more than money, preferring spiritual over material wealth!

In *And God Said to Angel: How to Transform Collectively*, I talk about Mohammad Reza Shah Pahlavi and how he became a major player in the Great Plan. Shah's story is worth telling, as it has shaped many world events, yet it has been kept secret out of fear of destabilizing global stability.

It is a shame that we had to first establish a Disunion structure and then transition to a union one. So many have suffered because of this decision, which, let us not forget, humanity made a long time ago, as the Book of Genesis tells the story, and we have continued to do so over the years.

It's amazing how smart the global managers have been and still are to have managed to keep us all alive amidst all our disasters. They've consistently balanced our accomplishments with a broader objective of stability for humans and the planet. They're incredible.

They've managed to fool humanity for more than a hundred years. They have become better and better at the game over the years, but unfortunately, their dependency on staying at the top and having enough money to support such a position has created a greater disunion structure throughout our global society, where the overall objective of the Western world and most humans on the planet has become:

TO BENEFIT ONESELF OR THE FEW
RATHER THAN THE WHOLE

It's been only a few hundred years since the new world began to form in the Land of Dreams that is the United States of America, bringing together so many collectives in one place to free themselves from Europe's religious tyranny and economic hardship.

For the State of Israel, it's been less than a century. Yet, already, it seems to me that these two collectives, the Americans and the Jews, are situated perfectly to influence the whole world to empower the Realm of Union to free humanity from the continual abuse and exploitation of the Realm of Disunion.

The Iranians have always been supportive of any transformation of disunion into union ever since the time of Cyrus.

The American people, the Jews, and the Iranians must realize the situation and try to team up with the English, the great strategists, in facilitating the Divine Plan. Today may be the right time for all the world's collectives to come together and unite in bringing about the formation of a new union structure on the planet that would continually follow the Realm of Union, not Disunion, and the benefit of all, not the few.

When Thomas Jefferson planted the seed of the Realm of Union with the formation of the new world, he said we would have to wait for it to grow.

Thomas Jefferson knew this because he was able to access the "Union Soul," which I describe in *And God Said to Angel: Toward the Divine Plan and Heaven on Earth*, as a strong spiritual force that can exist between two, three, or more individuals or collectives, influencing each member involved in the union regardless of time and space.

In 1858, Herman Melville declared, "We Americans are the peculiar, chosen people, the Israel of our time; we bear the ark of the liberties of the world... We are the pioneers of the world; the advance guard sent on through the wilderness of untried things to break a new path in the New World that is ours."

By the end of the nineteenth century, America's mission justified imperial expansion beyond the North American continent.

Since 1954, we have pledged that we are "one nation under God," echoing the Puritans' self-identification as God's new Israel and the special status that may imply.

On the first anniversary of the September 11, 2001 attacks, George W. Bush spoke of "the ideal of America" as "the light" that "shines in the darkness," identifying the United States as the chosen people destined to usher in the Messianic Age.

Before his first inauguration as the US president, Abraham Lincoln characterized the United States as the Almighty's "almost chosen people."

Yet the United States of America has been busy contributing to the Realm of Disunion through a sophisticated disunion structure that is now a pyramid, with the elites at the top, their advisors beneath them, and their compradors spread out beneath, all the way down to the victims.

I believe this book, in many volumes, is here not only to let us know that it is time to start coming together to heal ourselves, personally and collectively, but also to guide us on what to do when we do come together.

The bottom line is to stay positive and be thankful for all that has happened, including the entire system, subsystems, and projects God has proposed in *And God Said to Angel: How to Transform Collectively* as the key to Heaven's Door. I don't know about you, but I feel blessed and grateful.

It's time to learn and honor God's way, and to try to follow it rather than push and pull to get things done according to man's ways, which can drain energy and lead to other forms of disunion.

The next chapter provides a further explanation of why God's way is always better than man's way.

GOD'S WAY VS. MAN'S WAYS

We are told that in the Garden of Eden, we decided to live our lives according to "man's way" through the ego rather than "God's way" through the Divine Self, which is a part of God with infinite wisdom to know what to do.

These two distinct paths in life have been available to humanity ever since the beginning of time.

The first path follows God's way. It lets us learn how to witness the Divine Logos and interact with it in such a manner that we can become our Divine Selves and keep our connection with everything and everyone through God, according to His will and plan for us, so that we can each write our story as a co-creator of the ultimate story of God.

The second path follows man's way. It lets us live our lives independent of God, making our own stories without His help or participation.

Yesterday, I was talking to a follower of a spiritual guru. She said, "We have had misery in the past, and we shall have misery in the future. That is life!" I asked, "Why not try to do better?" She answered, "It's all God's doing, so why not leave it all up to Him?"

Just a few minutes earlier, this woman had intentionally given me the wrong advice on how to get something done. It was interesting to hear her now rationalize her disunion thoughts, words, and actions and put the blame on God. When we follow God or let God manage something for us, we must always do so in a union, not a disunion manner!

Her statement, along with all statements and explanations about spirituality, relates to the two approaches we may take in life. Man's way or approach in life versus God's way or approach in life.

We're told that Jesus Christ lived his life aligned with the first path, becoming the Logos (the WORD) in the flesh, and that no one else has lived fully on the first path as Jesus did. Most of us know how to align with the second path. We live our lives through our egos, while Jesus lived his life through his Divine Self.

Surely, living our lives through our egos has kept us in the Age of Disunion. Unfortunately, most people who try to follow Jesus' way and enter the Realm of Union don't stay there long enough to gain the pure energy to remain in this awesome realm for good. As they enter the Realm of Union, they get confused and promote the Realm of Disunion, which then takes them out of the Realm of Union.

Such people often rationalize that it's okay to sin because, no matter what, Jesus will save them, but in the meantime, they end up promoting the Realm of Disunion that can keep them in Hell rather than let them be in Heaven, which is the Realm of Union. That can naturally be very damaging to everyone and humanity.

The truth is that we can reach heaven while we're still alive. We don't have to wait until we die to reach heaven. This misunderstanding has caused people to suffer, surely wasting many lives. There is no question that it is possible to merge God's wish to be known with our wish to be in heaven, and that this has been the Divine Plan for humanity ever since the beginning of our spiritual journey.

I think we have misunderstood the meaning of it all. The reason for Jesus to be among us, as the Father, the Son, and the Holy Spirit, and the significance of his sacrifice and its miraculous power to heal us and show us the way to the Father and His Realm of Union through Jesus.

If what we've been told about Jesus and his story is true, then it means, through Jesus Christ, which is the same as saying through the Divine Eye, each of us can witness the Divine Logos, in other words, live our Divine Tale, one hundred percent, to become the Divine Logos in the flesh, and reach eternal salvation.

With the balance of oneness and uniqueness that dominates the Divine Logos, it doesn't matter how fragmented the whole is, for each fragment is in balance with the whole. That means the totality is present in the parts. That is a quality that exists throughout the universe of God, where we can perceive the ultimate order, in other words, the totality, from the pieces. Of course, today, very few can do that!

Those who can do it have an upper hand. The disunion people realize this and try to use this technique themselves while preventing others from doing it. For instance, they try to leave things disintegrated to keep others from seeing the whole, while they keep track of the different fragments so that they can see the whole, not because they're balanced, but because they're the wrongdoers who let each other know what they're doing wrong while deceiving others.

That, of course, gives them certain advantages that belong to the Realm of Disunion. But, at the same time, it can be dangerous, horribly dangerous, for they are positioned on the borderline of the Realm of Disunion. We should be careful not to go to a future so destructive to humanity that we may not be able to get out of the chaos!

As we approach the Messianic Age, which can be defined as a point in the space-time continuum, when a new spiritual path opens for humanity to transition from disunion to union, we will hopefully begin to learn this first approach, where we will walk with God on His Path for us, first personally and then collectively.

Some people will know how to do this better than others. For instance, those Jews who have learned how to keep the Sabbath holy are familiar with this to some extent; or those Muslims, who have learned to follow the Divine Will; or those Christians who have learned to go through Jesus to reach the Father; or those Buddhists, who have learned how to stay on the path of enlightenment.

However, for most of us, it's probably going to be our first time learning to take God's approach to life, where we witness and interact with the Logos personally and then together, collectively. And remember that anyone can do this. For instance, two partners can take the time to do this, and as they learn it, they can try it with their children, other family members, or friends.

If every person or group would record the Word, the Logos, Master Story, His Story, daily, and try to share it, perhaps pass it down truthfully, then it would allow us to view our collective humanity as an entity.

This recording will give us an accurate view of the Master Story, helping us know ourselves and see the Divine hand in humanity's destiny. Over time, people will be able to stand in Truth, witness the Logos, and learn how to interact with it, rather than be blind in a forest trying to find something a mile away.

As members of a collective strive toward the Realm of Union, they seek to benefit humanity, creating an open structure where all interested parties can participate to determine where everything truly stands, discuss issues at hand, and explore possibilities that would bring a better life for everyone. Humanity is destined to take this journey, if not in the past, due to the Age of Disunion, then someday in the future, hopefully soon.

The opposite of this path is what we have today, which has lasted for a few millenniums, where every collective is moving toward the Realm of Disunion, influencing its members to benefit the few.

That naturally adds up to our many myths filled with falsehoods. It drains everyone, for they now require exclusivity that demands: 1) secrecy because the less the opponent knows, the easier to take advantage of him or her; 2) control to safeguard the myths so that it is possible to continue to lie, deceit, cabal, or do whatever else to manipulate events and/or people, all done to benefit the few that is oneself and or one's collective rather than humanity as a whole.

Please note that when the overall intention is to benefit all, then there is no need for secrecy and or control.

But, so far, we've allowed the Realm of Disunion to grow in secrecy, employing more and more disunion attributes and techniques to achieve different goals that had to be kept hidden from the public, mostly to satisfy proactive history (according to man's approach), not God's approach or story. Many compradors who participated in such efforts became nonchalant, sometimes abusive, and often grabbed more money for themselves while strategizing on how to build a structure that would protect them and their goals. That naturally led to the current shadow government, which exists solely to reward those willing to support its structure.

After a while, we became so blinded by all the fragmentation and secrecy of the Realm of Disunion that we began to overlook future possibilities and potentialities! Most of us have forgotten about the Almighty God.

Looking back, the managers of the planet and their advisors may have had to wing it all since they had to depend on their compradors to get the job done. And most of the compradors who rose to the top became selfish, working for themselves and a few friends and family members rather than the actual plan, about which they often knew little.

In addition, some people at the top continued to rationalize that they had to keep people down and uninformed to manage them, which forced many to struggle in various conflicts within the Realm of Disunion, some of which were created by the rulers themselves. As time passed and the Realm of Disunion grew stronger, people just didn't have the time or energy to figure things out amid the escalating lies, deceptions, and secrecy.

But truly, we can no longer afford the Realm of Disunion, and so we need to get together and build a new union structure on the planet that promotes the Realm of Union. That follows God's approach.

The principles favored by the West are completely incompatible with what God's nature intends for humankind. The clash between ideals and reality has given rise to ever-increasing manifestations of the wickedness of the Realm of Disunion in Western life, affecting many societies worldwide.

Today, it is evident that the Western Judeo-Christian culture suffers from guilt because they know deep inside that they're far away from the teachings of their founders, and thus, not true Jews or Christians, following the "religion of love" as they claim and have been directed to do. The same can be said of most religions of the world: each religion is unique in its development, yet, overall, they lean toward the Realm of Disunion. Very few have remained pure enough to allow for the Divine manifestations among us.

The Western establishment has been terrorizing many countries around the world, often employing disunion attributes and techniques and taking from them their valuable resources. They have learned to incorporate many disunion tactics to achieve their goals, in which principles are made to benefit the few rather than the whole of humanity, but presented in the name of God and democracy.

Now that we have been given this book, we must take advantage of it and do our best to move toward the Divine Plan for us, because He plans to take us to the Realm of Union.

We should not let the Realm of Disunion and its people screw up our Divine destiny to reach the Realm of Union. God did show us how to attain individual salvation through Christ, and we will attain collective salvation through Christ when he returns the second time during the Messianic Age.

Let's talk about our personal and collective transformations and what they mean concerning our closeness to God and His way.

Individual salvation means we try to live in the Realm of Union with God, where disunion cannot exist, as we witness His Logos and interact with it properly to interface with people's Divine Selves rather than their egos while also watching people's egos dealing with their struggles caused by their egos remaining separated from their Divine selves, each Divine Self a part of God.

Collective salvation means we all learn to do this by collectively witnessing while interacting with His Logos, thereby dissolving the Realm of Disunion and all its conflicts and struggles.

Thus, to get to our salvation collectively requires the following tasks:

1. Every person and collective is to learn about union and disunion, how to differentiate between the two, and to employ union solely to

get closer to God and His realm, so that we can gain more knowledge about Him and His realm.

2. How to unite to share our disunion experiences so that we may finally see the many faces of evil, as we categorize them, understand each version, and learn to transform it from disunion to union, always through God, employing union attributes.

3. How to develop tools to use as an extension of humanity to transform disunion into union and keep on doing this until the Realm of Disunion is dissolved, always through God.

Studying these three areas, it is evident that we couldn't have completed tasks #2 and #3 until today, when we have the proper tools to do these two steps together. Now that we know the importance of these tasks and how to do them, we must get busy, collectively sharing and working together simultaneously to accomplish these and other tasks necessary to transition us from the Realm of Disunion to the Realm of Union.

But this hasn't been the only option available to us. We could have taken "God's approach," or path #1. In this first approach, it is possible to maintain a continual connection with everything and everyone through God, and to stay with God in His Realm of Union as we continue following His will, His way, and His methodologies that always employ union and never disunion to manage things!

Of course, the second approach, path #2, can take longer, requiring tasks #1, #2, and #3, slowly but surely, with the possibility of annihilation of humanity and/or destruction of Mother Earth, but also the possibility of success to reach the Realm of Union through our transition from disunion to union, as we follow this "man's approach."

My ex-husband, Duane, who is an atheist and incapable of believing in God, has often heard me talk about this book, but he has never read it. Yesterday, as he saw me struggling with *And God Said to Angel: How to Transform Personally,* to keep it from getting too long, he said, "Don't worry if this section gets too long. Just let it all come to you, as you've done in the past. What's important is to provide the best explanation possible for the most critical issue of all time."

I asked, "What is that?" He said, "If what you're saying is true, then humanity requires an apology from God the Almighty for letting the Realm of Disunion hang around and spread to bring the Age of Disunion."

As we began talking about it, I realized I had reached a dead end, with no answer to the most important question: "**Why has God allowed us to fall and suffer for so long?**" I prayed about it, and a day later, lo and behold, I received a few insights that may clarify things to some extent, and perhaps provide a partial answer.

I believe God has been with us all along, helping us reach a higher level of spirituality if we so desire.

But then, our mentalities aligned with the Realm of Disunion have kept us from attaining a greater perception.

Now that we're going to learn about the Realm of Union versus Disunion, it is time to recognize the many ways the disunion structure has kept us from seeing the Realm of Union.

Later in this volume, I will try to give some examples in the conclusion to show how the Realm of Disunion has often sought to draw us away from the Realm of Union.

So, here, let me just give a simple example.

Suppose in the Realm of Union, two qualities go together, like love and goodness. The Realm of Disunion then presents these two qualities in a way that can confuse people. Like showing someone who is always praying to look ill rather than shine, or showing a baby as evil rather than pure, always projecting things as their opposites.

Another example is when the elites and their advisors combine two concepts that do not belong together, like communism and atheism, to jeopardize humanity's potential to build true communities in the future.

Today, we can see such a disunion mismatch everywhere. For instance, in children's videos on YouTube, you can see people saying things like, "I love you and hate you at the same time," or girls fighting over a boy, or kids trying to deceive other kids to the point of hurting them and laughing about it. These are small stuff. When it comes to the drainage of bigger people and humanity, it can get complicated and nasty. The nastier it gets, the more people want to watch it. For many, it has gotten addictive, which is exactly what the Realm of Disunion wants.

In *And God Said to Angel: How to Transform Collectively,* I talk about the way the disunion structure uses many techniques to divide, confuse, and drain people. Hollywood and social media are filled with such examples. The disunion structure loves to support such avenues of hatred, division, and confusion. But then, this is the nature of the Realm of Disunion. And we cannot stop it unless we empower the Realm of Union, which each person or collective can do and must begin to do! Otherwise, we're all going to be in trouble!

My ex-husband's statement that God must apologize for allowing the Realm of Disunion to grow and make us suffer for such a long time opens up two options before us: 1) where we accept God's failure in letting us build a structure on the planet that is detrimental to humanity; or 2) where we don't accept it, because we realize that such an option is flawed and thus cannot possibly exist. After all, God dislikes disunion and never wants such a horrible disunion path for humankind.

The Story of God, the myth we create about Him, should align with Him and His Realm of Union, where He dwells, and truth resides to set us free. It shouldn't define God from a disunion viewpoint to allow a few to rule the many in a disunion structure that tends to promote disunion until its peak, almost its threshold, risking humanity's life. God will never build a structure that is aligned with the Realm of Disunion! He just wouldn't do that.

So, to answer the great question, "Why has God allowed us to go through the Age of Disunion?" we must try to look at it from a new angle. We must try to answer it from a Realm of Union perspective.

Our history demonstrates that God sent His messengers to guide us. They tried to show us the Realm of Union Story, but some elites and their compradors changed every such story to keep us in the dark so that we wouldn't get to the Realm of Union.

But then, again, why has God allowed the elites and their compradors to take us deeper and deeper into darkness? To tell us myths that would strengthen the Realm of Disunion? Perhaps because we chose the disunion route a long time ago, and we still do, and God has no wish to interfere with our wish to continue plugging away in the Realm of Disunion. Surely, all this has been our decision, not His. And, since we chose this path that formed the Age of Disunion, then we must now let it end naturally so that the Age of Transformation could unfold naturally to bring its fruits to the Realm of Union.

As I tried to explain all this to my ex-husband, he said, "Why don't you take a break and we watch Rian Johnson's film, 'The Brothers Bloom.'" I asked, "Why? Is it going to help me out?" He answered, "I don't know. I haven't seen it." Since I was tired and needed a break, I said, "Okay."

In this film, we're told that the perfect con is one in which everybody gets what they want, including the person who is conned.

The movie shows two brothers who grow up learning how to con people. The older brother, Stephen (Mark Ruffalo), is the mastermind, while the younger brother (Adrien Brody) follows. In Stephen's diabolically complex plots, he is often the only player who knows what is real and unreal. The younger brother, Bloom, is tired of playing games and wants to live a normal life where he can write his own story.

For Stephen, life is a con, and he's living it. For Bloom, the game is getting old.

The brothers meet a promising mark named Penelope (Rachel Weisz), who is rich, beautiful, and lonely. Stephen convinces Bloom to pull one final con, targeting Penelope for $1 million. The con game fails to play out as planned when Bloom falls in love with the irresistible Penelope.

The guessing games continue until the end of the film, when the older brother dies to free the younger brother from a written story. In other words, the younger brother can now write his own story to live life as he pleases with the love of his life.

At the end of the film, as I wondered why I had to watch it, I realized the similarities between this story and the human story. In humanity's story (our history), we left God (even allowed Him to die for us) so we could write our own story. We took the second approach, the second path. But we could have taken the first approach, the first path.

If humanity had remained on path #1 from the beginning, we would have stayed with God and let Him create the Logos (that part of the Logos belonging to each person), as we followed Him to become the Logos in the flesh, which Christ came to show us how to do. Now that we've taken the second path and learned how to do it, we must let it take its course as we try to learn more about the first path.

In the film, we're shown the Ace of Spades as the mark that trumps all other cards. I researched this and found: 1) it has been a symbol of good luck for hundreds of years; 2) it means unity, which is a noble quality; 3) it counts highest in the game of cards, outranking the king; and finally, 4) it refers to the soul's spiritual journey of sacrifice, not as punishment, but to forgo the need for adulation to acquire victory over the self, in other words, the ego.

This Ace of Spades reminded me of *And God Said to Angel: Toward the Divine Plan and Heaven on Earth,* showing us how the English, with the help of the Jews and the Persians, succeeded in shaping the twentieth century through proactive history to manage the growth of the Age of Disunion while safeguarding humanity and keeping the stability of the planet. Without it, anything could have happened, including the destruction of humanity.

Looking back, proactive history kept us all alive while it prepared us for our transition from disunion to union someday in the future. Through proactive history, the managers of the planet were able to facilitate: 1) the use of Iranian oil to fund and expedite the growth of the twentieth century; and 2) the Jews' return to their homeland, Israel; both of which can be beneficial to humanity's spiritual growth.

Some may object and say that we can't consider the Jews as one group wishing to return to Israel. Many Jews have declared this to be inaccurate, saying that they are against the Zionist movement and that many Zionists are not even Jews.

But, looking at the situation from a union viewpoint, it is clear that such a belief, "for the Jews to return to their homeland," became a part of the Jewish culture and identity, not only because of the Zionist movement but also certain events that had to occur to keep the stability of the planet, over the years, ever since the time of Cyrus the Great, toward the development of Western civilization and culture that has continually promoted the Realm of Disunion.

Fortunately, it appears that, as part of this disunion growth and our spiritual journey, we've been able to see the many faces of evil and create certain tools that we can now use to help us strengthen the Realm of Union to dissolve the Realm of Disunion, which means our transition from the Realm of Disunion to Union!

Surely, this is a miracle!

Hence, humanity must go through this spiritual journey to reach maturity, first personally and then collectively. That is a conversion process through which we will learn new things, new insights, and new techniques to live on the Divine Path of Infinity and use the Divine approach in life to transform disunion into union.

All this will show that we don't have to continue the Age of Disunion. We can work together to end it, but we've got to do it naturally. Later in this volume, the Chapter, *Union vs. Disunion Thresholds*, will explain this further.

For the Lord to fulfill His purpose and promise for us, both individually and collectively, we must take the time to:

1. Establish different methods of learning through which we may teach each other the differences between the Realm of Union and Disunion, and how to discern one from the other.

2. Strengthen the Realm of Union in and around us so that the Realm of Disunion can no longer touch us and live off us, thus gradually transforming every disunion into union through Divine guidance.

3. Identify the many faces of evil that can cause imbalances throughout our global society, and do our best never to let such imbalances take us away from the Divine Promise of the Realm of Union for us.

4. Take the union path toward our spiritual enlightenment, where we can become our Divine Selves free from all disunion, because as soon as any disunion tries to enter our domain, it is dissolved by the Divine presence and His power of the Realm of Union.

5. Safeguard our progress so we always move toward the Realm of Union. Later, in this volume, I will try to explain this further by providing some examples of how to balance everything in our global society.

6. Keep working together as a united front of union people who continue to do whatever it takes to improve humanity's health and balance to reach the Realm of Union.

As I said earlier, perception is the key, so we must first understand it and then expand it, while remembering that God loves us all unconditionally, for He has stood by us, always wishing to help us and never to harm us.

Fortunately, the Age of Disunion is destined to end soon, making way for the Age of Transformation. And God is now telling us to go to Him for guidance so that we can become whole again to experience the Realm of Union through our Divine Selves in all its glory! Alleluia!

No matter what pain and suffering we may have endured in the past, we must now try to stay positive, as negativity can pile up and drain our energy. So, it's best to obtain pure energy daily. The more energy we have in our bodies and around us, the easier it is for us to transition from the Realm of Disunion to the Realm of Union.

All this should be the foundation of our spiritual journey toward personal and collective transformation.

Here is a story that relates to this transformation.

A few years ago, I went to a spiritual retreat in Florida where a few hundred people had gathered to listen to a spiritual teacher. It lasted for six days, mostly in the afternoons, with time for meditation, dinner, and sitting together to ask the teacher questions.

In one of the Q&A sessions, after about three days, a man and his girlfriend showed up. He was huge, and his woman was also big, both Italian-looking. So far, the teacher had talked about individual transformation but not much about collective transformation.

So, I asked, "Shouldn't we try to transform both individually and collectively?"

As I began expressing my thoughts about the importance of collective transformation, which took less than a minute or so, the huge Italian-looking guy turned to me and loudly said, "We are not here to listen to you! So, why don't you just shut the hell up?" Many had shared their thoughts, some taking more than 3 minutes, and no one had been attacked this way! And I had tried to share my thoughts in the same manner, very peacefully, with no confrontation whatsoever, yet this man addressed me so rudely, and no one objected!

The teacher stayed quiet the whole time and later patted the big guy on his shoulder for a job well done! After that, I remained silent and even apologized to the teacher and the bully!

The reason I'm telling you this story is to give you an example of how the bully and other people in the gathering assumed that it was me expressing my ideas when it was the 'I Am' that is my Divine Self talking! So, in effect, the bully told the 'I Am' to shut the hell up, going against the event's teachings.

The funny thing is that I was showing everybody, unconsciously, how to communicate through 'I Am,' and no one realized it and thus allowed it to happen, which went totally against what the teacher was expressing at the time. It didn't bother me, for I was the 'I Am,' not my ego.

In such a state, where one is employing union attributes, not disunion, it can be a terrific opportunity to interface with the 'I Am' and learn from it.

Unfortunately, the bullying didn't give 'I Am' a chance to come out and explain why it's important for us to transform collectively.

So, once more, the reason we must care for our collective transformation is that if we don't, we may end up in a society so infected with evil that we may not even be allowed to practice spirituality, which can be defined as the freedom to live our lives according to our Divine Selves, the 'I Am' that is a part of the 'I Am Who I Am.'

It's time to free ourselves from all disunion so that we can witness the Divine Logos that can be potentially filled with billions of Divine Selves (each a balanced 'I Am'). That can make it easier for every Divine Self to come forward and speak out, helping us better understand things, since each Divine Self is more connected to the source. Wouldn't that be better than having a bunch of zombies and/or lopsided, unbalanced people walking among us and having no idea what's going on?

The empowerment of a person's 'I Am' rather than their 'ego' can be the first step toward collective transformation.

I know it's not easy to continually employ good thoughts, good words, and good deeds in and around us, but we must each try to do that. That is the way to get the Divine Light, His pure energy that can transform every cell in our body. When we are filled with the Divine Light, our intuition heightens, enabling us to recognize every trick and deception of the Realm of Disunion and to decrease its influence upon us, so that we can free ourselves to explore life and its many miracles.

Today, with the Divine Guidance and the many insights provided in this book in many volumes, it may be time to learn how to follow the Spiritual Formula to accumulate enough pure energy in and around us to transition humanity from the Realm of Disunion to the Realm of Union.

It is then that we can become our Divine Selves capable of witnessing and interacting with the eternal now, the Divine Logos, personally and collectively.

So far, most of us have learned how to live through our egos rather than our Divine Selves.

Living through our egos does not allow us to stand in the State of Truth. Like brother Bloom, we have no idea what's going on. Who is playing and who is for real? It's so awful to live in such an environment where we cannot possibly know the truth! Who wants to continually decipher every person, every move, every event, every minute of the day to figure things out?! To make sure we're not part of a horrible game played upon us by a bunch of disunion morons. Such a life is not worth living. But then, who am I to say? Maybe many would give an arm or a leg to live in any life, no matter how limited and/or insane.

We're rapidly approaching the end of man's way, that is, approach #2, path #2.

The question is: Would you rather take God's approach and be with Him in His Truth and see everything for what it is, or take man's approach, where it is not possible to trust the disunion structure and people? Surely, man's way won't be as good as God's way, where we can fully trust Him.

It's time to learn how to take path #1, which is God's way. It may take some time, with ups and downs, but not having to deal with disunion lies, deceptions, and mis/disinformation should make it easier for us, not harder, especially since we will be filled with the Divine Light, His pure energy.

My ex-husband asked me to describe God's way. But there is no way to describe path #1, because every person's path is unique, customized for the person at a "one of a kind" moment in the space-time continuum. The moment is matchless. There can be nothing like it in the whole cosmos. The person can live it, see it, and then share it with others so that, together, we can learn about it, categorize it, and define it to some extent, so that we can know it as a possibility that may have happened but will never happen the same way.

We can always record such moments and keep on recording, like an open book of insights into Divine Reality. Not like the Bible or other holy books described and interpreted in many versions, where each version remains constant and often misinterpreted and misunderstood to keep us in the Realm of Disunion. But an open book that stays in the Realm of Union and gradually lets us get to know God and the true interpretation of His words. And, through this process, humankind reaches Heaven on Earth, an infinite path full of wonders and miracles.

If we were to wait for the Messiah to come and do everything for us rather than take the initiative ourselves, then the Messianic Age may not gain the momentum that is necessary for its arrival.

Also, when the Messiah comes, we need to be prepared to help him out. We need to be knowledgeable about our global environment and what it may take to aid the Messiah in ushering in the Messianic Age.

We need to understand that God gives to the just and the unjust, but the unjust rejects His gift due to a lack of knowledge of the invisible world (including the Realm of Union versus the Realm of Disunion). Such knowledge will, of course, help us understand how the Kairos works.

Kairos means the ability to align with God in such a way that everything comes together perfectly to open the right, critical, opportune time and place for action.

When we align with God, we realize: 1) we can stay with Him in His presence permanently through spontaneity and purity and that we really should try to do that rather than push and pull to control things; 2) we can become fully conscious of the moment being the right, critical, and opportune time for us to act upon what God has already arranged for us; and 3) we require the awareness and responsibility to aid the situation and what is about to transpire, so needing to acquire the necessary knowledge to know the timing of God and Man working together to make the moment right for action. It is then that we can witness the Logos, recognize Kairos, and fully profit from it.

Jesus said, "When Kairos is fulfilled, then the kingdom of God is at hand."

In history, we have always had periods of crisis. In the end time, we're going to have another crisis. Every crisis usually creates an opportunity and, indeed, demands an existential decision, where humanity's knowledge of Kairos and how to handle it properly can become crucial for seizing the moment and fully benefiting from it. The second coming of Christ may be an example.

When we can "witness the Divine Logos," we're in tune with God and prepared to interact with Kairos to allow God's miracles. We're continually conscious and aware of the qualities of every moment. We become experts at turning every disunion into union, so there is no way to take away from the moment, the Kairos. And, we have the knowledge, tools, and expertise to be with God and follow Him in each moment, serving Him and letting Him act through us.

Of course, this may take some practice, but maybe not. I've seen some people get the hang of it much faster than others. For instance, it took me years to remember my dreams and use them as a tool, but my dearest friends in Switzerland (Elise, a Jewish woman from South Africa, and Erve, a Frenchman) were able to do it in a few weeks! The three of us even learned how to dream together. So, one never knows!

The key is to learn to witness the Divine Logos and gain the ability to interact with it, as it guides us, for God is manifesting throughout His creation and is available to every person.

However, due to the Age of Disunion and its darkness, most of us have not yet learned how to witness the Divine Logos and let it interact with us. But this Age of Disunion is now ending to allow for the Age of Transformation and its unfolding.

There is a kabbalistic tradition that the seven days of the week are based upon the seven days of creation. It teaches that the seventh day of the week, the Sabbath day of rest, corresponds to the seventh millennium, the age of universal rest, which is the messianic era.

The Jews believe that the year 6000 is the latest time the Messiah shall come to begin the Messianic Age.

The reason for the Shabbat, whether on a personal or collective level, is for the Jews to try to keep everything holy, at least for some time, to bring about the Divine presence. On a personal level, this period lasts for one day and takes place at the person's home. On a collective level, naturally, it is a longer time and a greater space.

Of course, this is not that easy to do, and so many may fail, but the thought of wishing to make a day holy for God surely pleases Him, and now and then, people do get to see His sparks. The goal is to get closer to the Realm of Union, where every day can become a Shabbat!

Also, learning how to keep at least one day a week holy will most likely help the Jews to try to bring the same holiness to Jerusalem so that it can hopefully become the City of God as it is meant to be at the end of the Age of Disunion and the beginning of the Age of Transformation.

Let me just mention a few things about the importance of Shabbat as it relates to God's Plan.

God blessed the seventh day and sanctified it, because on the seventh day, God rested from all His work, which He created and made.

God's rest was a purposeful stop. He looked at His creation. He declared it to be "very good." So, He ceased His activity. That tells us that God was active until He was done, and then a period of rest followed for contemplation.

Since man is created in the image of God, we must also be active, then rest and contemplate what we have done. This period of rest is important for man because it is a time of contemplation, when we try to synchronize with God; in other words, we make sure we are in alignment with Him through prayer and holiness, as is done on the

Sabbath. This way, we can witness the Divine Reality, His Logos, and let it interact with us, guiding us to come to the next period of acting together with Him, according to His will for us.

Here, Kairos brings everything together to open the right, critical, opportune time and place for action.

We align with God by empowering the following:

1. We stay with Him in awe and humility in His presence, recognizing certain attributes we must gain and keep (as the Jews have tried to do on the Sabbath), rather than push and pull to control things.

2. We become fully conscious of the moment as the right, critical, and opportune time to act on what God has already arranged for us.

3. We gain awareness and responsibility to aid the situation and what is about to happen, thus coming to know and understand the timing of God and Man working together to make the moment right for creation. It is then that we witness the Logos, recognize Kairos, and fully profit from it.

So, by activating the Kairos, we allow for the Divine Logos to interact with us. That is a crucial area of exploration. It's like playing the piano. The more we do it, the better we get at it. So, practice is the key!

Truly, it is now time to recall that God would rather be with us as we go on living our lives to fulfill our Divine destiny. Every religion has directed us toward the Divine way rather than man's way.

Judaism has directed Jews to perform the required mitzvot to achieve holiness and spirituality. Christianity has emphasized love. The love between man and God and the love between a man and his fellowman together form the cross. Islam has guided every Muslim to submit to the Divine will and plan for us.

Jesus made it clear, showing us how to do this by becoming the Divine Self that is the Logos in the flesh. That has enabled us to align ourselves with Jesus and His goodness, being purified in an instant. That's why we've been told that it is possible to reach redemption through Jesus Christ. But, for this to last, on a personal level, we must do our best to stay in the Realm of Union, where we can continually obtain the Divine Light and Love to lead us to God and His way and keep us with Him in the Realm of Union for good.

However, at the collective level, the Realm of Union requires the participation of all citizens and stakeholders. The reason is that evil forces can affect each person differently. We each need to share this information to help us see the many faces of evil and come up with ways to minimize its influence upon us. In our battle against the Realm of Disunion, there is no other way but the "We the People" way! Together, we will succeed because every person is a part of the solution, with a unique role to play in our planetary destiny. Our primary objective should always be to transition all of us, without hatred or rancor, from the Realm of Disunion to Union.

What we need is a system that would always let us know humanity's problems, understand them, and contribute to their resolution if we so desire.

In *And God Said to Angel: How to Transform Collectively*, I have dedicated a few chapters to describing a system in which we each can participate in the areas we most desire and are best suited for. This approach will reduce implementation costs and increase each person's contribution to the whole Realm of Union structure. Besides, this process would make people much happier than today, when they are often dissatisfied with how things are developing but unable to make a difference.

As we make the necessary changes, both personally, as it is explained in *And God Said to Angel: How to Transform Personally*, and collectively as it is shown in *And God Said to Angel: How to Transform Collectively,* we will discover that every person, having a piece of the solution, will be motivated to come up with new ideas toward a Realm of Union structure that is tailored to bring improvements for all, not just for him or herself or a few groups or collectives.

Life feeds life as the cycle of change for the better continues. Humanity is strong when united. Given a chance, we can together surmount mountains of obstacles. What seems unattainable right now would become possible.

I feel we need an overall framework, a structure, to which we could each contribute. As the Realm of Union structure develops, I'm sure people will bring more details, each person in their own area of expertise.

This book tells us how things should be in the Realm of Union, and together we can decide whether a project follows the union principles. If so, then we include the project as one to develop and monitor its growth. If not, we leave it aside for a later examination.

We must understand that even though God has given us free will, we cannot go against the Divine Creation when everything in the universe coexists in harmony. We are not alone. We need to acknowledge our interconnectedness and interdependency and reconnect with our Creator and His creation, each in our own way.

Some may wish to remember Him, and some may wish to forget Him. Both options are okay if we all work toward a life in harmony with the Realm of Union. Remember that God the Almighty dwells in the Realm of Union, so when we finally get there, we will naturally be with Him.

Throughout history, we have been warned to follow God rather than Gold! For our atheist friends, one could say, to follow the Realm of Union rather than Disunion. Not that the use of money promotes the Realm of Disunion, but the misuse of it does, like telling lies to confuse others, so that it is easier to deceive and abuse them, all to take from them toward the benefit of oneself or one's group.

If we don't follow the Realm of Union, where there is a balance of oneness and uniqueness, then selfishness naturally grows, causing us to misuse money. The situation has become crucial. If we want humanity to survive, we must begin to cherish the Realm of Union above our selfish materialistic desires.

Some have asked, "Why now?"

The reason is that we had to grow up first and experience the Realm of Disunion until its peak so that we may learn from it.

We had to gain the maturity to gradually become aware of the many faces of evil and its possibilities of destruction. We will soon get there, especially since the disunion influence has grown worldwide, bringing greater manifestations of evil and its many faces that we can talk about, analyze, and gradually diminish to a point of no return. Total elimination! But, in the meantime, I'm sure most of us have become tired of it!

Second, we had to develop the necessary tools to employ as an extension of humanity to put an end to evil. We now have all kinds of digital gadgets, like cell phones, computers, tablets, audio and video recorders, telecommunications, voice and pattern recognition, natural language translation, the Internet, artificial intelligence, and other tools to use to finally see evil, indeed its many faces, and how it has drained us all to keep us away from our oneness, our connectivity, and our uniqueness, our diversity, and the balance between the two.

Third, we had to wait for the right time when God would bring everything together to begin the age of enlightenment for humanity. The End Time of the Realm of Disunion drainage and sufferings. The beginning of the Realm of Union, the Kingdom of God, and its establishment on Earth. Only the Divine can decide at the right time. The End Time. So, we've been waiting for His decision, approval, and guidance.

I believe this book is here not only to let us know it is time to start coming together, but also to guide us on what to do when we do. However, even though I am almost 100% convinced that this book is from God, we must realize that, right now, it is not possible to know for sure.

The only way we are going to be certain is to go ahead and plant the seed of the Realm of Union, implement the projects detailed here, and watch the results for ourselves.

If this book is from Him, then we would know by the fruits. That's why I worked very hard to finish this book. That's why I feel the only option left for us is to act and observe the results. There is no other way. I hope you understand what I'm saying here.

It's like saying, "Love everyone. Love yourself. Love God. Love His creation. Love. Love. Love." How can this be bad or result in anything but goodness?!

In any event, let us not forget that there is pride, not a bad pride, but a good one, in such an accomplishment, a sense of purpose, and overall direction of our human effort toward a Realm of Union structure for all, which can be gradually built side by side with our current Realm of Disunion structure. A legacy of a life well-lived, left by each generation for the next.

What are the characteristics of such a mature social order? We can give an example as something to consider.

When we ask young people anywhere in the world what they plan to be when they grow up, what do they say? If they answer with confidence, then it means their environment is safe and balanced, that there is a future to be made and to contribute to, and that hope and opportunity are ever-present.

Today, unfortunately, this is not the case. Most children in the world have no answer to this question. They may instead give us a strange look, making us wonder if they understood the question.

Our poor children need a better future, filled with hope, clarity, beauty, and other attributes of the Realm of Union. Not a future of despair and other Realm of Disunion ugliness.

In the past, we often rationalized, and for good reason, that we need a common language, a common standard of measures, and the like, instruments that mirror our agreed intention to walk the path of maturity and unity. I believe the Realm of Union provides us with that language. The language of eternal love. Unconditional love. For all parts of the universe. All parts of humanity. The union of all things, including every true self, the Divine Self, which is waiting to be manifested in the image of God.

It is solely through this union that we can finally look at the whole Earth and begin to manage it appropriately as spiritually mature entities with the sole responsibility for its future. We are trustees in charge of a great endeavor; let's act like it. It is time to leave behind our childish ways!

We must unite and help each other reach the Realm of Union that can dissolve the Realm of Disunion. That is a goal we can all achieve by employing union attributes solely to get things done so that we may reach the Realm of Union. It is only in the Realm of Union that we can obtain the Divine Light and Love to dissolve the Realm of Disunion in and around us.

The next chapter discusses union versus disunion attributes and explains why we must enhance union qualities to dissolve disunion qualities.

UNION VS. *DISUNION* ATTRIBUTES

I had a dream last night where I was with an old boyfriend of mine, who was moaning and complaining that most women are not interested in sex, whereas a lot of men are desperate to have sex. He told me that it is often difficult to discuss sexuality without feeling awkward in today's society. It was a strange dream.

When I woke up, I realized how women often try to take advantage of this lopsidedness between men and women to get things out of men and how men often give up and do what women want. Of course, in this process, many women and men become actors, pretending to be this way and that way to get what they want, where most men want sex and women want goodies!

So, the two sexes don't get to know each other. They are too busy making the right impression to figure out what is happening.

Relationships between men and women can get screwed up. The feelings of love and sexuality, with the ego always expecting and resenting, and everything else does not let men and women relate to one another as human beings.

That is unfortunate, since it can result in a weak foundation for building a family, which is often based on the relationship between a woman and a man.

Furthermore, sexuality can be a great source of pure energy if it is done properly and if it is filled with love and other union attributes, as has been intended for us, always in union manners, never disunion.

Such imbalances and misalignments in the most basic unit of our global society can hurt humanity unless we take the time to understand them and discuss them in union ways that can dissolve our disunion shortcomings. Everything has been affected. A lot of people seem to be suffering from this disunion of separateness, either directly or indirectly. We don't see things as they truly are. We try to change things, often in disunion manners, where we are constantly screwing things up!

Unfortunately, many societies around the planet have no idea how to address this and similar imbalances, sometimes even adding to these deficiencies by promoting more disunion rather than union.

In general, most societies are so ignorant of the balance between oneness and uniqueness, and of the true definitions of success and failure in what we may do personally and/or collectively, that they tend to ignore or hide their shortcomings, sometimes even feeling shame.

They don't know the way to equilibrium, and the importance of balancing our disunion attributes and events with union attributes and events, where we try to transform everything from disunion into union through God and a deep understanding of concepts, many of which may have been defined inaccurately to confuse us and keep us in the Realm of Disunion.

Let me explain this and other disunion qualities; some of which may affect our personal growth, as explained in this chapter; some may influence our disunion threshold and some our union threshold, as explained in the next chapter; some may build up and shape our society, as explained in the chapter that follows the next; and some may impact the spiritual light in and around us, as explained in the Chapter, *Eternal Light vs. Darkness*.

Next, I wish to explore what it means to succeed or fail, not only personally but collectively.

SUCCESS VS. *FAILURE*

In the film It's a Wonderful Life, a penniless George Bailey dies, thinking that his whole life has been a failure. But then an angel comes and takes him back in time to show him that he had indeed succeeded in helping his friends and family to have a better life, saying to George, "Strange, isn't it, George? Each man's life touches so many other lives. When he isn't around, he leaves an awful hole, doesn't he?"

Anthropologist Margaret Mead said, "I must admit that I measure success in terms of the contributions an individual makes to her or his fellow human beings."

When we live in the Realm of Union, we do what we love and are inspired to do. We are not afraid to experiment with life. As we continue this course, of course, we get better and better at what we do. We end up, in a way, competing with our old selves every day, as our capabilities exceed those of the day before. We're all successful, no matter how much money we make or how high a position we attain.

In the Realm of Disunion, as the ego and its desires drive us, we often try to compete, and in the process, we may hurt others just to succeed. Competing, honestly, should not hurt anyone. It would be like having Mozart and Beethoven compete—each of them bringing us unique music that is part of the Divine Kingdom. Competing, dishonestly, keeps the Divine Plan from materializing, for we feel another person's success may be our failure.

In our Realm of Disunion world, many steal other people's work and benefit from it without properly acknowledging the originator or creator of the work. Most geniuses are surrounded by people trying to take advantage of them.

Remember the film *Amadeus*? Salieri cannot stand Mozart's genius. So, he devises a plot to poison Mozart. He succeeds in killing Mozart, taking his final work, and making it his own!

Our society must build a certain support structure to safeguard our talented individuals against such disunion attacks. Most of the time, this happens because the attackers have not found their unique talents through which they could manifest their creativity.

That is unfortunate because there are always reasons for something to happen in a certain way; for a certain individual or collective to be the creator, originator, or owner of an asset. By not allowing the Divine Logos to unfold naturally, we prevent the manifestations of God and His will for humanity from occurring as planned. That is an unholy act with consequences beyond our imagination. Our history is filled with comparable stories, all due to misunderstandings about the distinction between success and failure.

Heidi Wills said, "When you're confronted with a problem, don't get depressed, get excited, get involved. A problem is an opportunity to do something generous or positive for the world." In other words, take advantage of moments of conflict and try to practice your ability to transform people and/or events from disunion into union.

In my life, especially during the past fifteen years, ever since I became aware of the battle between the Realm of Disunion and Union, I have tried to take advantage of such times of conflict to bring resolution and transformation in ways that would heighten everyone's awareness and understanding of the Realm of Union, always democratically and harmoniously.

Of course, I have not always succeeded in my attempts to convert disunion into union, but each time, I found myself getting better at it as I let God manage it for me, watching and learning more about His ways.

Competition causes us to see people as obstacles, mere blocks to something we are trying to achieve or win, and this way of thinking is dehumanizing. Greatness comes from going at one's own pace and letting others do the same, not from forcing oneself to do better than others. As I said earlier, such acts can come from an imbalance of oneness and uniqueness, often caused by our inability to perceive totality, the wholeness of things.

When we see someone with a special gift, we should not envy them, for we are too small to fully comprehend the whole picture. We should respect the person and cherish their talents and capabilities as God's gift to humanity, to which we all belong. Believe me, if we would only look deep inside ourselves, we would find our unique gifts.

The same goes for a collective that may possess something special, like the Iranians, who have oil and wish to share it with the rest of the world, but are, in many ways, misunderstood and not allowed to do so properly.

First, the fact that Iran has so much oil may be due to the Iranians' union ways throughout history and to the country's accumulation of pure energy. The land's overall pure energy may have influenced Mother Earth to produce oil and other precious resources.

Second, we have disregarded such a possibility and, as a result, have done our best to hurt them rather than appreciate them and their union ways. We have not acknowledged their precious gift of oil to humanity, even killing half of their population in the early twentieth century to keep them too weak to stand up against the aggressions of the Western world and its exploitations. It's very sad!

We must learn to acknowledge people's contributions to humanity, whether they come from individuals, groups, or collectives. The key is to empower the Realm of Union, where we can truly respect one another and see each person's potential and actuality. That lets the individual's Divine Self feel comfortable enough with us to come out and greet us!

RESPECT VS. *DISRESPECT*

Every person and entity must be respected as part of the universe, which is a Realm of Union place and requires it. When we disrespect another human being, we often feel pride that we're perhaps better than our brothers and/or sisters. I have also seen many bring others down so that they may stand higher.

Going against this rule (or any other union attribute) can cause the spirit of God to depart.

Pride is a trap in the Realm of Disunion. And the only way out is to get rid of it through attributes of the Realm of Union, such as humility. That is the manner through which we may gain our true power that the Realm of Union supports.

We must let go of haughty opinions and behaviors. We must stop being so full of ourselves as to disregard others. When we pass judgment on someone else, we need to remind ourselves of the differences and variations as manifestations of God's Law of Uniqueness, rather than black-and-white, right-and-wrong, which can then lead us to the Realm of Disunion.

The respect that we gain through attributes of the Realm of Disunion—such as moving up and down the societal status ladder by controlling others or allowing ourselves to be controlled, or let's say, through public works or office, or recognition for our talents and/or gifts, or through shocking the world into respecting us—cannot belong to the Realm of Union. Such disunion acts are all rewards for earthly accomplishments to satisfy the ego.

In the Realm of Union, our heart leads us with joy and genuine interest, feeling gratitude for being alive and experiencing life and letting others do the same, always reminding ourselves that we must respect every person's right to be a human being, in the image of God, with the potential of becoming the logos in the flesh, in other words, the Divine Self. It is then that we can love others freely, care for the world unconditionally, and become like a magnet, attracting union attributes to ourselves.

Human arrogance or pride can never be a container for God's greater work. The universal plan dictates certain conditions. When a person, a group, or a structure lacks humility, employing the attributes of the Realm of Disunion and failing to keep in mind the powers of God and His Realm of Union, then they can no longer be guardians of God's plan, for they have dissociated themselves from its higher enfoldment. Only individuals, groups, collectives, and structures in the Realm of Union can participate in the Divine Plan and share in its blessings.

Pride can blind any person to witness the Divine Logos, where the Divine Light, the truth, resides. Logically, with greater pride, everything becomes more complex, requiring greater powers of the Realm of Disunion to maintain one's pride. That can apply to all disunion qualities, where the greater the disunion, the greater the complexity, keeping us from seeing things as they truly are.

We remain in the Realm of Disunion, resenting each other and creating more drainage that may bring our destruction or even extinction. We need to learn how to forgive and allow each other to exist through our

Divine Selves. We shouldn't let anything or anyone stop us from learning how to do this. How to make it easier for God to manifest through us, in other words, through our Divine Selves!

FORGIVE VS. *RESENT*

Studies show that people who can forgive are happier and healthier than those who hold resentment. They suffer less from anger, hurt, stress and a wide range of illnesses. They feel more compassion and self-confidence, are optimistic, and experience increased vitality.

The process of forgiveness is to balance the bad with the good. It is a transformation of a bad event into a good one, from disunion to union.

Thus, it requires the following:

1. We recognize and acknowledge the offense.
2. We commit not to repeat the offense.
3. We do whatever is necessary to rectify the offense.
4. We pray to God and hope that abusers are forgiven and transformed from disunion into union, remembering that the bullies and the victims both suffer because they cannot be in the Realm of Union.

It's easy to recognize the offense and pray for forgiveness (1 and 4 above). However, it is often difficult to commit not to repeat the offense or to do whatever is necessary to rectify it (2 and 3 above). Many are unwilling to do these last two, which are required to transform from disunion into union.

Their unwillingness to do two and/or three is because they wish to continue with their bullying and exploitation of others. Indeed, this habit may be extremely hard to break, especially since it has taken years for such people to learn the many techniques of the Realm of Disunion and the know-how to advance within it!

Often, such people have inherited the disunion existence from parents and/or grandparents, observing every aspect of it while growing up! They have learned how to promote the Realm of Disunion by trying: 1) to show union events as disunion when others try to promote the Realm of Union, or 2) to project disunion events as union when they are trying to promote the Realm of Disunion. So, the reverse of things!

In the first case, an offense may often get repeated due to misunderstandings, but sometimes done to drain another person, group, or collective. Let me give an example.

Once, I was at the UU Church when a man in his late sixties approached me and started a conversation. We soon learned that we both shared an interest in encryption. He had developed some algorithms he wanted to market, and I knew how to do so. So, we got together for over a week to see whether I could help him. Soon, it became apparent that his encryption algorithm could not be marketed as he had intended. However, during one of our meetings, I learned of his wish to relocate from Massachusetts to Lynchburg to be near his son and family. He asked for my help, and I agreed to assist him, not realizing at the time that it might later cause problems!

To make it short, I did a lot for this friend, but later found that his family not only did not appreciate my help or anything else I had done for him, but also considered it an intrusion.

Through this experience, I learned that people can make wrong assumptions and convert union events into disunion, either consciously or unconsciously, thereby promoting the Realm of Disunion. At the time, I was confused, not understanding the situation.

But afterward, I realized that it's best to explain to such people that they should stop their attempts to convert union acts into disunion, especially since one's intention has been to help, not to hurt! Such conversions have sometimes destroyed lives. So, we must be careful! It's best to investigate every situation and bring clarity to it to diminish any negative effects in the spiritual realm.

The second case happens often in politics, where politicians try to project a façade of union activity to the public while promoting the Realm of Disunion, thereby spreading falsehoods.

Of course, it may take a while to learn how to confront such people in a loving, union way, so that there is greater understanding and less strain for all involved.

This ability, like any other, can be acquired through lots of practice. And, I believe, every union person must try to learn it well to weaken the Realm of Disunion kindly. Because if it is not done right, it could create more negative feelings among participants, promoting the Realm of Disunion, which we do not need.

In the second case, the issue of rectifying an offense must be addressed on a case-by-case basis. Often, we face this issue because it may take away from our greed and future success, especially since people who have succeeded in the past through disunion means have often done so.

Such people don't know much about the Realm of Union and its great powers. If they knew, then they would be in the Realm of Union, and there wouldn't be so many disunion attributes in the world. They've become accustomed to taking from others by first damaging them while on their path to success. They don't want to give away what they've taken, and many times, it may not even be possible to do so. Yet it's crucial to study such disunion events and address each properly; otherwise, we will remain in the Realm of Disunion.

It's best to simplify concepts and agreements so everyone can understand them, as this can help remove the Realm of Disunion noise.

SILENCE VS. *NOISE*

The Persian poet, Shams Tabrizi, wrote, "Be silent that the Lord who gave thee language may speak." Only in silence can we hear our soul, our fellow men, God, and His creation.

When we are comfortable with ourselves, we are quiet. We don't need to be loud. People who make a lot of noise are looking for something outside themselves, usually to gain acknowledgment or to convince others. Unless the Realm of Union benefits from us talking, what's the use?

Life always teaches us silently while weak men utter their instructions in loud voices. Noise is often an attribute of the Realm of Disunion that keeps us from feeling the Divine Will. But sometimes, we do need to speak out against misrepresentations of the Realm of Disunion, which are often done in the Realm of Union clothing! Especially when the Divine wills it!

What if the Realm of Disunion causes the death of our child? Do we watch in silence, or do we make lots of noise? It's important to analyze the consequences of our shouting. Will it benefit the Realm of Union or not? If it does, then we shout, but if it does not, then we remain silent.

In today's Realm of Disunion, one of the best tools for generating a lot of noise and distracting people from feeling the visible and invisible worlds is television. By creating negative thoughts and visions on TV, daily, it is now possible to drain masses of people at once. When we watch television, we can observe energy drainage. People are watching too much of it, especially since we're now living in a disunion structure filled with falsehood and mind control techniques trying to brainwash people on a mass scale. It's nice to relax and watch television occasionally, but not all the time!

As the Realm of Disunion grows more aggressive, it will be natural for its establishment to install large TVs in public places. I've seen this happening in Europe, even in beautiful parks. Not that TVs are bad. But the misuse of television, like any other tool, belongs to the Realm of Disunion. In this case, people are forced to hear disunion advertisements and propaganda, sometimes brainwashing them and depriving them of the chance to listen to nature around them, which can often bring them Divine Guidance.

As we move toward the Realm of Union and its structure on the planet, TV can become a powerful tool to offer people insights and truth about each other and the forces here to promote the Realm of Union and Disunion.

We must have respect for humanity and never force people to listen to continuous noise generated by a humongous TV in the middle of a park, of all places!

These days, anywhere we go to wait for something to get done, we're forced to sit and listen to TV, often the Fox News Channel. Why not just let people rest in silence? If they like, they can bring their own entertainment (e.g., a smartphone or tablet).

We need to silence our minds and our environment at least half of the time. Otherwise, we may never get to hear our inner voice (with no sound), which may come to us with our instructions from the invisible world. It is through our instructions that we can discern the Divine Will and the many patterns unfolding before us.

Sometimes in a meeting, we can see one person talking the whole time and not letting others participate, as if they know and others don't, all because of ego. Such a meeting can often be a waste of time unless we try to learn from it, which is always possible. One way contributes to the Realm of Disunion, the other to the Realm of Union.

You need your space, your silence, and others need theirs. When you are afraid of it or uncomfortable with it, remember not to confuse it with isolation, which would further distance you from it. Welcome it as an opportunity for reflection and regeneration.

Too much noise can cause agitation and prevent us from staying calm. Agitation can cause accidents, which we don't need.

CALM VS. *AGITATED*

We can get filled with either pure or polluted energy, but never both. At any moment, the degree of our purity depends directly on the quality and quantity of the energy we have in our bodies.

Pure energy is eternal. It is Divine Energy, which we can obtain directly or indirectly from the Source. So, when we are filled with it, we feel calm and strong for a long time. When we are filled with polluted energy, we may seem energetic and strong, but this is temporary. The polluted energy tends to deplete very quickly, forcing us to constantly look for our next refill from others rather than learn to draw pure energy from the source.

That can naturally make us agitated, for we're desperate to find more polluted energy that can be gained solely through draining others. It's like a sugar fix that easily burns and constantly needs a refill. Once we know how to extract pure energy from the source, we never have to go to another person for a refill.

I knew an executive of a major corporation who was filled with polluted energy due to the daily disunion activities that he felt he had to do to succeed in the business world, which is truly a disunion place. He could have taken the time to fill up with pure energy, but he didn't know how to do it.

Some corporate executives understand the importance of energy and how to obtain it, whether from the source or from others.

There are stories about Steve Jobs meditating and getting pure energy from the source. There are also stories about him draining other people. Unfortunately, he didn't have enough energy in his body to sustain him at the end of his life, for he died young! He reached a point where he didn't want to take people's energy, and, at the same time, his input of energy became less than his output, forgetting how to get pure energy on an ongoing basis as he used to do when he was young.

In any event, this executive, who was a basket case, managed to make a lot of money. Fortunately, these days, he's trying to change and become more balanced. But in those days, he was so filled with agitated energy that he had a tic, which I'm not even sure he realized. It was hilarious.

I've seen some executives and politicians so filled with polluted energy that they just can't stop laughing almost uncontrollably—a laugh from the belly and very unnatural.

It's easy to tell whether someone's energy is pure or polluted simply by observing their life. Polluted energetic people cannot just relax and enjoy this vast network of things for very long. They are either asleep or busy running around doing this or that task, not as a helper of the Realm of Union but as a vampire of the Realm of Disunion to get their next refill.

I've seen some people get so agitated and exhausted that they turn to alcohol, drugs, sex, or other types of addiction to calm down and reconnect to the world, even if for a short time, artificially done under the chemical influence. Watching television, movies, or other forms of entertainment can also help such people, but this calmness is temporary, gone in a few hours.

Some executives get their energy from their partners, who may know how to get pure energy from the source.

I have noticed that when the agitated energy is high, children feel it and get disoriented, either falling or having other accidents. I'm sure it must have similar effects on some adults. We must try to bring calm to our surroundings by learning to replenish ourselves with pure energy.

People who are filled with pure energy do things with ease and calmness, and of course, great rewards come their way! Rewards of the Realm of Union, not Disunion!

I've seen some people continually look for a refill of their energy through one sexual act after another. Some men force young women to have sex with them, even raping them, to get the young person's energy. No doubt, if the sexual act is done properly between two adults, where there is union and appreciation, then pure energy can be obtained from the source with love and calmness. Otherwise, one body gets depleted while the other gets filled through the transfer of polluted energy. It's best to go through the source to connect in a union way. That is true, not just in sex but in everything else that can cause your chamber of spirit to become dense rather than hollow.

Since we've been living in a disunion structure for more than two millennia, we have continued to operate under a global structure that leans toward the Realm of Disunion rather than Union. That has created and empowered the Age of Disunion. But this age is now ending. The Age of Transformation is coming to bring us unity.

I've noticed that I can follow the Realm of Union effortlessly when I'm living in the present moment with no interference from the past or the future. Because I can witness the Logos and try to follow that portion of the Logos that is intended for me, which is what Jesus tried to teach us by becoming the Logos in the flesh.

When we finally come together and follow the Divine Will for ourselves and humanity, we will reach our maturity to become whole, where God's wish to be known and Man's wish to be in heaven will merge into one to be fully satisfied. Otherwise, the Realm of Disunion will continue fragmenting our lives, making us miserable and depressed rather than happy.

HAPPY VS. *DEPRESSED*

Do you recall Tom Cruise jumping up and down on Oprah's couch on the Oprah Winfrey show on TV? He had just fallen into the Blob of Love with Katie Homes, his future wife, and was so excited about it that he had to tell the whole world.

It was an awesome scene for all of us to watch and remember that when two people who are meant for each other meet, it can be the most incredible experience upon which a couple may build a great union, becoming the foundation of a great society based on real togetherness. Alas, Tom and Katie had to part ways. But their union produced a beautiful daughter, Suri, who must be special to both Tom and Katie.

Unfortunately, only a few of us have experienced such togetherness on the planet, and we often lose it due to all the garbage that goes on in our society, but there is no question that it's better to experience it than never know it! It's the best thing that could ever happen to anyone or any couple.

Each of us is a part of the Divine Universe. When we are integrated with it, we become a whole person in the Realm of Union, receiving full support from this realm to live a fulfilled life. The biggest support is the Divine pure energy that is the essence of life to fuel our bodies to allow us to be active, experience life fully, witness the Divine Logos daily, and interact with it in a way where we can see the many manifestations of God in and around us to feel good about being alive.

That's why Tom Cruise became an activist against taking drugs to heal depression. He knew firsthand from experience that depression comes from the lack of pure energy, and really, nothing else.

On the other hand, when we are separated from God's union universe, we can't draw on it, such as getting the pure energy required for our daily activities. It is then that depression can sneak in to take us to a dysfunctional state of low energy and aversion to activity, where we stop living life, slowing down our spiritual growth. That includes the inability to get pure energy. Depression may sneak in to take us to a dysfunctional state of low energy and aversion to activity, where we stop living life, slowing down our growth. We become sad and unfulfilled. We are on a path of decay, moving toward death. It is the Realm of Disunion.

In the Realm of Union, even if we were to sit like a cat for hours and do nothing, we would still feel great and fully aware of the Divine Logos, the universe in and around us, and obtain the pure energy required to have a greater journey in this magical place. There is so much love and energy in the Divine universe to support us and let us experience and learn. Infinitely! Never-ending! But we must learn how to enter this blob of love, filled with light.

The Divine pure energy is the key to living a happy and fulfilled life, gradually moving us toward the Realm of Union. God wishes us to enjoy life. Cherishing and enjoying life can be a way to express our ultimate gratitude to God. That is how children act.

We need to become like children, happy and eager to live life, without resentments and worries that can weigh us down so heavily that we may feel guilty to set our minds free simply to enjoy life for a moment, a day, or the rest of our lives. We must free ourselves from expectations, preconceptions, judgments, and other dogmatic behaviors.

These are disunion attributes that we so often use to define our identity. We need to transition from the Realm of Disunion to the Realm of Union, where we no longer fear looking foolish to be a happy child, totally integrated with the universe and in harmony with our surroundings and the people around us.

So many people worry about what others may think, say, or do to them that they stop living their lives. If whatever they wish to say or do slightly differs from the standard, they don't let it be. They may think about it, but after a while, they may stop even doing that. In effect, they stop BEING. They forget who they are because they haven't spent any time being who they are, their real self. What a shame!

Rabbi Harold Kushner said, "The happiest people I know are people who don't even think about being happy. They just think about being good people. And then happiness sort of sneaks in the back window while they're busy doing good." And doing good means promoting the Realm of Union, not Disunion.

When unhappy events occur, or stress becomes more of a fixture in our lives, we need to stop and take a long, hard look at what we can do to readjust and reposition ourselves in an environment where we can bring in more pure energy to our bodies and surroundings, allowing us to move away from the turmoil and closer to peace.

You must let go of everything that makes your chamber of spirit dense. It's best to become hollow.

HOLLOW VS. *DENSE*

When we are hollow, we expect nothing. We are flexible, ready to receive, and follow the Divine Will. With no expectations, we end up living a stress-free, happy, and contented life. We let others be. We are optimistic, and we don't get discouraged.

It is only when we expect things that we become dense, following our own will and plans without any consideration for the collective will and the Divine Will. Such a life can be a stressful and empty existence because things don't usually turn out as we expect. Also, many try to manipulate others to accomplish their plan. We can become negative, pessimistic, and discouraged when our plans fail to materialize. And all along, we have failed to perceive what the universe has in store for us and our parts in the universal plan.

Failure is an attribute of the Realm of Disunion. In the Realm of Union, there is no such thing as failure or success. Whatever God wants is what we feel may be best for us. We don't judge events. We study and learn from them. We realize that eternality comes to us when we are hollow. When we are dense with the temporal, then there is no room for the eternal. No room for the soul.

You may ask, "How can the eternal or the soul enter?" And the answer to this important question is that hollowness makes an urgent space for the new, surprising, and unexpected. When we're hollow, we have no expectations. We do not judge. We realize that only God can judge. And, without judgment, we remain calm, for there is nothing to agitate us and take us from our centers, one within us and one outside of us, as I explain in the Chapter, *The Spiritual Formula*, in *And God Said to Angel: How to Transform Personally*.

There are many tools available to us to reach this peace, but unfortunately, not all of them have remained natural and close to the Divine order. For instance, every religion has come to help us in this process so that we may reach peace and heaven on Earth, but most religions of the world have been infected over the years, often promoting disunion rather than union.

However, we still have spirituality and so we can now use it to figure out the sacred teachings of every religion and bring them all together through a process of integration to help us better understand our religion as well as our state of spirituality and, if possible, let the two merge to provide us with a foundation to live in the Realm of Union, where there is only happiness and no depression.

Such a state of being can lead us to higher consciousness, where only God reigns and nothing else. And God always leads us to happiness to live a fulfilled life. That is what He has wanted for humanity ever since the beginning of time. Unhappiness and depression can only come to us from our separation from Him and His Realm of Union.

The Realm of Union is always sending us messages and insights to help us reach our wholeness and functionality. The key is to be awake, aware, and ready to see the many invitations that come to us from the Realm of Union to bring us the Divine Light and Love that can move us away from the Realm of Disunion that is slow death, so that we may enter the Realm of Union that is filled with life and thus eternal.

Every person can promote union rather than disunion to increase the overall pure energy, knowing that there is a threshold of purity above which we can reach redemption and a threshold of existence below which we can get dissolved. In the middle of these two levels, there is a spectrum of union versus disunion, where we can gradually move from the lowest to the highest level of purity, from finite to infinite.

The next chapter discusses these levels and thresholds, providing examples. The goal is to manage the climax of disunion versus union so that we can survive the Realm of Disunion's continual attempts to destroy us all.

UNION VS. *DISUNION* THRESHOLD

T hroughout this book, I discuss how the Realm of Union dissolves the Realm of Disunion and why we must learn to employ solely union attributes.

This chapter explores the thresholds of accumulated pure energy and accumulated polluted energy, and how these thresholds can affect our existence. It shows us how to monitor our overall energy and the benefits of such an approach in life. It explains why humanity has not yet learned this path.

Some of the benefits of employing solely union attributes to influence our union threshold are:

1. When we employ union attributes, we activate the Divine Light and Love to flow through and around us, dispelling the darkness of the Realm of Disunion and allowing us to see more clearly. The best way to see this is to experience it and learn to practice it daily in your life. Like everything else in life, the more you do it, the better you will become at it until you no longer want to employ disunion attributes. Only union attributes!

2. If we were to take this approach in life, the Divine Light would accumulate, forming bubbles of pure energy around people that would gradually spread throughout the world. This light takes away the darkness. Hence, it can make it easier for humanity to witness the Divine Logos and to properly interact with it, as Jesus did and tried to tell us about it, so that we could all do the same.

The opposite of all this can apply to the disunion threshold, which can be set through polluted energy and the use of disunion attributes and techniques, yielding the exact opposite results.

We can accomplish everything through union attributes and techniques rather than disunion. But, for some reason or another, we do the opposite. We employ disunion attributes to get things done because it often seems easier. We are used to doing things this way. You could say we are conditioned to do it this way. As a result, most of us have become addicted to it.

The time has come to let go of the Age of Disunion and embrace the Age of Transformation, but this transition must happen naturally, not artificially.

Why is it important to let the Age of Disunion unfold naturally?

A long time ago, when we chose a certain approach, we had no idea where it would lead us. How could we have known this?

When people in the nineteenth century made secret plans, they aged and died. New people arrived, unaware of the details. Then, they grew old and retired or died. As everything changed and new people got involved, there was a time when the people running the show didn't even know how it all got started. I mean, they knew, but not in detail, according to actual accurate history.

So, they came up with their reasons for doing things! Not because it necessarily made sense, but because it allowed the money from Iranian oil and other resources around the planet to flow with ease. And remember that many people and organizations were fed, so they didn't want to interfere.

For instance, the individuals and/or groups who participated in the formation of Israel are no longer around, and the new groups do not share the same knowledge and/or interests. But they still do their best to stay aligned with God's mission to safeguard humanity and maintain the planet's stability, even when it is difficult at times.

I'm sure many elites and their advisors had to wing it, since they depended on their compradors to get the job done. Most of the compradors who rose to the top became selfish bullies, driven to work for themselves and a few friends and family members rather than the actual plan, which they often knew little about.

That's why some people at the top continued to rationalize that they had to keep people down to manage them, which forced many to struggle in various conflicts within the Realm of Disunion, some of which were created by the rulers themselves. As time passed and the Realm of Disunion grew stronger, people just didn't have the time or energy to figure things out amid the escalating lies, deceptions, and secrecy.

Today, most of us are so addicted to using disunion attributes to get things done without any consideration for the collective, all the way to God, that we employ more disunion than union attributes daily. We could have followed God's way rather than man's way a long time ago, but we didn't. Now that we have taken the disunion path, we cannot just stop it in the middle of its course. We must wait for it to dissolve naturally through a process of transformation from disunion into union, while we rely solely on God employing union attributes, never disunion.

There is no other way!

We must try to align ourselves with the Divine Plan, following the Divine's Way, rather than push and pull to do whatever is possible according to man's way, no matter union or disunion, to get our plan to succeed.

The reason is that God's plan always leads us to the Realm of Union, but our plan may go against God's, which is not good, creating all kinds of disunion, disharmony, and chaos.

We're hopefully approaching the Messianic Age, the time of our maturity, when we will learn at last how to handle the Realm of Union versus Disunion, becoming aware and mature adults.

With this maturity comes a sense of responsibility, not just to ourselves and our collectives but also to humanity as a whole and the Divine creation, which is the collective union society to which we all belong. We can either grow up and join the Realm of Union or continue with our childish behaviors, allowing the Realm of Disunion to grow and dissolve us all.

We must understand that, in the twentieth century, because we leaned toward man's way rather than God's, we failed to do things the right way.

But fortunately, those who understood all this naturally helped, and so every collective seems to have been involved in some way or another to keep us all safe. As we approach the Age of Transformation, we will see more about each collective's role and contribution to this effort.

Unfortunately, a few unlucky people have been so infected and blinded by the Realm of Disunion that they've decided to sabotage the Realm of Union and not let it unfold, even getting paid to stop its natural flow. But this is the nature of the Realm of Disunion and its structure as it grows and infects more people. This draconian approach to life must stop!

Today, the old world, which has mostly followed the Realm of Disunion, seems to be ending; and the new world, which is destined to bring about the Realm of Union, seems to be unfolding. We need to get together and weaken the Realm of Disunion, which is now increasing its totalitarian powers globally, to prevent its death. Otherwise, the Augustinian refuge of the City of God, as I explain in *And God Said to Angel: Toward the Divine Plan and Heaven on Earth*, may not be possible.

Modern humans may now face the final challenge of history: whether we create the next millennium or go down into the lake of fire.

It's time to replace today's proactive history, which began around the time of Thomas Jefferson, with God's Plan, which has no end. In the Messianic Age, there is no need for proactive or reactive history, which existed before the nineteenth century, because we will finally learn how to let God rule rather than man. These two methods of managing history may have worked before, but now that the Age of Transformation is approaching, they won't work because any system of governance must align with the Divine Plan for us, where we are all protected and cherished.

I'm sure most of us have wished to live in the Realm of Union. Many individuals and groups have come together and tried to build a union structure for humanity. Still, so far, we have not succeeded because this process requires tools and understandings that were not available to humanity. It was not yet time for our transition from disunion to union.

Evil, just like weeds that take over a garden or cancer that takes over a body, must be removed or, if possible, eradicated; otherwise, it can spread and destroy the garden or the host. Our leaders are just doing what they believe they must do to continue keeping their positions, whether personally or collectively. They're not to be blamed. It is the disunion structure that is flawed and needs to be dissolved to end the Age of Disunion.

In an imperfect structure, many feel driven to leave the Divine path to keep everything running. Not realizing that it is possible to rely on God to dissolve evil for us, as explained in the Chapter, *How to Rely on God*, in *And God Said to Angel: Toward the Divine Plan and Heaven on Earth*.

No doubt, the Israeli government treated the Palestinians horribly over the years, and a lot of what has happened is unjustifiable.

But let's face it. In the Age of Disunion, where the Jews had to work extremely hard to manage the growth of the Realm of Disunion while keeping the stability of humanity and the planet, evil's tentacles spread pretty much everywhere. No one or place has been safe or unaffected. That is especially true as we move up the ladder to the higher echelons of our society and study those who lead our current disunion structure.

It's important to read this book, understand the Realm of Union versus Disunion, and then try to look at the total picture from a refreshed union perspective that can let us see our leaders for who they truly are. Human beings who are as much in bondage as everyone else existing in the Realm of Disunion!

The key is to end the Age of Disunion in a way that relies solely on union attributes, not disunion ones. That is difficult to do when most of us have not yet learned how to dissolve disunion through union however after you read this book that is here to teach us all the techniques of the Realm of Union, it's going to get easier and easier, which can become essential in building a union structure on our planet that can make it possible to follow the Realm of Union rather than the Realm of Disunion, the Divine way rather than man's way.

The Jewish collective and the Persian collective (especially the Bahá'ís) must get together and help the Palestinians and other collectives on the planet to accept Israel as a nation of God's chosen people who have been destined to empower God's Plan for the redemption of humanity. The Israelis must take the necessary steps to include the Palestinians in the land of Israel with love, equality, freedom, and justice for all.

The Persians have always been lovers of God and the Realm of Union, as well as great teachers of spirituality. However, as it stands today, the Persians are strong in oneness but very weak in uniqueness, lacking the ability to appreciate one another deeply and to let one another be without much comparison. This imbalance between oneness and uniqueness has sometimes prevented them from uniting as a collective.

That's why, throughout history, the Persians became victims of the Realm of Disunion. But then, each time, through God's grace, they learned how to transform events and people from disunion into union, gaining greater expertise in this area. Today, there is no question that the Persians are the greatest transformers of disunion into union on the planet, but right now, they're suffering from this lopsidedness of oneness and uniqueness, where they are driven to compare people and not honor each other's uniqueness. As a result, they have become weak, carrying too much ego.

The Persians' immense earthly pride has prevented them from working together to accomplish their divine assignment. That's why the Persians are not equipped for certain tasks, especially since they can't balance oneness and uniqueness. They can function as great teachers, insightful providers, and creative master builders. But they cannot manage the growth of something that requires the building, allowance,

185

and appreciation of all pieces coming together, changing and exchanging ideas every day, while integrating different pieces toward the building of a future structure.

The Jews, on the other hand, knew how to keep this balance of oneness and uniqueness, but solely within their collective. This ability allowed the Jews to be united in oneness and, at the same time, appreciate each other's uniqueness, with enough balance between the two to get things done in the Age of Disunion, even though they may have suffered from other disunion attributes, like not knowing how to appreciate the rest of humanity, who may be non-Jews.

The key is for humanity, especially these two collectives, who are destined to aid us all in our transition from disunion to union, to understand the meaning of equality.

What does it mean when we're told that we're all equal?

Each person or collective possesses a unique set of attributes. Some qualities are strong and some weak, together summing up equally to a value common to all humans. Attached to this value is the person's or the collective's mission or purpose in life.

Beauty, intelligence, or any other trait that may be considered valuable can also become a weakness, depending on circumstances, bringing down the person or collective. The minus and the plus always balance out in pieces that are unique to the person or collective, but when placed together, they can beautifully fulfill the functionality needed in the Divine Plan to lead humanity's destiny, with equal contribution and value.

Just to clarify things, please imagine an antique weighing scale where, on one side of the balance, is the summation of all your weaknesses, and on the other side, the summation of all your strengths, both sides balanced by a pendulum on zero. Now visualize all people having these exact balanced (minus and plus) attributes, with the pendulum at zero. Then, add to all this the dimensions of time and space, which depend on different circumstances.

Conclusion: All men are equal, which is what we've been told in our holy books.

That's why we need to stop comparing each other and uniting one group against another group. Instead, we need to learn the integration process to balance our oneness and uniqueness. This balance can take us to a level of maturity that enables us to comprehend true equality and to try to abide by it.

The Persians, who have been blessed with broad oneness, can now help the Jews expand their circle of inclusion (their oneness) to the whole of humanity, not just the Jews. And the Jews can help the Persians to consider and empower the uniqueness of their Iranian brothers and sisters!

All collectives should come to each other's rescue to balance oneness and uniqueness, which is a requirement of the Messianic Age.

Right now, all collectives lack this balance due to the Age of Disunion.

However, everything has so far worked out, surely with Divine assistance, with the Persians generously sharing their insights, teachings, and oil with humanity and its collectives, and the Jews remaining united among themselves as they helped each other take part in carrying out the Divine Plan.

We must be thankful for this and try to take advantage of it by understanding where we are, how we got here, and what we must do to move toward a better future for all.

Cyrus the Great was the last ruler to try to follow the Divine Will. After Alexander conquered the Persian Empire, we adopted the Greek mentality, which leaned toward fragmentation and division. So far, we have continued plugging away on this second path even though the Divine path has been available to us all along. That has naturally forced us to go deeper into the darkness of the Realm of Disunion.

In this darkness, it's natural that we reach a point like the coronavirus pandemic of 2020 to 2021, where we cannot tell what is true and what is false, or what is real and what is unreal, just like the Brothers Bloom Story!

How can we trust what we're told when we know for a fact that our global politics, media, and other aspects of our current disunion structure have been targeted for years and most likely hijacked a long time ago by the disunion people?

Today, we've come to the most insane point where the disunion people are trying to figure out:

1. How to cut down the global population (the poor, the old, the unhealthy, the unwanted, etc., all according to their insane standards and specifications).

2. How to make more money off humanity by making everything more costly (thus, going against God, who has given us everything for free, but wants us to honor and protect what we've been given to pass it on to our children and grandchildren, something the disunion people cannot possibly do unless they transform and become union people).

3. How to find the best technique for mass manipulation that can easily be done at any time to control everybody in such a manner that the disunion people could benefit from it, and no one else, preferably taking us all to a new level of disunion manipulation that is better... stronger... etcetera.

Unfortunately, most people are isolated with no understanding, no support, and no money to protect themselves from such manipulations and exploitations of the Realm of Disunion and its current structure.

The key is to recognize the union people and bring them together to transform victims into union people. It is then that we can build a humongous network of union members who can unite against the Realm of Disunion, which is here to drain us all. It's best not to even say "against" for we should never go against the Realm of Disunion. So, even though I may mention this word here and there when talking about the Realm of Disunion, please note that in life, it is best to learn how to go through God and His Realm of Union to dissolve the Realm of Disunion. In other words, according to the Divine approach or way rather than man's approach or way.

In the past, we have had many people who came to unite us against the Realm of Disunion to reinforce the Realm of Union, seldom with success, because the old approach (man's approach) and path can often add to the polluted realm that is the Realm of Disunion. Instead, we must try to increase the pure energy around us to dissolve the Realm of Disunion, according to the Divine approach and path, since it works and is more pleasing, even allowing for a long-lasting relationship with God.

It's in your best interest to learn this new approach, which will lead you to your Divine Self, a part of God tailored to every person and collective. Your Divine Self knows everything that God wants for you and from you to live in the Realm of Union with Him. You need to believe in God and your power to reach the Realm of Union, even if you only get a glimpse of it, for it is truly the way to dissolve the Realm of Disunion in and around you.

We must appreciate and support our union people. They're like pearls, sanded down and refined through time (even karmas), to be full of God's love and compassion—His oneness and His uniqueness, totally balanced—to help every person and/or collective to reach the Realm of Union.

We must make it easier for everyone to understand the areas of the Divine Plan that relate to their share in God's work to establish the Kingdom of God on Earth. In other words, we must help every human being discover their true purpose in life.

We should never be unhappy to see another person happy! My God, we must learn to enjoy seeing everybody and everything fulfilling their potential. We must work toward building a great life for humanity and all its members. We must reach a level of spirituality where we can be super glad to serve the collective, to see people get healed and allowed to live their unique lives in the Realm of Union with no drainage. A life fully balanced and filled with miracles of God.

189

The Chapter, *How to Rely on God*, in *And God Said to Angel: Toward the Divine Plan and Heaven on Earth*, shows you that God, as Bearer of Burden, never employs disunion attributes. He always adds to the union attributes that promote the Dissolution of the Realm of Disunion.

Let me give some examples.

Suppose some people are caballing against you and trying to hurt you. You can either deal with them through the second approach that takes you on the second path, which can be draining and difficult with the possibility of failure and getting hurt, or you can ask God to take you to the first path that is aligned with the Divine approach.

In such a scenario, where you ask God for help, you must make sure you don't employ any disunion attributes, only union, while you wait and watch God in action. I usually try to shower everything and everyone with Divine pure energy and love as I follow His will for me.

Soon, everything naturally comes together, new people arrive to help you, and before you know it, even those who wanted to hurt you end up going either against their wishes and goals or completely out of the picture. The reason for all this is that when God operates, there is so much pure energy that most people's Divine Selves come out following the Divine will rather than their own will. After it is all done, most people don't even know what happened to them. They go, "WTF just happened?" They're too blind to see and figure things out. It's hilarious!

That takes practice. So, you've got to do it with no fear until you gradually learn how to do it. You can start with smaller tasks and slowly build up to bigger tasks.

I have always tried to take God's approach rather than man's, solely employing union techniques in my life, and I must tell you, it does work. You've got to see this for yourself.

Sometimes it can get difficult, especially when we're dealing with people who are close to us, like those who mean a lot to us. On a few occasions, I remember praying to God and asking Him not to punish someone for hurting me, but then seeing them get hurt, not by God, but by other entities in the universe that are in love with God and against injustice, imbalance, and inequality.

We must come to realize that it is not God who brought us to a disunion structure that continues to keep us in bondage. We did, and we still do. From the top echelon of our global society to the first unit of our community, in other words, our families, we now have disunion attributes and imbalances generated daily. All done to make it easier to steal money or other assets from each other, so that we may feel more secure to be able to take care of ourselves financially. We forget that such behaviors can take us away from God and His awesome existence.

And God allows for such behaviors because He prefers not to interface with a bunch of robots. He wants us to reach maturity to recognize: 1) He is in full control; 2) He made us and knows us intimately; 3) He loves us unconditionally; 4) He is aware of our wish to continue experiencing the Realm of Disunion without the ability to use our free will properly; 5) He allowed for the Realm of Disunion to continue so that we may learn from it as long as certain requirements are met to prepare us for our transition from disunion to union at the end time of disunion.

These requirements are 1) we each experience evil and try to learn from it as we do our best to transform every disunion into union through Divine guidance; 2) we share and record our experiences of evil and the effort taken to transform it from disunion into union; 3) we unite against evil by trying to figure out its many faces; 4) we develop the necessary union tactics and technologies that can work together, as an extension of man, to reduce the effects of evil in our individual and collective lives; 5) we build a structure on the planet that promotes the Realm of Union, side by side, our current disunion structure, gradually dissolving all evil; and 6) we continually maintain the new union structure to keep the balance of oneness and uniqueness so that the benefit of all is considered rather than the benefit of the few as it stands today.

Plus, we need the appropriate tools to make all this possible with minimal drainage. For instance, telling our stories without necessarily divulging people's names or other identities, thus respecting confidentiality and recognizing that, as a story grows, it can naturally lead us to its truth.

That's why God allowed us to live in the Age of Disunion for more than two millennia to learn from it, so that one day we could see the many faces of evil and have the tools to put an end to it. This time for good!

He also arranged for Jesus to die for us, so that each of us could redeem ourselves personally, if we so desire, through faith in Christ to have eternal life in Heaven. It is then that the Holy Spirit can enter our domain to remind us of "all that God has given us" and to let us know that God loves us so much that He wants to be in our lives.

So, please pray to God and ask for His guidance as you seek personal salvation through Him.

Think about it. When you ask God for help, then you are allowing Him to be near you and show you His glory! And, when God is with you, supporting you, who can be against you? So, go to Him, dig into His Word, and begin claiming the divine guarantee that Christ's death can wash away your past wrongdoings to help you feel worthy again to be in God's presence in the Realm of Union.

You must understand that God does not interfere with things, for He honors our free will, which He has gifted to us. But when an event is in direct conflict with His plan, God does interfere. God can stop anything He wishes.

We must try to employ union attributes to dissolve disunion, always through God. Otherwise, we cannot stay with Him in the Realm of Union, where He dwells, where His presence alone can dissolve the Realm of Disunion.

His light is pure as spring water. It is the essence of life. This pure energy sustains everything and everyone in the universe. His love is unconditional and infinite, with so much caring behind it that it is endless and ready to support all. The key is to take time for a Soul Day to learn how to continually receive the Divine Light and Love to stay in the

Realm of Union, and to learn from Him His approach that leads us to the Divine path, which is the first, not the second.

So, again, why did God and His messengers wait and allowed for disunion to begin and continue rather than let humanity understand: 1) the way of union (paradise) versus disunion (hell), 2) how to obtain pure energy, 3) how to align with our Divine Selves, 4) how to remain our Divine Selves, and 5) how to be in the divine presence, all of which would have allowed us to live in the Realm of Union, individually and collectively, hence no need to wait for Christ's return to help us reach our collective salvation?!

Attar's Story of Simorgh, which I described earlier in the Chapter, *How to Rely on God*, in *And God Said to Angel: Toward the Divine Plan and Heaven on Earth*, is all about this. But then, why did it have to be this way? Why the delay? Prophet Mohammad even directed the Muslims to cover women, half of the population, so that our transformation from disunion into union would be delayed. Why?

To most people, this is the dead-end of the exploration toward an adequate explanation of our spiritual journey. I came to this dead-end as well. But I didn't give up. I continued to explore, as always, through God, and I found that those who have seen the reason for such delays expressed their insights, as revelations, like the mystics and messengers of God. Not as explanations. Humanity is waiting for explanations, which they believe only the Messiah can deliver.

The Christians have tried to practice what Christ showed us the last time he came. In brief, they know how to transform on a personal level through Christ. But most of them have learned how to do this temporarily, not permanently, primarily due to their inability to stay in the Realm of Union for good. That is why they are now waiting for Christ's return to show us how to do this on a collective level, which, to me, could happen through the first or the second approach, or through both approaches simultaneously.

Let me explain this further, as it is a crucial issue that needs a better understanding.

To reach collective salvation, every person must have already reached personal salvation so that they can, together, experience the Realm of Union. It is often difficult to remain in the Realm of Union when everybody around you is in the Realm of Disunion. Thus, a union environment can help a person to stay in the Realm of Union.

The disunion structure has done its best not to let people remain in the Realm of Union by telling them that they are not worthy enough, pure enough, righteous enough, or strong enough to live in such an existence.

The disunion structure has developed many stories over the years to teach us that it is not possible to live in the Realm of Union with God for good and continually receive our daily union instructions.

That is a conflict that goes against humanity, where every human has an innate need to contribute to humanity to which we all belong. If this tendency to empower conflicts continues, then people will gradually lose their connection to humanity and their collective, thus becoming less human.

The same applies to every collective needing to contribute to the whole, a formidable quality, which we must all acknowledge, honor, and protect. Otherwise, we will all lose our humanity, which can be detrimental to humanity and lead to our extinction as a species.

Some people are ashamed to be righteous and clean. There is nothing wrong with regaining your cleanliness so that you can feel refreshed to witness the Divine Logos again. Get up every day, eager to learn from Him, His ways of the Realm of Union to dissolve the Realm of Disunion with the Realm of Union and its many union techniques. If you have not yet learned these union techniques because you've been too occupied with the Realm of Disunion, then go to Him for guidance. Believe me, he is here, waiting to help you. You must BE SINCERE as you ask Him to guide you.

Sometimes, I feel, God is disappointed to see so many of us promoting the Realm of Disunion, or collaborating with it, rather than trying to safeguard His creation against it. But it's okay because, in the past, most of us didn't know much about the Realm of Union versus Disunion, but soon, we will learn how to properly handle these two realms and employ such knowledge in everything that we do.

That will naturally reduce our tendency toward disunion. It will help us gain the wisdom to realize that our world religions are here, not to be compared, but to be integrated, so we can see the many sacred teachings they offer.

It is our destiny to come together from different collectives to complete this integration process of unification toward the realization of the Realm of Union, the Kingdom of God, on the planet. That is part of humanity's spiritual development and growth during the Messianic Age. Hopefully, we will take every necessary step to improve humanity's wellness and wholeness.

Without the Messianic Age, our disunion qualities will undoubtedly grow and promote the Realm of Disunion on a collective level, which will surely destroy humankind. It's crucial to come together and build a global union structure that can dissolve our current disunion.

This new union structure will promote certain union qualities that will grow every day more than the day before, empowering humanity's potential, now crushed by the Realm of Disunion and its people.

In Hollywood, we have developed a formula to keep the audience glued to the television. This formula is so detailed and followed that every filmmaking student must learn and abide by it. We can see this formula in most American and European films. These films tend to employ sex, violence, and other aspects of life dealing with disunion, often telling stories that can contribute to people's fears and the transfer of polluted energy. However, channeling pure energy from the source through good old storytelling can be an awesome art and a great tool for accessing it.

Thus, we must be careful not to tell stories in ways that can drain us. We can find many examples of this drainage throughout our society, like when people can't differentiate between storytelling and gossiping or any other disunion manner of telling stories.

STORYTELLING VS. *GOSSIPING*

Have you noticed how certain people love to gossip? I've learned that it is not necessarily gossiping that turns them on. It's the storytelling. We've been telling stories for thousands of years. Our holy books are full of stories. Remember when people gathered around a fire and told stories to each other?

We instinctively love stories. We are attracted to each other's stories. It's ingrained in us, for we each are a part of humanity and connected. We enjoy hearing about one another. Take any project that deals with storytelling, and people are drawn to it. People want to see movies that tell stories, especially Realm of Union stories like Titanic. So many people, including me, saw this film many times.

We have a desire to know about each other. So, talking about one another is an attribute of the Realm of Union—if it is done in the form of storytelling without draining anyone. When we provide information about each other that could drain someone, then it's not good. It becomes gossiping rather than good old storytelling.

Why not honor and respect the people around you by gossiping about their positive qualities and protecting their privacy? I must admit, it takes lots of practice. So, be careful of what you say about other people. Sometimes, your stories, which you may tell to get closer to those who are listening, could damage the characters involved and even isolate them. Don't distance someone from the same people you wish to get close to. Wish for others what you wish for yourself.

I know a guy in our community who tries to act gently and kindly, but whenever he hears a story, he broadcasts it without any thought for the outcome. That's his way of connecting to others at another person's expense! He doesn't realize that this approach offers short-term closeness that may not even be worth it. To establish a long-lasting relationship, it's best to let the universe naturally take us to it.

Some time ago, I worked on a film project for more than a year without charging. I did it as my contribution to the City of Lynchburg and the African American community. While working on this project, I learned that this guy tried to damage my contribution by gossiping about me and my work. Can you imagine? To try to undo or weaken someone's effort done in a loving, positive manner in the Realm of Union! The poor guy must have suffered doing it.

All of you out there, who can't help but gossip, please stop! Realize that you're gossiping because of your inadequacies as a person. You don't feel you're worthy. That is your way of building and growing your friendships. Calm your mind, sit in silence, and tell yourself, "I'm worthy. I don't need to buy others' love and friendship through the destructive means of the Realm of Disunion, which damages lives. People could love me for me, for the person that I am, without the gossip and secrets that I may provide about others. And anyone who requires such disunion acts from me to love me is not worth my friendship."

Let's not be careless with the information we may have about others, as it can harm them and prevent them from reaching their future potential. Please, stop! What if what they're doing is connected to what you're doing, but you are too blind to see it? Try to look at everything and everyone in a union manner. Don't keep people from knowing the Divine Will and serving their purpose in life, even tampering with their ability to see life's opportunities and future paths.

SEEING FUTURE PATHS VS. *FORTUNE-TELLING*

Telling people about their future can be dangerous. Fortune-telling can cause trouble. It can be an attribute of the Realm of Disunion if done improperly. The future is not fixed. The Chapter, *Recognizing Patterns*, in *And God Said to Angel: Toward the Divine Plan and Heaven on Earth*, explains how the future can sometimes be modified and that we often have a few paths to choose from, which are dependent upon our own free will, the collective will, and the Divine Will.

When a fortune-teller gives us information about one of our futures, then we tend to go toward that future without realizing that there are other possibilities in addition to the one described. That is not good because, in a way, we could be reinforcing a future that may not necessarily be the best one for the person, in other words, their optimal spiritual path.

However, if we were to tell the person about all the paths and help them choose the most comfortable one, the one closest to God's Realm of Union, that could be beneficial. But again, we must always go through God to proceed.

I try to do that for my children. I also try to show them how to obtain Divine Guidance and His pure energy, helping them travel on their true path in harmony with their true essence. I guide them. I don't force them, for no one knows but the person. However, with my assistance, they have a better chance of reaching their goals, for I try to describe some of the signs to them—signs they could follow—as well as convince them that it is possible.

So, showing various paths and describing them to our children or whoever, scientifically, as in probability theory, is educational and beneficial. But when we try to predict the future in a way that may drain or limit the person, then it's not good.

When we are serving humanity and the Divine Will, sometimes, we may have to project ourselves into the future to figure out how to perform our duties best. That's fine. It's part of our intuitive abilities, where we try to see our potential futures and how the present can affect them.

It's always easier to live life when many happy union paths are open to us. Otherwise, one may feel cornered, causing stagnation and/or helplessness.

A friend recommended that I leave this part out. In other words, don't talk about "future telling" because she said, "Most people do not believe in seers who can foretell the future." But then I thought, I don't want to leave out all those people who do believe. That won't be fair!

Seeing future paths and learning how to empower one over the other can be a powerful tool and exercise. *And God Said to Angel: Toward the Divine Plan and Heaven on Earth* shows us how to recognize and empower the most miraculous union past so that we can come to the most awesome present from which to go to the best future for humanity. That can be done on a personal or collective level. Those who know how to do this can see unity, whereas those who cannot remain fragmented, leaning toward duality.

Since we've been living in a disunion structure for more than two millennia, we have continued with duality rather than unity because the disunion structure always leans toward the Realm of Disunion rather than Union. It tries to promote disunion attributes rather than union, primarily to survive. That has created and empowered the Age of Disunion. But this age is now ending. The Age of Transformation is coming to bring us unity.

Earlier in this volume, I addressed the concept of duality versus unity. I mentioned in the Chapter, *To Unity vs. Duality*, the reason we're still in duality. I explained that the word "duality," along with many others, should be redefined to minimize confusion and maximize clarity.

The key is to understand different concepts according to the Realm of Union. That is a process that simplifies things, not makes them more complex. Knowing that simplicity is closer to the truth, that is a part of the Realm of Union.

SIMPLICITY VS. *COMPLEXITY*

We must redefine the word "complexity." When we design a system and try to keep it modular, if done properly, we end up replicating similar modules, which keep the system simple to see, monitor, and maintain. Whereas, when a system is not modular, its true nature and relationships among its various parts are not properly seen or defined. So, complexity often occurs when we don't understand the whole and the parts well enough to keep the system simple.

Life is simple. It is we who insist on making life complicated through disunion means. Little is needed to make a happy life. The higher the truth, the simpler it is. The price we pay for life's complexity is too high.

The Realm of Disunion encourages complexity to keep us from living a fulfilled life. By living a simple, calm, manageable life, we maximize our energy while minimizing our worries. It is then possible to keep ourselves away from the complexity and imbalance of the Realm of Disunion that can blind us to drain our energy so that we cannot live life fully.

The time has come to stop the waste by making things easy to use, understand, and feel—just all-around easy. In the Realm of Union, we simplify our lives so that our energy does not get wasted.

That's why I am trying so hard to write this book simply. We all know that it's easier to understand things when they're made simple rather than complex. Simplicity is a key property of the Realm of Union. As the Realm of Disunion grows, so does the complexity of things, because in a complex environment, it is always easier to confuse and, consequently, trick people. So, whenever you see things getting more complex, watch out!

Take politics, for instance, which has become so complicated that most of us don't know what's going on. The other day, I was listening to a political expert on TV. As she tried to explain a concept, she used so many acronyms that I was lost by the end of her speech. Some people think it's intelligent to talk in complicated terms. I believe the whole reason we talk is to establish communication and understand one another. Otherwise, what's the point of talking? So why not try to make things simple, use simple terms and simple explanations?

I used to get drained when paying bills, spending hours to figure out why I was being charged a certain amount. I was surprised to learn that many companies have purposefully set up complex billing systems and procedures to confuse, frustrate, and drain us into giving them more of our money. Every few cents added together on a large scale can amount to millions of dollars, especially since most of us are too tired and drained by the Realm of Disunion to complain or try to stop them. This drainage is happening on a large scale, affecting many people trying to keep up with their bills, which then depletes their pure energy, making them weak and thus targets of the Realm of Disunion.

Poor humanity! If we don't do something about it soon, we'll be living in such a complex structure that it will no longer be possible to participate in any decision-making; we would either not understand it or become enslaved by a structure of lies accumulated over centuries of caballing and manipulations. A friend told me, "Angel, we are in such a structure right now! We need to set up projects that simplify things in our homes, schools, workplaces, and any medium that can affect us."

Another friend said, "But what can one person do?" Indeed, one person can't do much. But together we can move mountains! In *And God Said to Angel: How to Transform Collectively,* we're shown how to do that.

These days, some of us try to accumulate so many material goods that we end up becoming slaves to our jobs. We are often drained because of our jobs, but we still get up each morning and go to work because we need to pay our bills and support our families. It's better to cut down and regain our energy than live in a mansion and be drained. What's important is to have a nice home that's just the right size, not too big or too small for our needs, just enough, with lots of plants and flowers and pleasant things around to increase pure energy.

We must strive for a simple yet beautiful life. Sometimes, there is more pure energy stored in one of your children's drawings than in a painting purchased from an art gallery for thousands of dollars. Unless, of course, you enjoy looking at the expensive picture, in which case, through appreciation, the picture can become a source of pure energy. Also, you may buy the picture as an investment, which is okay as well.

If you were to surround yourself in your home with items that hold pure energy—and with thoughts, words, and actions that bring pure energy—then, over time, the accumulated pure energy would make your home glow with the Divine Light, turning it into a healing place!

Today's engineers must construct large-scale systems with complexity exceeding the comprehension capacity of the individual human mind. The modern jumbo jet has over six million parts.

Many current software systems consist of millions—even tens of millions—of lines of high-level language code. While some have argued that we should not build systems on this scale, for better or worse, our society has made that choice, and, in some ways, it's part of our growth.

However, even though extreme complexity has become a necessary aspect of many modern engineering projects, simplification can be achieved through modularization and other techniques.

I've seen some experts create systems so complicated that only they can understand and work with them. That way, they would be so needed that they would be employed no matter what.

My husband was one of such people, perhaps not intentionally but unintentionally, since he was unique in his ability to perceive and his great curiosity. He was the only one who could fully understand the system wherever he worked. When he took a leave from his job due to sickness or other matters, everything stopped working until his return.

The next chapter discusses the union versus disunion buildup of energy, influencing the global structure.

Building Union vs. *Disunion*

I n nature, all things constantly interact, and energy flows throughout, allowing us to observe energy transfer from one body to another. It is difficult to see this energy transfer with our current limited vision. Nonetheless, it is happening, and we can measure it through observation and experimentation.

In the Realm of Union, it is possible to obtain the Divine Light, His pure energy that can accumulate to affect our threshold of enlightenment and higher spirituality.

In the Realm of Disunion, on the other hand, we tend to obtain polluted energy from others by draining them. This energy drainage and accumulation of polluted energy can also affect our threshold for dissolution.

So, we must all work together and help each other to obtain pure energy rather than polluted energy. *And God Said to Angel: How to Transform Personally* explains all this in detail. Here, I wish to explore the attributes that can affect a society's overall health.

When a society is filled with pure energy and closer to the Realm of Union, everything becomes less costly and more productive and efficient, benefiting humanity as a whole. Naturally, this makes people serve each other and the structure rather than try to rule others. Also, they tend to trust the structure and each other.

Let us explore these attributes, starting with freely vs. costly, and showing the disunion attribute in italics.

FREELY VS. *COSTLY*

In 1998, Shawn Fanning developed Napster, one of the first popular peer-to-peer file-sharing platforms. A year later, Sean Parker co-founded Napster, offering a free file-sharing service for music that drew the ire of recording labels and the Recording Industry Association of

America. Lawsuits by various industry associations eventually led to the service's shutdown.

When I first heard about it, I thought, Great! The wave of the Realm of Union is coming, bringing freebies! The reason is that as the Realm of Union grows, the number of free things naturally increases. When stuff becomes too costly, it is a sign of disunion growth. We need to support those entities that give us free products and services, for they are often from the Realm of Union. Not that what Napster did was good! For it was hurting some artists, but if done in a way where no one can get hurt, where it is good for all, like Craigslist, it would contribute to the Realm of Union.

In God's creation, we don't get charged for breathing the air, drinking the water, smelling the roses, swimming in the ocean, watching the sunset, playing with the cat, dancing in the rain, experiencing the richness of the Earth, the softness of the grass, and so on. We don't have to pay for anything. Everything is free! Even our connection to the universal life force and the abundance of pure energy we can receive from it!

The word 'freedom' is close to the free kingdom; this Kingdom of God we have been given for free to cherish and hopefully protect against all aggressions of the Realm of Disunion.

Look at what the Realm of Disunion has done to this free kingdom. It has gradually taken it from us, piece by piece, forcing us to pay for things that were given to us for free! Every few decades, they come up with new ways to make us pay for things that were free before. They have become so blinded that they don't realize their greed is now endangering our planet, our home, without which no one will be around! So, with their disunion optimization, they're succeeding in turning whatever that's free into costly!

Our freedom is important to us, for it allows us to live in this free Kingdom of God as He intended it! In the Realm of Union, where we can live our lives freely. Not in the Realm of Disunion, where we are controlled and forced to live a life that is expected of us, often filled with falsehood, for which we end up later paying big time! I know some may have difficulties imagining such a union world—in other words, Heaven on Earth—but believe me, it could happen if we were to follow the Spiritual Formula described in this *And God Said to Angel: How to Transform Personally*. It is then that we can build the union structure proposed in *And God Said to Angel: How to Transform Collectively*. It took me twenty years to finally comprehend this concept of freedom!

Right now, people spend money they don't have; they purchase or take things they don't need to impress people who don't care, and they dislike! We need to learn how to properly handle the gifts that have been given to us, in a sense, loaned to us on Earth. These do not just belong to us. They also belong to our children and grandchildren. It is only then that we can experience the freedom of spirit that is in store for us.

We must release our attachments and experience detachment to achieve the following:

1. Be one's true self through the Divine Self and live one's true story.

2. Let others be their true selves and live their true stories.

3. Let our life stories be gathered to see the Mythos that we have built and the reasons for each.

4. Let our transition from the Realm of Disunion to Union begin, so that every story is finally transformed from disunion into union, hopefully facilitating our ability to witness the logos. Divine Reality, and properly interact with it so that we can remain in the Realm of Union.

In brief, all lies come from the prevention of 1, 2, 3, or 4. Freedom is to allow for the above 1, 2, 3, and 4, to bring all of us closer to the truth.

As people try to live their true stories, they bring events into the light that were once invisible. With freedom, we can live our true story and share it with others, finally seeing the full picture of this reality, God, the Divine Logos, while understanding our Mythos. The Realm of Disunion prevents us from living our stories and often gives us lies to keep us from seeing the truth.

Today, it has become evident that we don't understand the meaning of freedom or how to attain it. Freedom comes when we are allowed to learn the truth about ourselves, live according to our true selves, and be members of a society that permits and promotes the development and sharing of our true stories so that a true history of humanity becomes available to every person. True history, not false history full of lies!

We need to strengthen our spirituality that can enhance our perception. It is through this greater perception that we can gradually perceive and restructure our reality so that it is filled with miraculous and Realm of Union attributes.

Furthermore, this ability allows us to select and empower the best past to bring us to the best present from which we may potentially move to the best probable future, as explained in other volumes of this book, always toward the Realm of Union. Not to empower the worst disunion past, present, and future, always in conflict with God, humanity, and our freedom to meet our Divine Destiny!

It takes a lot of effort to keep this freedom alive and well! "We the people" must continually care enough for it to protect it against all aggressors. Otherwise, the Realm of Disunion tries to minimize our freedom to take advantage of us.

Why do we take advantage of each other and/or hoard more than our share?

A great question and difficult to answer, except for the fact that we do it to make it hard for the victims to see the wholeness of God's universe as a testimony to His Realm of Union power that is here to support us all. Thus, there is no need to feel insecure and try to protect ourselves through material accumulation and wealth, which the disunion people have learned how to do, hoarding for generations.

The disunion people figure, why not create a drive to pursue Gold rather than God across the whole society to entice everyone to compete, a disunion way of life that tends to weaken the union people and the victims.

Plus, they reckon such an approach may be best for them since they do have the upper hand when it comes to money, and so far they've been successful at it!

I just cannot imagine what in the world could be so special or precious that we would go against the universe and God to have it. At the end of it all, we may miss out on what truly matters, which may be summarized in a few words: "To witness the logos," so that we may accumulate spiritual wealth.

In my own life, I have found that the more I serve, the greater my access to the Divine Information Network. That is the way to greater perception and, consequently, closeness to God.

Thus, everyone must learn how to serve rather than rule.

SERVE VS. *RULE*

A true servant of God tries to serve Him and His creation, which is the Realm of Union, through the balance of oneness and uniqueness.

No doubt, it's in every person's best interest to maintain this balance as they serve God, their collective, and themselves, knowing that it can empower the Realm of Union and every person's ability to live in it.

Brokers don't care about this balance of oneness and uniqueness. They want to benefit themselves and a certain limited group. Such tendencies to care for a few at the expense of many tend to follow the Realm of Disunion. In the Realm of Union, we want to serve God who loves all unconditionally. So, we strive to benefit all, not just a few. We honor and practice the Spiritual Formula, which clearly shows that we cannot have masters or affiliations. Only the Divine and His will should matter to us!

Jesus came to show us how to serve God, humanity, and the Realm of Union. And he served it fully to the point of total sacrifice of his life, becoming the Divine Will in the flesh. Unfortunately, more emphasis has been placed on Jesus coming to take our sins away, which is also true and significant. But what about his demonstration of servitude to the point of giving his life for God and humanity? When we focus more on our sins, we bring ourselves down, rather than emphasizing that we've been created in God's image with great potential and the capacity to serve like Jesus.

One may ask, "How are we going to know what God wants?"

The answer is simple. God wants the Realm of Union. So, we must analyze everything according to His realm and determine in advance how to best serve Him, His cause, and our cause as a subset of His cause.

This understanding of service, however, must permeate the organization, the entity, or the group and become the servant leader's role. After humanity learns how to do all this, people will be able to work together and decide how to fulfill the overall purpose, which will be close to approving everything the servant leader does.

Such an environment naturally exists in the Realm of Union, where people are relaxed, with full trust in the structure and in each other to follow the principles of the Realm of Union. That means people will serve one another and humanity with respect, honoring God as the Master Leader who knows everything and everyone, as well as the best path for all.

Humanity has been quiet, watching different people function as leaders who are more interested in fulfilling their egos and, often, in the benefit of the few rather than acting as servants of God and humankind, serving all. So, we all need to come to humanity's rescue and help each other transform from the Realm of Disunion into the Realm of Union so that we can begin to benefit all rather than the few!

John C. Maxwell said, "A leader knows the way, goes the way, and shows the way."

Now, try to imagine "the way" to be Christ's way, as in "the Way, the Life, the Truth." That tells us that the leader is in the Realm of Union and that he follows the Divine will and plan that always belong to the Realm of Union.

So, a great leader must already know how to recognize and follow the Divine Will, and to help others do the same, personally and then collectively. A person who cannot do that is not a leader; they are an administrator.

In history, we have had good leaders who tried to lead us to the Realm of Union and bad leaders who misused and abused their power, leading us in the wrong direction toward the Realm of Disunion.

The Bible tells us about Cyrus the Great, who was such a great leader that he became the Divine Messiah, doing everything God had asked of him during his lifetime and after his death.

Another example given in the Bible is King David, who did his best to follow the Divine will.

But the greatest leader of all time is Jesus Christ, who became the Logos in the flesh, and founded a movement that has lasted to this day: Christianity.

Jesus knew how to respect every person as a potential dwelling of God's manifestation on Earth. With this understanding, other union attributes always follow.

For instance, when we go to a meeting, we all participate. We don't allow one person to tell everybody else what to do. Of course, all this takes discipline and practice. But so what? We can do it, and we must do it because when we finally succeed, which is not going to take more than a few years, our rewards will be magnificent. And I'm sure God will be pleased!

We need to help each other avoid distractions, remain humble, love one another, and learn to cooperate and collaborate as servants of God and humanity.

All this requires a new mentality, as Einstein suggested, where we try to benefit the collective. Such an approach will make us all feel good about ourselves. But we must be careful, because the balance between oneness and uniqueness must always be maintained, where we are neither selfless nor selfish.

Divine pure energy will be extremely important to all who wish to live in such an environment. The more pure energy we have in and around us, the easier it is to see things and prevent energy drainage, so no one gets drained or drains others.

Simply put, to serve each other and the purpose of our union, we must learn to work together, avoid internal politics and protectionism, and share our ideas and resources more freely, with total trust and faith in each other's abilities to figure things out, always with the Divine guidance.

Some people have trust and faith in God, but not themselves. Others have trust and faith in themselves, but not in God. Here, it is important to have trust and faith in both to empower our creativity. It is then that we feed such a Realm of Union environment to produce the impossible.

If you're an atheist, then you can always believe in the Realm of Union because by reaching this realm, you're going to end up with God naturally. The bottom line is servitude to the Realm of Union, where God dwells, and Truth resides. We should change the word "leadership" to "stewardship" to better describe the role of someone who will be more Christ-like or Buddha-like.

Since Jesus was a guardian of God's natural ways, coming solely from Him, he knew how to listen not only to others, because he loved everyone through God with perfect, unconditional, and infinite love without being condescending, but also to his conscience and to the promptings of God.

As a union person, Jesus knew who he was and why he was here on this planet. Knowing his mission from God, which meant following the Realm of Union and God's natural way perfectly, he could lead from strength, based on the fixed principles of the Realm of Union rather than on uncertainty or weakness, making up the rules as he went along. Consequently, his stewardship style was eternal.

So many secular leaders today are opportunists; they change their hues and views to fit the situation, allowing their egos and self-interests to come before the collective, humanity, and God, which only tends to confuse the followers who cannot be certain what course the collective is pursuing. Those who cling to power at the expense of the principles of the Realm of Union often do anything to perpetuate their authority.

Jesus, on the other hand, was a true empath. He could feel others. He knew why they were driven to do things in ways that went against God's natural ways. When Jesus said, "Come and follow me," He didn't mean "do as I say." He meant "do what I do." In other words, try to serve the Realm of Union!

This quality of empathy allowed him to be humble and to show mercy and compassion toward others, enabling him to walk and work with those he was destined to serve. That's why he was not afraid of close friendships. He was concerned that his nearness to others might disappoint his followers.

Being an empath is like a mirror that intensifies everything. So, when Jesus upheld the balance of oneness and uniqueness and recognized its importance as a prerequisite for being in the Divine presence, where disunion couldn't exist, those who followed him could see his awesome qualities and tried to do the same themselves.

It is important to note that when he was here two thousand years ago, he had to let the Age of Disunion continue its course because he knew the reason for such a path, but when he returns to fulfill the goals of his second coming, it is going to be the end of the Age of Disunion and the beginning of the Age of Transformation, where he is going to be able to help us all to better understand the Realm of Union and the Realm of Disunion and why it is so crucial to remain righteous so that we may be in the Divine presence, where the Realm of Disunion cannot take hold.

So, in the second coming of Christ, we're going to have a greater reflection in the mirror because of the Age of Transformation, allowing us to see everything so clearly that we're going to move rapidly toward God and His Realm of Union, whereas in his first coming, the situation was very different, where we were given a choice to either reach personal salvation through Christ, to move us toward the Realm of Union, or continue to stay in the Realm of Disunion, a dark place filled with falsehood and secrecy, where it is difficult not to sin.

Jesus knew all this. As a result, even though he saw sin as wrong, he didn't condemn others for sinning because he could look deeply enough into the lives of others to see the basic causes for their failures and shortcomings while living in the Age of Disunion. That's why he tried to help people by offering himself to God and His Realm of Union, where people could stop sinning.

The Savior's stewardship was perfect, where nothing came before God. He put himself and his own needs second and ministered to others beyond the call of duty, tirelessly, lovingly, and effectively, while always promoting the Realm of Union.

In the next hundred years, we will have innovative technologies in artificial intelligence, cognitive science, nanotechnology, genetic engineering, and other areas of exploration that will allow human beings to transcend the limitations of the human body. We will learn how to use these technologies and tools as an extension of man to redesign ourselves and our children in ways that push the boundaries of "humanness."

We must be careful to never go toward the Realm of Disunion. We must do our best to go to the Realm of Union, personally and collectively, where the Divine natural way is honored and easily followed.

Of course, all this requires people's beliefs and wishes, which must then be integrated into the master system that seeks to incorporate all stakeholders' opinions into the union structure.

A disunion government, which is what we have today, is a destroyer of liberties by its very nature. We need to establish a union government for humanity that does not interfere with our peace of mind, expression, or existence, and that doesn't continually seek ways to bother us and control us.

If we let the Realm of Disunion stay, we're going to end up with higher taxes, bigger government, and less freedom for the people until it gets so complex and unmanageable that it kills us all.

I assure you, the Realm of Disunion has tried to erase every collective's identity and culture over the years, primarily to weaken every part of humanity to keep us from seeing our totality. We need to help each other find our personal and collective identities that together make up our humanity.

That is not going to be easy because most of us have not yet learned how to rely on our union soul, our Divine Consciousness that comes from our Divine Selves. Instead, we have been used to seeing the fragmented parts of the whole rather than the whole itself, the Realm of Disunion rather than the Realm of Union.

But, through practice, as we learn to bring all the fragmented pieces together, it's going to get easier, over time, to gradually come to perceive the whole, which will then aid us to move closer to the Realm of Union, where we will get to reach wholeness that is going to allow us to experience our Divine Selves, each blessed with the Christ or Buddha-nature.

Some may say, "If we were to regain our Christ or Buddha nature, then why not just relax and let everything unfold as we keep on living in the present moment?" Well, this is something we could do; an easy path to a Realm of Union environment where there is no conflict or resistance to keep us down and in bondage as slaves in the Realm of Disunion.

But, unfortunately, today, the Realm of Disunion has become very strong, victimizing almost everyone and everything, so it's best to be proactive rather than passive while we learn how to handle the Realm of Disunion through God by 1) relying on Him to handle the Realm of Disunion for us, always through the Realm of Union; 2) living in the present moment to allow for the Divine manifestations through our Divine Selves rather than our egos; 3) learning how to continually obtain the Divine Light, His pure energy, to keep us strong and awake to witness the Divine Logos; 4) believing in the Divine Love for each of us and trusting it fully; 5) having faith in ourselves and our abilities to make the world a better place for all.

The bottom line is that we've been checkmated. That means we're at a crossroads where we must decide between the Realm of Union versus

Disunion. If we choose the path that leads us to the Realm of Union, then we will be free to grow and reach our potential. If we choose to continue with the Realm of Disunion, then we will surely die.

In the Realm of Union, we let God rule as we serve whatever takes us closer to God and His union way, whereas in the Realm of Disunion, we are busy serving ourselves and maybe a few others, always trying to rule through any means possible.

A long time ago, in the Persian Empire, kings tried to serve the people. There is a story of a Persian king who dressed as a beggar and went out at night to check on the welfare of his people and kingdom. Before anyone could take on a job as a public servant or administrator, he or she had to learn, and even memorize, the ways of servitude described in Persian books and pamphlets, detailing the union structure of governance in the Persian Empire. These were designed by Cyrus the Great and based on Zoroastrian teachings to promote goodness, cooperation, and servitude rather than to rule, which is an attribute of disunion, since no one but God should rule.

Our leaders have forgotten how to serve. Sometimes, even if they want to serve, they can't, for the current disunion structure won't allow it. In a prayer breakfast in Washington, DC, on February 5th, 2009, President Obama said:

> "Democracy as a political system and capitalism as an economic system are compatible with each other. Suppose the capitalist system consists of opposing vested interest groups/classes. Wouldn't the corresponding democratic system, too, contain different opposing pressure groups/classes, which would fight to protect their respective group/class' interests? In such a situation…can we achieve harmonious existence when the basic premise…is self-interest…? Doesn't it seem unconvincing and mere utopias to think that though nations/societies consist of different opposing self-interest groups/classes, they would work harmoniously in the interest of the others?…when the vested interest groups deliberately misguide the masses by creating false consciousness among them by diverting their attention from the real

issues, i.e., poverty and inequality, by dividing them based on caste, creed, gender, region, religion, state, nation, language, faith, political alliance, etc.?…The philosophy of Buddha can flourish…only on the strong foundation of good Samskaras that teach selflessness. But how far will it be viable to be selfless in a selfish society?

"God wanted all of us to mitigate conflicts, nurture goodwill, accept each one's uniqueness, and co-exist in peace. Following Jesus means that submitting to Allah's will means surrendering to Krishna, and every faith subscribes to this idea."

Please note President Obama's above statement, "But how far will it be viable to be selfless in a selfish society?" In other words, could one be a union person in a disunion society? And I agree with President Obama that it is difficult, especially when one is working in the higher echelon of our society.

That is why we must change our current structure on the planet from the Realm of Disunion to the Realm of Union, always through the Divine Guidance employing His transformation approach of dissolving all disunion with union attributes.

Around the globe, we can now see many politicians who have taken the political path as a lucrative way to get rich, not to serve their people. That has attracted many greedy, hardened people! The field has become so polluted that when a caring politician enters it, he or she has a tough time getting anything done!

A few years ago, a young politician told me that when they went into a back room to decide on various bills, the older politicians would tell the younger ones, "Well, you know how things are. It's no use fighting it because it has already been decided, so let's get it over with." This woman was a newcomer and upset to see the unhealthy environment around her. Many politicians have gradually become like Mafioso, working secretly to get stuff done rather than openly. And the media is forced to support this type of operation.

President Obama said, "I'm asking you to believe. Not just in my ability to bring about real change. I'm asking you to believe in yours."

President Kennedy said, "Ask not what your country can do for you; ask what you can do for your country."

They both emphasized us, the people. That is okay if our leaders do their share of public service, especially since we're paying them to do that for us, whereas nobody is paying us!

They're supporting a disunion structure that is taking from us what belongs to us, gradually and steadily, and giving it to a bunch of disunion takers, which is not right. We've hired our politicians to care for us and protect our interests, and instead, they're collaborating with a bunch of takers to take from us. Come on! Let's get out of our disunion path and move toward the Realm of Union!

The key is for all of us to serve the Realm of Union regardless of who we are and what position we hold. And the Realm of Union has only one clear-cut rule. We must first serve God and His awesome creation, including humanity through Him.

A few years ago, I told my ex-husband, "I love the U.S. and its people. They have something unique that cannot be put into words."

He asked, "What?"

I answered, "Well, look at Bob; he is almost seventy years old, and yet he comes here to our home every day working hard to renovate our basement, even though sometimes he is annoyed by the fact that he won't be making enough money for the hours put in. A persistent fellow!"

Bob was a contractor who had come and taken the job of renovating our basement, but due to his mental disability (he couldn't see a straight line), it took him almost two years to finish the project, which he had estimated to take two months! My ex-husband and I, along with his son-in-law, finally had to come to his rescue to get the job done.

I continued telling my ex-husband, "You, yourself, when you used to go to work, you always woke up without any complaints and went to your job."

Most Americans are this way: good workers and ready to accept their instructions. Another quality is that the American people are not as conniving as those in the rest of the world. Look at the Persian, English, and Jewish collectives; they are always strategizing and caballing!

Americans are simple and young, trusting their fellow men and their government. They've been conditioned to be good little boys and girls and naively follow orders, which so far have not been beneficial to humanity, but one day, they are going to become aware and then watch out! Anything can happen. That's why today's disunion structure wants to take away their guns!

My ex-husband asked, "What would you say to them?"

I answered, "I would say, first, grow up and realize that you cannot trust the current global structure of the Realm of Disunion that has grown and taken over everything. Things are not what they seem or what they used to be. Second, now that you know what's going on, don't try to strategize like some others to the point of caballing. Try to become aware of the Realm of Disunion and stop it from draining you and the rest of humanity. Be careful; don't take the path of becoming a Realm of Disunion comprador, conspiring against others. Stay on the side of the Realm of Union."

America is a nation of good kids, still young and naive, not yet able to recognize the enemy, yet strong enough to handle anything. Wouldn't it be something if they end up being the collective that saves humankind, with the Jewish collective as the day-to-day facilitator and the Iranian collective as the spiritual advisor and transformer of disunion into union?! That's why God brought me to America. To be here when it happens! Nothing would make me happier!

All the collectives in the world have gathered here in the US with families abroad. We call ourselves Americans. The day of our spiritual awakening will be a new beginning for humanity. With God's grace, humanity will then have a chance to survive. Otherwise, our government will continue bullying other nations and taking from them until it's too late to save humankind.

It's time to wake up and put an end to all the drainage that we're causing other nations to benefit ourselves. We must begin serving the Realm of Union rather than the Realm of Disunion. The benefit of all rather than the few! In the Realm of Union, we try to serve rather than try to rule. Thus, to rule can be an attribute of the Realm of Disunion. To serve is an attribute of the Realm of Union. It's impossible to rule in the Realm of Union. Only God rules.

Over the past 2500 years, as our planet became more polluted and disunion increased, leading to less spirituality, our teachings became more selfish and individualistic, taking us away from the balance between oneness and uniqueness and promoting and strengthening the Realm of Disunion. As we move toward servitude to the Realm of Union, we will naturally become aware of many events in our history in which one collective, group, or person may have, intentionally or unintentionally, abused another.

It's important to balance such disunion events with Realm of Union acts and transform them from disunion into union through God and deep forgiveness. Otherwise, we will remain in the Realm of Disunion, resenting each other and creating more drainage that may bring our destruction or even extinction.

I'm sure he felt good about that in some ways, but we must try to serve the Realm of Union, not Disunion. We should try to simplify things while also knowing why we are simplifying and who stands to benefit.

Trust is the key.

TRUST VS. *DOUBT*

In Iran, as children, we were taught to recite Surahs from the Quran whenever we were scared, asking God and His creation to come and protect us in the event of danger.

When we stayed in our village, I remember that every night before going to bed, we used to chant different Surahs. In one Sureh, I asked wolves, and in another Sureh, I asked tarantulas to be my friends and not harm me. And we slept without fear in the middle of the desert, where there were hundreds of small, medium, and large animals that could hurt us. We trusted God and His universe. We did not doubt that we would be protected.

When we have doubts and thus cannot trust, then we try to control things; we're afraid. It's as if we were to lock ourselves in a room and stay there rather than go out and experience life. It's more secure and predictable inside the room, but my God, it's like an early retirement from life, a spiritual suicide. Why would we want to do that to ourselves?! It does not make any sense.

When we try to cover for ourselves through hurting others, not realizing that what we gain, if any, may add to our material wealth, but never to our spiritual wealth, which is the main purpose of being alive—every human's raison d'être.

The universe around us is changing at every moment. There is no way we, as limited beings, can know the full picture or where we fit into the scheme of things to optimize our path. Only God knows. So, why not trust in our Creator and His creation for guidance and stop pretending that we know everything?

In a meeting, we need to trust the attendees and allow everyone to participate, because they are all there for a purpose too deep for us to see at first. When everyone is allowed to communicate democratically, we may have a better chance of knowing the participants and the reasons they may be in the meeting. Not only the reason established by man but also by God the Almighty, especially since every person has the potential of being his or her ego as well as the Divine Self. The former belongs to the Realm of Disunion, while the latter belongs to the Realm of Union, both of which may be necessary to get us closer to the truth.

Most of us, unfortunately, live such busy lives that we are often so out of tune with our true selves that we have lost our connection to our centers and thus to ourselves and the universe around us. We need to reconnect to our centers for our instructions. So, it's important to strengthen our connections with these centers and to have more faith in the Divine and His creation, which guides us.

Think about it. What would have happened if Adam and Eve had continued to trust in God directing them? Would we have been in the mess we are in today? Surely, not! We would have learned from God how to live in the Realm of Union and leave the Realm of Disunion to God to manage it for us. Let's pray and believe in God. Let's work together to regain the faith we lost a long time ago.

And for those atheist friends out there, who don't believe in God, it's okay. Just believe in the Realm of Union because it is almost the same, except for the fact that God is the creator of the Realm of Union, while allowing for the lack of it, which is the Realm of Disunion.

Life happens spontaneously if we let it and trust it. So, if in doubt, take a walk. Be spontaneous. Practice this spontaneity, and you can regain your trust in life. After a while, no more doubt! No more fear! You stop controlling life. Some people plan their whole lives and are so busy implementing them that they don't let God or His creation give them any instructions, miracles, surprises, or other gifts. They function as if they know what the higher powers have decided for them, and 'whatever that is' never changes!

When we control things, we do not trust or listen to God and the universe to show us what to do. The universe is changing every second. We need to stay in tune with it. And the only way is to try to receive our instructions from it daily through witnessing the Divine Logos.

It takes time to overcome your doubts and fears to practice spontaneity. Just try it now and then and see what happens. As you act freely and see for yourself how things just come to you, you will regain your confidence and learn to live spontaneously. Believe it or not, in the Realm of Union, you can live this way all the time!

The question is: How do we uplift humanity to better understand its relationship with the Divine? That is the challenge of our time— to heal this relationship that can help us build a union structure on the planet.

OUR RELATIONSHIP WITH GOD'S EXISTENCE

God's existence is magical and mystical. Divine mysticism is something about which all the great mystics have spoken.

A mystical relationship to existence implies an opening of the heart. It is when a breath of Divine Love enters us. When this happens, we find that we can see the whole as well as the parts in everything and everyone. That lets us find a much deeper level of relating to the world than we can imagine in the normal course of life.

Such a relationship allows us to relate to both the feminine and masculine sides of life, expanding our mental, emotional, spiritual, intuitive, and sensory aspects, and truly feeling a sense of divine union. That can be the first step in finding a relationship with Divine Sophia, where we learn to pray, meditate, and practice devotion to God and His desires for us, at both personal and collective levels, taking us into a mystical dimension.

We gain the wisdom to know the essence of things. That means everything—even every flower—becomes a work of divine wisdom. We're so filled with Divine Light and Love that everything becomes clear. Soon, this clarity begins to speak to us and guide us to a deeper relationship with God and His awesome existence, where we begin to witness the Logos, the Divine Reality, and experience the living power of thought.

This kind of knowledge can bring us daily insights that go to a deeper level of understanding aligned with Divine Reality. Gradually, we learn how to interact with it. That is very different than an abstract level of knowledge. It involves an elevation of our whole mental, emotional, and spiritual state, with greater intuition and senses, where we are in pure awareness with no thought, yet our desires of the heart are manifested. Everything is God and filled with union attributes, with no disunion in sight!

One of the magical aspects of this relationship involves aligning our will with the Divine Will, in service of the good, the true, and the beautiful, where oneness and uniqueness come together in balance, allowing us to enter the Realm of Union.

In the spring of 333 BCE, when Alexander conquered the Persian Empire, the Persians honored the balance of oneness and uniqueness; thus, the Realm of Union reigned. As far as we know, this is the last time we lived in the Realm of Union as a collective.

Of course, this phase was not the complete union phase that is the Age of Union to come someday in the future. It was the "Wishing Union Fearing Disunion (WUFD)" phase, for we still feared the Realm of Disunion taking over our existence. But it was still a great time for humanity, as explained in many books, including Cyrus' Cyropaedia and the Book of Esther in the Bible.

Throughout history, many leaders around the world were drawn to Cyrus' approach to governance because they were lovers of the Realm of Union, and Cyrus tried to follow the Divine will that is always aligned with the Realm of Union. Thomas Jefferson, who owned a few copies of Cyrus' Cyropaedia, wished to implement Cyrus' style of government in his own country.

The Persian Union that existed in Cyrus' union empire, was influenced by Zoroaster for Cyrus was a Zoroastrian King of Kings who tried to be righteous and follow the Divine will, where he was able to rescue His Chosen people, the Jews, care for his people, the Persians, and build the Persian Empire with enough union attributes that could empower humanity for years to come.

However, this phase had to end to allow for the Age of Disunion, as I explained earlier in the Chapter, *God's Way vs. Man's Way*.

Consequently, Alexander defeated the Persian King Darius III in a battle. Darius fled, causing his army to collapse and leaving behind his wife, his two daughters, his mother, and a fabulous treasure. He offered Alexander a reasonable peace treaty, but Alexander declined, saying that, since he was now king of Asia, it was he alone who would decide territorial divisions.

On entering Persepolis, Alexander and his troops looted the city for several days. He stayed there for five months. During his stay, a fire broke out, burning the city.

In 330 BCE, Alexander first chased Darius into Media and then into Parthia. The Persian king no longer controlled his destiny and was taken prisoner and later killed by someone other than Alexander.

Alexander buried Darius' remains alongside his Achaemenid predecessors during a royal funeral. He claimed that, while dying, Darius had named him as his successor to the Achaemenid throne, and so, Alexander declared himself King of Kings of the Persian Empire in its entirety. However, the Achaemenid Empire is considered to have fallen with Darius.

That was a great victory for Alexander, and a time to rest, so he rested in the capital of the Persian Empire, enjoying what was left of the Realm of Union. Throughout history, the Persians have tried to intervene whenever possible to transform disunion into union. So, King Darius' daughter, Princess of Persia, became Alexander's wife and, together with King Darius' mother, succeeded in transforming Alexander.

Soon, Alexander's calmer side came out, allowing him to perceive the world in a way he had never seen before. Aristotle had trained him to be perceptive, logical, and calculating with a great desire for knowledge. He was also highly intelligent and quick to learn. All this together helped him to wake up from years of disunion and brainwashing.

Soon, Alexander was on a journey of self-discovery, moving toward the Realm of Union. He began to respect Persian ways and adopted many Persian social and administrative customs at his court. His countrymen could not understand, for they were still in the Realm of Disunion. They were upset at Alexander for having forgotten the Macedonian ways in favor of a corrupt oriental lifestyle.

But Alexander was smart and could perceive what others could not. He trusted his feelings, so he stayed and experienced Persia's culture, with its many union attributes.

He took the Persian title "King of Kings" (*Shahanshah*) and adopted many Persian social and administrative customs at his court.

As Alexander's union attributes flourished, he became fulfilled, and his comfort reduced his drive for power gained through disunion and bloodshed.

He formed strong friendships with women, including Darius' mother, who adopted him and supposedly died from grief later on, upon hearing of Alexander's death.

His generals couldn't understand why his behavior had changed so much in such a short time. He no longer seemed as bloodthirsty as before. He was moving away from the Realm of Disunion and getting closer to the Realm of Union.

Unfortunately, before he could gain the full wisdom of the Realm of Union, his generals began complaining and asking Alexander to leave again to conquer new territories. They wouldn't let him be, but his craving to conquer had diminished this time. He couldn't succeed as before, for he had transformed disunion into union. It's hard to kill when one has had a taste of the Realm of Union.

It had taken the Persians more than 224 years to build an empire in the Realm of Union, where the balance of oneness and uniqueness was honored and continually maintained, where every king tried to behave in a Realm of Union manner serving his or her kingdom, where Cyrus, the King of Kings, did his best to safeguard every kingdom under his empire while serving the interests of its citizens, just as a Father would protect his children.

Surely, Alexander could not possibly fulfill his role as King of Kings, managing the Persian Empire in a Realm of Union way, when his countrymen were still heavily in the Realm of Disunion.

The Greeks had no idea of this balance and how it worked. As a result, they were disappointed in Alexander for wishing to support the Persians. All this, I'm sure, brought a lot of stress to Alexander. He didn't know what to do. For a while, he probably oscillated back and forth, from union to disunion, back again to union, not knowing how to maintain an empire structured so differently from what he was used to in Greece.

Those who misunderstood Alexander's behavior considered him a megalomaniac, which cost him the sympathies of many of his countrymen. However, by this time, he must have realized the difficulties of ruling culturally disparate peoples, many of whom lived in kingdoms where the king was considered divine.

Alexander's life ended in 323 BC at the age of 32 in Babylon, the city he planned to establish as his capital. It has been suggested that Alexander's wine-pourer, who was Greek and a long-time family friend, may have been instructed to spike Alexander's wine with Veratrum album, poisoning him.

Firdausi's Shahnameh ("The Book of Kings") includes Alexander in a line of legitimate Iranian shahs, a mythical figure who explored the far reaches of the world in search of the Fountain of Youth. Later Persian writers associate Alexander with philosophy, portraying him at a symposium with figures such as Socrates, Plato, and Aristotle in search of immortality. These three philosophers shaped Western thoughts and beliefs.

Here, the "Fountain of Youth" or "immortality" may be Divine Pure Energy, which is explained in detail in *And God Said to Angel: How to Transform Personally.*

When we begin to comprehend man's relationship with existence and the possibility of empowering the Realm of Union in and around us to dissolve the Realm of Disunion, then everything may fall into its right place to let us see the whole as an integrated version of the parts, each part playing a role in the balance of oneness and uniqueness that leads to an existence filled with union attributes, and no disunion whatsoever.

Those who are stronger in this union can help others who are weaker, so that together we can reach the Realm of Union. That is what the Jewish people have believed and often tried to do over the years, surely sometimes succeeding and other times failing, but always praying, hoping, waiting, and working toward its completion.

God created the world in harmony, but it has since fallen into disharmony, mainly due to humanity's improper use of free will. Even though we may believe that the Messiah will bring harmony and align us with God and His universe, it's best also to have faith in ourselves and the powers we can derive from God and His will to make the world a better place for all present and future generations.

In the Realm of Union, the most important factor in achieving any goal is cooperation; in other words, knowing how to work together as a team to get the job done. Not to expect one person to have it all and to make it all happen without anyone's help. To allow for teamwork, where a group can, together, become miraculous and do wonders.

And the second most important attribute is hope, in other words, to stay positive. Without hope, it can be difficult to get up each day and keep plugging away when the path isn't clear. That's why the disunion people always try to take our hope away right upfront before the start!

So, we have to be careful not to let anyone discourage us. When positive energy is high, the impossible becomes "I'm possible."

The next chapter explains this further, providing many examples. The overall goal is to promote the Realm of Union, which can bring us eternal light and take away the darkness.

ETERNAL LIGHT VS. *DARKNESS*

E verything is interconnected. Nothing can stand alone except for the Almighty God. In life, it is crucial to see the whole of things and not just the parts. I have noticed that I can see the whole effortlessly when I am living in the present moment with no interference from the past or the future. Because I can witness the Divine Logos and try to follow that portion of the Logos that is intended for me, which is what Jesus succeeded in doing by becoming the Logos in the flesh.

No doubt, Jesus was good at this and tried to show us how to do the same. But most of us misunderstood him and still do. We haven't learned how to serve God and His Realm of Union in a manner where we could become our Divine Selves and stay with Him in the Realm of Union for good, in other words, how to become the Logos in the flesh!

When we finally learn how to come together and follow the Divine Will and Plan for us, we will reach our maturity to become whole, where God's wish to be known and Man's wish to be in heaven will merge into one and thus be fully satisfied. Otherwise, the Realm of Disunion will continue fragmenting our lives.

All prophets of God and mystics were able to witness the Divine Logos, God's Reality, which is the Realm of Union, and how to act through Kairos to get things done successfully for humanity and the Almighty God.

These precious people could access the Divine Information Network (DIN, which means 'religion' in Farsi) on a need-to-know basis, according to the level of their servitude. Jesus tried to show this to us on a personal level. And he will soon return to show this to us on a collective level. The first deals with personal transformation, and the other with collective transformation. Knowing that the more we do this, the easier it will get, as we learn through practice.

Truly, it is now time to recall that God would rather be with us as we go on living our lives to fulfill our Divine destiny, and that it can often get difficult to have hope in a better world when we're deep in the darkness of the Realm of Disunion.

That's why we've been shown the possibility of redemption through Jesus, where we align ourselves with Jesus and His goodness to get purified in an instant, but for this to last, we must do our best to stay in the Realm of Union, where we can obtain the Divine Light and Love to keep us strong to continue serving God, His creation, and our fellowmen.

These are invitations for us to take at any moment to move away from the Realm of Disunion that is slow death, so that we may enter the Realm of Union that is filled with life and thus eternal.

LIFE VS. *DEATH*

Life and death are the roots of all the attributes of the Realm of Union versus Disunion. Today, most adults have chosen a path of slow death rather than life. Very few adults are among the children enjoying life. It's as if life has not much to offer or is too dangerous for us to experience it!

What has happened to make people so negative, keeping them from living their purpose in life and reaching their potential? Why have they chosen death rather than life?

And when I say life, I mean the ability to truly exist in the universe, not just in this reality, but in all forms of existence. So, here, death means decay until there is no life. It does not mean a transition from one state to the next.

If a person is occupied with death, then all disunion attributes tend to follow. On the contrary, if one is occupied with life, the best aspect of the Realm of Union, all union attributes follow.

Most people who have been victims in life, when they finally lie down on their deathbed, will probably be thinking, "It's time to die and leave this abusive world finally." But the union and disunion people, most likely, won't be feeling this way. They will think, "I'm just getting started to live life."

Imagine life as a journey where one is continually making decisions, hundreds to millions of them, on an ongoing basis. If one were to make each decision in harmony with one's heart, then one would stay on the right track close to one's true self. One would easily process every experience into an open system of thoughts, harmoniously growing into a beautiful being, never straying from one's true path or the balance of oneness and uniqueness, and always in the Realm of Union with God.

However, if along the way, the Realm of Disunion comes to trick us and take us away from the Realm of Union, the best thing to do is to recognize it for what it is and try not to get entangled with it. Instead, we can ask God to manage it in His Realm of Union way and just wait and watch to learn from such an experience, every time getting smarter about how to employ union attributes to dissolve the Realm of Disunion. The worst thing to do in such a situation is to feel sorry for oneself, condemn others, or begin getting entangled with the Realm of Disunion that is here to deceive us, hurt us, and, if possible, destroy us. Let's not get fooled by the Realm of Disunion ever again!

It's time to learn to recognize these two realms and to handle each life situation in a way that fills us with pure energy rather than drains us or others. Every decision can be easily made if we were just to ask, "Would the outcome of my decision serve the Realm of Union or Disunion? Would it drain or bring pure energy?" If there is any drainage, it will benefit the Realm of Disunion, so we shouldn't proceed. If there is no drainage, then it's going to benefit the Realm of Union, and so we must proceed. That's all.

One could say that when we are unable to interact with life—in other words, witness the Divine Logos and allow it to manifest itself through us—then we are not in the Realm of Union, where God dwells. Something is keeping us from seeing the Divine Reality. One may ask, "How does one become occupied with death rather than life? Does this attribute of disunion come through abuse by force? Or through conditioning by one's parents or society? Or something else?"

Today's TV news and shows are all about killing, bringing death right to our homes, intending to occupy people's minds with fear of death or a certain numbness to it. Both conditions prevent people from exploring the Realm of Union and the innate powers it offers, making them either victims or mercenaries of the Realm of Disunion.

The media has become a tool of the Realm of Disunion, manipulating the masses to think, talk, and act the same way, making them very predictable under the Realm of Disunion's limits and control.

As we create a reality, either a bad one or a good one, the outcome is always dependent on the winning realm. If the winner is the Realm of Disunion, the negative attributes rule. In contrast, the positive attributes rule if the Realm of Union wins. And as the world grows smaller with the advent of the information age, bad traits can easily spread, ruining all the good we have worked hard to achieve over the years. People can no longer isolate themselves and think that they are free from evil. So, all of us need to work together to maximize good news while studying and evaluating bad news in ways that cannot drain us further, always working with God to dissolve evil for us.

These days, in most developed countries, people watch TV and are manipulated by corporations to buy their products and services. Corporations are manipulating governments to control us through the media. People are complaining, and a few courageous groups are suing some corporations for manipulating us and lying to us. Not remembering that these corporations are just doing their jobs. To make more money!

We repeatedly witness different governments around the world taking the side of the international corporations and their major stockholders, loving money more than humanity, spreading the deadly cancer of "benefiting the few rather than the many" everywhere around the globe.

Money! Money! Money Makes the World Go Around!

That is a natural growth of the Realm of Disunion, where money is worshiped before anything else. Remember the Golden Calf Story in the Old Testament. It teaches us that there are no other powers but God alone and that the source of all blessings, including wealth, must come from God and His Realm of Union, not Disunion. When we forget such teachings, then we become unaware and blinded by the Realm of Disunion, as we are today riding on the death train that is taking us rapidly to our destruction and possible extinction! Yes, we are going to die! Unless we wake up, get off this train, and learn how to live life again.

When we are born, our soul has a chance to manifest itself in this reality. Our body is an aspect of this manifestation, a projection or materialization of our soul in the third dimension. We exist in this dimension so we can see our bodies. However, there are other forms of manifestation that most of us cannot see. Among these are the fourth and fifth dimensions. The motion of all three-dimensional entities through time constitutes the fourth dimension. The reasons behind these movements lie in the fifth dimension, which concerns the purpose of every entity. A seer is someone who can perceive the invisible world and consequently some of the manifestations of the soul that are not apparent to an average person.

When we can perceive information through these higher dimensions—such as how a person has moved through time from birth to the moment, the purpose behind their actions, different events in their life, etc.—it becomes easier for us to perceive the individual and understand what's happening on a large scale. With this understanding, we can be detached from any personal or temporal issues that may bring us disunion attributes. That allows us to get closer to the Realm of Union.

When things are unknown to us, it's best to go with the universe's flow, respecting our place in it. Imagine seven billion people living together and sharing this planet we call home. It's awesome and magical that I can pick up a phone, talk to other citizens of Earth, and get to know them! So many stories! So many mysteries! Through reflection and acceptance of the mystery, as is, we can get closer to the true meaning of life. If we go against it or refuse to accept it, it becomes harder for us to receive insights!

Most insights come from our soul, which is a part of the Divine, holy and eternal. When we die, we lose our body, but our soul moves on, manifesting in other forms in accord with the Realm of Union. Our soul is not like our body, which is under the burden and control of space and time. It is free; neither time nor space hinders it. That's why the soul has incredible knowledge about other dimensions.

Our body is our temple. We must keep it healthy, for it is through the physical that we can contact our higher self. If we are in poor health, fatigued, or overstressed, we cannot be pure channels for higher consciousness, for the Holy Spirit. We need to take care of our bodies and our souls.

No doubt, suffering can sometimes become an opportunity for spiritual progress. So, people can experience immense suffering and, at the end of it all, convey superior spirituality. So, it all depends on how they handle suffering. Some may get lucky to learn how to go to God and ask Him to dissolve the Realm of Disunion for them. Some may get weaker and not be strong enough to figure things out. That's why it's important to have union friends who can help you when you are down and under.

As I was writing this passage, I took a break to have dinner. The TCM Channel was showing the film, Violent Saturday, with Richard Egan playing the role of a husband whose wife died in a bank robbery. As he stood outside the hospital talking to the nurse, he mourned his wife's death. He said, "Just this morning, I watched her alive and healthy, drinking her coffee, and now she is dead! Just this morning, she finally decided to have a baby, not knowing that her wish would only last four hours! Why does it have to be this way? One morning, alive and well, and before the day is over, dead and gone!" And then he began crying!

The story made me think of how fragile life can be for some people and yet robust for others! Life becomes fragile when we can be damaged or destroyed by the Realm of Disunion, and robust when we can withstand its attacks.

When we can transform our lives from fragile into robust, then it is in our best interest to do so by aligning ourselves with the Realm of Union, where we can serve God and live life happily through Him, rather than be mercenaries of the Realm of Disunion whose lives are robust yet empty and unhappy.

The overall goal in life is to allow our true selves to experience life through Divine Guidance, which is often referred to as the voice of God within, and yet these disunion people waste their time doing everything but that! They can't honor life! They instead honor death! And when they finally die, they can't take their accumulated wealth or otherworldly possessions to the other side for nothing, but our spiritual gains can benefit us after our death.

Powell Davies said, "Life is a chance to grow a soul."

And what we leave behind is not worthwhile, for our material wealth has often been gained and accumulated through disunion means, thus bringing the same cycle of destruction to the lives of our descendants!

This process of taking more than one's share, of dishonoring life and the balance of oneness and uniqueness, not only drains us personally but can also drain us collectively, preventing humanity from reaching the Realm of Union. Today, we may have advanced in many of our fields, but unfortunately lost our identity. Most of us have no idea who we are and where we are going.

Elie Wiesel said, "When you die and go to heaven, our maker is not going to ask, 'Why didn't you discover the cure for such and such?' The only question we will be asked in that precious moment is, 'Why didn't you become you?'"

If the Realm of Disunion continues to grow, without intervention from the rest of us, it is possible that one day, the disunion people may become so blinded to cooperate with the Realm of Disunion wishing to kill most of humanity!

In 2006, while traveling in Goa, India, I met a young man, half English and half Iranian, from Oxford, who said that it would be okay to kill 90% of humanity so that the other 10% could live in harmony, not realizing that any attribute of the Realm of Union, including harmony, can only occur through a Realm of Union act. Killing people is a disunion act that could not bring us harmony in the Realm of Union. Why have such beliefs spread in our society?

Perhaps because we have allowed the disunion people to gradually bring us principles and doctrines that are false, that go against God's universe, that honor disunion rather than union, which propagate separation and fragmentation rather than unification and integration, which promote competition rather than cooperation, and that are closer to death rather than life!

The reason for this is that, over the years, the disunion collective has unfortunately lost the spiritual sight to recognize that spontaneity promotes life while excessive control promotes death.

SPONTANEITY VS. *CONTROL*

When we are spontaneous, we are too busy living life and having fun to be bothered by fear, criticism, or expectations. Even though we may have plans, we keep them open and flexible so that they can easily become a subset of the Divine Plan for us. In other words, the Divine Plan takes priority, with our plan becoming a subset of it.

There is less control, allowing us to freely interact with the universe and get closer to our true essence, our divine selves.

For example, if we were busy getting ready to take a trip to London and then suddenly received an incredible urge and/or sign to go to Costa Rica instead, we would change our plans and go there. Think about it. How many people can do that?

Individuals who can change their plans at the drop of a hat are often perceived as blithely uninhibited, almost crazy. Such people make wonderful characters in novels and movies because they dare to go where most of us only dream of going—into the dangerous, enticing realm of the unknown. But having lived this way most of my life, I wish to assure everyone that not only has it not been dangerous for me, but it has brought me incredible accomplishments, love, and joy, and has brought me closer to the Divine Spirit.

Living life through the divine self is unbelievable. It is the most awesome existence because the Divine Self is the holy twin partner of every person. It is possible to reach a level of spiritual understanding where one lives a life free from all disunion and aligned with one's twin partner, one's soul, which is a part of God. The twin partner knows the Realm of Union versus Disunion and how to successfully move away from all disunion toward the Realm of Union, where there is tremendous support from the Realm of Union for everyone to reach their potential.

Today, humanity's growth in consciousness has made many aware of the power of spontaneity. I recently heard David Icke explain this in detail. Of course, every person's experience is unique, but together, I'm sure, we're all destined to move toward the same spiritual destination.

The only problem for me is that it is sometimes difficult to promise I'll be at a party a month from now when I live day to day. People used to get upset at me, but not anymore because I have learned to tell them, up front, how I live my life.

But that doesn't mean my brain has been scattered, jumping around without any purpose or mission in life. I've been able to focus and accomplish much more in life living this way. Because when we serve God and are in tune with His will, things become simple and structured with definite purpose and priorities that allow us to reach our destination without getting drained.

We're blessed with faith and the power of the Realm of Union that can protect us against the dangers of the Realm of Disunion. Things often change to make it easier for us to travel the path. And it's a lot of fun living life this way. Plus, it's amazing how much we can learn in a day following God's will as we try to exist in the Realm of Union, witnessing His logos.

I always make sure to explain to my friends that when I live spontaneously, it does not mean that I do not have a plan. It means I am ready to align my plan with God's will and thereby enter His Realm of Union. A friend once asked me, "Angel, why is it that I never get the urge to change my plan?"

The answer came: "When we restrict our lives to a certain plan and nothing else, then we are not listening to our center or the universal center for our daily instructions. After a while, our links weaken, and we can no longer be reached by God, our soul, and/or other agents of God's creation wishing to direct us toward the Realm of Union path."

But then, if a person is always following the Divine Will, they have a better chance of staying on their true path with minimal change, because God's plan doesn't need modification! I'm sure Jesus lived this way!

However, someone like me can make mistakes, but no worry, if I listen to the Divine Instructions and am ready to make changes!

Suppose that you walk home every day, taking the same route. Then one day, your best friend, whom you have not seen for years, happens to be sitting in a park near your home. If you always take the same route, not allowing any spontaneity in your walking, if you don't spiritually connect to trees, birds, dogs, winds, or any other element in the universe that could bring you to the park, then you most likely would never get a chance to see your friend who is sitting there.

As you live in the present to the best of your ability, you go toward the future you are meant to have! Your potential path. The future that best aligns with your purpose in life in the Realm of Union. The reason is that by being spontaneously in the present, you act closer to your essence, your true Divine Self, which, in turn, helps you walk your true path rather than a false one chosen by expectations and/or outside influences.

Some people are so full of themselves that not only do they inhibit themselves from experiencing life, whatever the reasons, but they also try to control others to live their lives. How can they know another person's path when they can't even figure out their own? Who has given them the right to inject their own opinions and fears into someone else's story? Don't they realize that only the person himself or herself is equipped to decide through God's guidance? How arrogant!

We can find this type of control in many relationships. In life, whatever we chase, when on a disunion path, usually flies away, often to teach us a lesson. But it's all automatic, built into the system.

Why chase and/or try to change people when such efforts seldom work in the end, even if we were to gain something? Because whatever we may gain cannot have the seed of the Realm of Disunion in it, taking us away from the Realm of Union, our Divine Destiny. Surely, there are exceptions, but why not extend an open invitation to those we love, with constructive advice, if necessary, to show them more examples of the Realm of Union versus Disunion and let them decide for themselves?

We must make ourselves available to receive by freeing ourselves from all preconceptions and letting God write the definitions. Our divine story toward our destiny! As we learn to behave this way, discovering the basic goodness in our own lives, we can improve others' lives by being a good example for them to follow instinctively. We are all magnets drawing people and situations to us through the powerful energy force of our thoughts and belief systems.

Some Hollywood people who have made it on their own have guts. They have gone and spontaneously done what most of us would not do. As a result of their courage to just go and try these rare fields of art to express themselves and live in the spontaneous world, they are much less controlled than we are.

These stars and other union people have managed to live their lives in a way that allows them to tap into the Realm of Union's creativity and positive energy flow without letting the Realm of Disunion drain them. They have reached a certain balance where there is more positive energy than negative, helping them to accomplish their goals and dreams. They are the people who know the magic and power of spontaneous living, like Oprah Winfrey, Whoopi Goldberg, Michael Keaton, Bill Murray, and so many others.

An important aspect of the Realm of Disunion today is that it has become strong everywhere on our planet, increasingly preventing us from living creatively and spontaneously. The current structure does not lend itself to a carefree life. Even though most of us must work so hard to financially support ourselves and our families, with no chance to let our hearts sing, it is still possible to take time to become more spontaneous in many aspects of our lives, especially with our children.

This exercise of control, directing influence over others, always acting for the benefit of the few while claiming to wish the best for all, is done to cage humanity or a part of the population in the Realm of Disunion. On a large scale, it can become a manipulative oscillating cycle of population management where victims are added to or deleted from targeted collectives, depending on different circumstances, like in Africa where millions of people have died in the past few decades, or the Katrina Tragedy in New Orleans, or the wars in Iraq, Afghanistan, and Syria, or the present ban against Muslims.

Sometimes the whole exercise is planned, and other times, when an event occurs that could advance the agendas of the current disunion establishment, no action is taken to stop it. Moreover, the union people are always targeted by the Realm of Disunion to keep them busy protecting themselves rather than supporting the victims of such disunion attacks on humanity or other union people.

If everybody loved one another, then nobody would have to live anywhere but the present moment. Both past and future are necessary when we feel insecure and want to protect ourselves. When we feel secure, we can live in the present.

Over the past 20 years, I've felt blessed to have enough money to support myself and my family. This financial independence has given me the security to live in the present so I can better serve God and fulfill my mission to write this book!

Most people are so busy trying to support themselves financially that it becomes difficult for them to live in the present. That's why the Realm of Disunion often drains people through money. This drainage even affects the rich, for they are so preoccupied with optimizing their future gains that they are unable to live in the present. Again, there are exceptions!

The freedom to be in the present is a precious quality that only comes to those people who don't need to involve themselves too much in the past or future. Unfortunately, the number of responsible adults who could live so freely has diminished in today's global society. The reason for this is that most adults are either getting drained or draining others.

It appears that the whole of global society is confused, just running around trying to get somewhere better, often relying on leaders blinded by selfishness. We're wasting so much money and time on things that cannot possibly benefit humanity in the long run. And no time to relax and think, to find out where we are and where we are going. We could get together to work and create, socialize and play, meditate and pray, etcetera, all in balance toward the Realm of Union. To witness life itself! The logos. That is the reason we're here.

There is often a lack of love and appreciation for what there is, what we've got, right here, in the present! All caused by our lopsidedness. In their songs, the Beatles and Elton John said, "All we need is love." That's why young adults get high with marijuana (MJ) to get into the present moment. That is okay if it is done in moderation.

People who have been abused as children have a tougher time living in the present, for they spend most of their time dealing with the past and the future rather than exploring the Realm of Union in the present. God dwells in the present, where truth resides. When we cannot be in the present, then we are more inclined to be blinded to the truth. These days, many people are discovering the truth through research rather than living it. The truth is right here, waiting for us to perceive and live it! All the Divine Manifestations. The Divine Reality. The logos!

When we allow for God's way rather than our way, then we are permitting the power of God, the logos, to reign freely without controlling its flow. Many religions limit God's power by directing people to go through different channels to reach the Divine, mostly through control exercised by affiliated religious leaders. This kind of limitation, which promotes a bunch of brokers to help us access the Divine, diminishes the power of God and humanity, placing it in the hands of a few who may be controlling it for their own benefit.

Of course, this is not always true. There are great spiritual leaders out there who truly help their followers. You can tell by watching their ego and degree of servitude. Christ was willing to wash a union person's feet!

Jesus said, "I am the way, the truth, and the life. No one comes to the Father except through me." Here, Jesus is saying that the truth comes to us when we live our lives in His way, which is the same as saying "to allow the WORD, the Divine Will, the Divine Thought, the Divine Story, to become FLESH in the person."

That is a topic that has been misunderstood, which has contributed to the growth of the Realm of Disunion.

Some Christians, who understand the true meaning of the Trinity, go to Jesus, the Lord, to stop getting drained by the Realm of Disunion. The first time they do it, they're surprised because they feel so good. They call it 'Being Born Again.' In effect, what they're doing is aligning with the Holy Spirit through Jesus, which happens to be one of the Trinity's three expressions.

But then, after a while, they start doubting the experience, which then ends their bliss.

Instead, they should continue to follow the Holy Spirit and let it manifest through them so that they may learn from it. After a while of watching it do its work, each time in a new way, they may come to realize that it's best to have faith in God and themselves. Soon, their trust in God may grow to allow them to seek Divine Guidance properly.

It is then that they finally learn that any disunion thought, word, or deed can cause God to depart, thus keeping them away from the Father and the Holy Spirit and leaving them solely with Jesus Christ to help them out, which is surely possible and doable. But then, why not do what it takes to remain in the Realm of Union for good?

If not now, then when?

Unfortunately, most people who follow Jesus' way and enter the Realm of Union often rationalize that it's okay to sin because, no matter what, Jesus will save them. However, in the meantime, they end up promoting the Realm of Disunion rather than Union, which can then be very damaging to themselves, others, and humanity.

The Christians are this way because they don't realize that we can reach heaven while we're still alive; we don't have to wait until we die to reach heaven. This misunderstanding has caused people to suffer, surely wasting many lives.

The Christians have misunderstood the reason for Jesus to be among us, as the Father, the Son, and the Holy Spirit.

The concept of the Trinity, where God's wish is manifested as:

1. **The Father** wants to guide us to live through our Divine Selves in the Realm of Union, where we follow Him and His will for us rather than ignore Him and His will to satisfy our own will. So, a dense and noisy state on one side keeps us disoriented and confused, whereas the other is a state of silence and hollowness, allowing us to hear the Divine Instructions and Plan for us.

2. **The Son** wants us to believe in Him, the purest of all people in history, so that through Him, we may experience the Realm of Union and its balance of oneness and uniqueness to reach personal salvation rather than forget about Him and let others convince us that there is no hope, for we're all sinners.

3. **The Holy Spirit** wants to flow through us to lead us to our Divine Selves, always living in the Realm of Union, which allows for greater spontaneity in being our true selves, remaining on our true paths rather than more control that keeps us from who we truly are.

This concept of the Trinity has become an essential part of Western Christianity, where Jesus is primarily seen as God who came to take away our sins.

We are told that Jesus was the only human ever who lived his life so close to the Divine Will that the Divine Logos, the Word, became flesh in Jesus. And he abided so closely to every will of the Divine that he agreed to die for Him and humanity. For every one of us! This part of the story is significant and should not be ignored.

When we do live our lives aligned with the Divine Word and Will, then we can be our true selves, living on our true paths, witnessing the

Divine Reality, which is the state of truth, the Divine Logos. This is every person's raison d'être in life. So, we're all destined to get there. And I believe humanity is now at a turning point, where we could each reach this state of existence as we transition, personally and collectively, from the Realm of Disunion to the Realm of Union.

Do not listen to those who wish to profit from Jesus' statement, taking it out of context and twisting it to suit their own purposes. You can tell who they are, for they try to control humanity and serve the few. Any type of control takes us away from God and His powers. And when God's power is diminished, humanity's power is diminished as well, preventing us from reaching our potential.

We need to become creative and find ways to free ourselves from any personal and/or collective control so we can be more spontaneous in receiving the Holy Spirit.

The main technique for manipulation and control has always been through lies, not telling people the truth, so that they remain ignorant, confused, and/or unaware. That way, it's easier to drain them and keep them from reaching the Realm of Union.

Thus, the key is to be in now and witness the Divine Logos, the Realm of Union, where God dwells and the truth resides to set us free.

The state of truth is the most incredible place that I'm sure Jesus and other messengers of God must have experienced. The question is, why didn't they tell us about it in a way where we could experience it ourselves? I believe they told us, but we didn't get it, so it never materialized. Hence, it was not recorded.

In *And God Said to Angel: Toward the Divine Plan and Heaven on Earth*, I discuss my 2006 trip to India and how I learned to experience the present moment through Vipassana Meditation. Every person can reach this state of truth by witnessing the Divine Logos daily and properly interacting with it. Jesus showed us how to do this by becoming the Logos in the flesh. We should all try to do this since it is every person's raison d'être.

TRUTH VS. *LIES*

Here, the word "truth" is singular, whereas "lies" is plural. The reason for this is that other lies always follow a lie. We cannot have one lie as we have one truth. For the truth is a state of awareness.

The Hindus believe that the name of God is truth. Since we are in the image of God, truth is within us. It is one of our attributes, whether we live by it or not. We all know it instinctively. Thus, loving God and loving the truth are the same.

These statements may seem inconsistent with the last section. So, before I continue, I must explain that these are in accord with what I said before.

In the last section, I said that one must live in the present to see the truth. Here, I'm saying that the truth is within us, no matter what!

So, the question is, "Where is this truth? In the present or at any time within a person?" And the answer is that the truth resides within us at any time, because even though we may be too occupied with the past or the future to witness the present, our subconscious mind is still registering everything that is happening.

That is why, under hypnosis, it is possible to recall events that occurred years ago, even though our conscious mind has no memory of them. So, everything gets recorded, not only in this reality but in all realities. However, we are unconscious of this recording, which is happening not just through one person but the whole of humanity, even the whole of the universe. This recording is part of God's super-consciousness!

As we learn to live in the present, we become more aware of the Logos and how it operates and interfaces with everything and everyone to maintain balance. So, naturally, we try to continue witnessing it consciously and interacting with it. We exist in the present moment.

When I first became aware of now and tried to live in the present as much as I could, I was able to see the truth as it was happening and, at the same time, replay past events that had been recorded in my subconscious, slowly making a record of the real events that had happened in my life. This process tends to move the unreal events, which are the false impressions of the past events in one's life, from the storage of actualities to the storage of false impressions in the brain. Gradually, the domain of actualities fills with truthful events and no longer allows false events to occupy it. So one begins seeing the truth in everything.

What's interesting here is that it's possible to access events that haven't been witnessed, because everything is recorded and available for download once a person becomes a seer.

It is fantastic to reach this state, which has been experienced by prophets, saints, and highly spiritual people in our history. It is a journey worth taking, especially with tools such as the subconscious mind, the universal consciousness, and the Divine Information Network, which record and store everything for later access. I hope this clarifies what has been said.

When we lie, we try to cover or change the truth. But this truth never goes away. It stays on in the Logos, as we store a dismantled version of it in our perception. This version is naturally fragmented, gradually helping us see the whole. Sometimes, we lie repeatedly to prevent the truth from coming out. After a while, we build so many layers of lies that it becomes difficult to see and study the many patterns that exist in our lives and the universe around us. These patterns can bring us information about ourselves, humanity, God, and His creation. Lying is an attribute of the Realm of Disunion, blinding us to God's Will. We lose touch with our inner selves, our Divine Selves, which can collectively give us a glimpse of the Divine Plan for us.

We must always be true to ourselves and willing to be truthful with others. Our true self recognizes union versus disunion and knows the situations we want to be in. Not telling the truth can drain our energy, for we must continually keep track of the dismantled version of the truth. How to keep it organized? How to express it properly in different circumstances? After a while, people may even forget the whole thing.

Telling the truth often promotes the Realm of Union, making it easier for us to remain in it. But, sometimes, it can aid the Realm of Disunion. So, we must be careful.

Consider the example that has often been given. A Gestapo officer comes and asks whether we have any knowledge of Ann Frank's whereabouts. What is the correct thing to say? Do we say, "Yes," aiding in sending Ann to the gas chamber and her death, or do we act as if we don't know? I think we all know the answer to that. We tell the officer, "We have no idea where Ann is!" We lie because, as helpers of the Realm of Union, we try to protect Ann's life and not cooperate with the Realm of Disunion.

In such circumstances, it's best to rely on your true self (your Divine Self) and ask God to come to your rescue. It can help you decide whether to lie. It appears to me that this whole exercise may be quite simple.

We know that the Realm of Disunion is always in opposition with the Realm of Union and vice versa, where helping one is always hurting the other. We cannot help or hurt both realms at the same time. So, there are merely two conditions: 1) where telling the truth helps the Realm of Disunion and hurts the Realm of Union, and 2) the opposite, where it helps the Realm of Union and hurts the Realm of Disunion. And the best path to take is always to help the Realm of Union. That's why it's so crucial for us to understand the Realm of Union versus Disunion and the properties of each.

Another consideration is when we are lied to so that it's easier to take advantage of us and drain our energy to strengthen the Realm of Disunion. These days, most of us experience this kind of drainage. Our only solution is to unite against the Realm of Disunion and stop it from draining the Realm of Union, but this must always be done through God's guidance since He uses union to dissolve disunion.

However, we need to realize that, even though most of us yearn to be truthful to reach the Realm of Union, it has become increasingly difficult to do so because the Realm of Disunion is powerful today and can harm us if we disclose sensitive information. It's possible to build a structure that would enable us to protect our privacy while telling the truth. *And God Said to Angel: How to Transform Collectively* shows us how to do that.

But, above all, it's time to recognize that there is a state of truth that one can reach to see things as they truly are, with not much effort, but to stay in this state.

We say that the reason for all the lies we have today in our current disunion structure is for the Realm of Disunion to control us, but then why do disunion people want to control us? Perhaps to take from us what belongs to us and does not belong to them! Everything they could put their hands on! The disunion people are continually finding new ways to control us and take more from us! Until they have everything and there is nothing more to give. And, in this process, they can take what matters the most. Our freedom to live in the Divine Kingdom as our Divine Selves! Notre raison d'être.

Every prophet and mystic has experienced this State of Truth and tried to tell humanity about it. But most of us have not understood it because there is no way to know it unless you get there and can see it for yourself. Fortunately, the Messiah is destined to come soon, and one of his functions is to help us gain greater perception so we can do all this and more.

And God Said to Angel: To Greater Perception goes into detail about this topic and describes the tools currently available to help us gain greater perception.

Hopefully, if everything goes our way, the new perspective will make it easier to see the many interdependencies. That will help us increase our oneness and uniqueness equally, on individual and collective levels, a crucial step toward balance and harmony.

The Kingdom of God, the Realm of Union, will then be established on our planet. However, the Realm of Disunion will do everything possible to keep us in darkness so we won't reach the divine kingdom.

Think about it. Every few years, we have a new war. It never ends because this is the way we've been kept in bondage. Why would true union leaders agree to having so many wars, just so that they could take the victims' assets to provide a better standard of living in their own country?

These leaders must know that God loves all and is against such injustices in the world. But they remain quiet because most organizations currently benefit, financially, from such wrongdoings around the world, not directly but indirectly. They all belong to the same disunion pyramid structure that has grown through years of scamming and looting others' assets.

It's heartbreaking for most of us to witness our country, our leaders, and our organizations living off the wealth taken from other countries. I'm so sorry for talking this way. The disunion way of the Age of Disunion, with its many disunion games, where the Realm of Disunion tries to weaken and exploit others whenever and wherever possible. Nobody can win in such situations because God departs to allow us to use our free will. So, the Divine presence is gone!

And without God, people suffer because they end up building a fake world for themselves, which they don't really like, sometimes even hate, but they avoid making changes because they're unwilling to acknowledge or test the fakeness of their existence.

Through their use of language, you can sometimes tell how resistant they may be to finding the truth! For example, they're often vague.

I've seen the following responses:

- They may say, "We don't have the time, or now is not a good time to talk about this."

- They may say, "We have more crucial, important matters to resolve right now."

- They may bring up crisis after crisis to avoid addressing the issue at hand.

- They may mention other topics that have nothing to do with the discussion to confuse the issue.

- They may present false representations of the concept, making it difficult to view the issue clearly (due to deliberately created confusion) and to dissect it.

- They may say, "You mean, you don't trust us," and suddenly, your patriotism is questioned!

- When they are caught in the act of the Realm of Disunion, they may either say, "Screw you all, there is nothing you can do about it," or explain the situation, but in the process take the issue to the Realm of Disunion rather than the Realm of Union.

- They may just fall asleep or get up and leave!

This entire process is meant to ensure that everybody ends up in the Realm of Disunion. Sometimes, they're so afraid to get a glance of the Realm of Union that they don't even want to talk about it! It's a shame.

Because we do need to talk about the Realm of Disunion and how it has kept us all in bondage, and/or the Realm of Union and how it can aid us in reaching its real peace and balance; otherwise, nothing ever gets resolved! This whole game can easily be seen in how we deal with individuals, here and there, when they're trying to handle smaller problems that need resolution.

But all this can change with the arrival of the end time, which is the beginning of man's effort to repair the world through the guidance of the Almighty and the Messiah as His vessel.

It's going to be a great time for all of us, when we will be able to feel, for the first time, the heart of the mystic, allowing us to see the Truth as it is revealed to us moment to moment.

The mystics are open to what is in the process of becoming because they live in the moment in the Realm of Union, where God dwells and everything is whole and holy. They're His true lovers who know that the path to God is not about self-improvement. It's about God's wish to be known and man's wish to be in heaven, coming together to become one.

Mystics have always stood at the forefront of consciousness because they are not attached to the past or the future and can witness the form and fragrance of the present NOW manifested in the Divine Logos.

They know the ego and how it can fabricate a false path for everyone to take toward the total annihilation of humankind. Yet they're naturally inclined to remain silent and withdraw within their devotion.

That's why many mystics go into isolation to be alone, where no one can interfere with their ability to witness the Divine Logos, the Realm of Union in NOW.

That's why many mystics are reluctant to live among us so that we can see them and learn from them. They are often reclusive, introverted, and looking inward towards the Source. They cannot stand our collective activity that is often in the Realm of Disunion, smelling to high heaven with attributes of disunion, like the benefit of the few rather than the benefit of all.

The mystics would rather live their truth inwardly in the solitude of their devotion, where the power of the Realm of Disunion cannot reach. But today, there is a need for the secrets of the heart to be made public, for the music of the soul to be played.

The mystics feel love for all. At the same time, they wonder how anyone can be transformed to love when love is so free to be packaged and so potent to be forced.

Surely, there is truth in that. But today, we're approaching a new era. The Age of Disunion is ending, and the Age of Transformation is coming, desperately needing the Infinite Unconditional Divine Love and Light.

For centuries, God's lovers have held the secrets of Divine love within their hearts, sharing them only with initiates. But now, this knowledge needs to be made public. Otherwise, life will lose its meaning. There are signs of this happening right now. We have forgotten our oath to remember Him. His signs are all around us, yet we can't see them.

How can we return to Him when we can't recognize and understand His signs? Who will help us discover His signs and then translate them for us?

Our spiritual teachers, leaders, and brokers are no longer showing us the sacred path to the Beloved. Even when we do see the signs, we can't read them. We've been so conditioned and occupied with all of the ways of money and how to get more of it by employing disunion and promoting the Realm of Disunion that we no longer know where and how to look and see the Realm of Union and its awesome attributes and tools.

We need a new quality of consciousness to recognize and read the signs of God. His lovers can come forward to act as Helpers and Comforters of man and Servants of God, helping us all open to this new consciousness. It's time for it to be born; to be established in our collectives. His lovers must now work together to assist humanity.

What does it mean to work together?

It means consciously recognizing and sharing the purpose beyond each life, and then letting it manifest through the person who holds it, so that together we can find our collective purpose.

That is an urgent matter. Humanity has forgotten spirituality. We've been too busy collecting material rather than spiritual wealth.

His lovers need to work together to give humanity what it needs. The soul of the world is weeping for the Divine Light and Love. It probably senses the way to get rescued, somewhere beyond Man's Mythos to meet God's Logos, where we can experience the Divine consciousness within the heart and witness His wonders and miracles in the Divine Logos.

It is only then that we can regain our purity to be in His presence and comprehend His essence. To be able to read His signs. To come to know who we are. To return to Him and once again see His face reflected in His Logos. In everything and everyone!

I hope the mystics and other lovers of God come together and make this new quality of consciousness accessible to humanity.

Let's read God's recommendations detailed in this book regarding His Realm of Union. Let's wake up and recognize the signs God is giving us to embrace the Messianic Age.

For miracles to appear, we must first believe in miracles. Similarly, the belief that it is possible to create a better future for humanity could, in itself, be productive, even facilitating the coming of the Messianic Age.

When exploring the future of humankind, it would not be a good thing to say, "I don't care, or what can a little bitty person like me do to make a difference!" or to stop ourselves from imagining that "Justice will prevail." Instead, we must try to have faith in humanity, in each other, working together toward a better world, while trusting God to get us there.

In the eschatology of the world's major religions, this phase is described in great detail as a period of change, leading to a time of peace and greater harmony with nature, with each other, and with God, and ending all human suffering. True happiness brings lasting peace.

We must recognize that the Realm of Disunion is truly weak and can easily be dissolved in the presence of God and His Realm of Union. We must resonate with every story that can help us and get away from every story that can prevent us from building a better world for all.

Any negative attitude would add to our apathy and complacency and take away our "Cause to Fight" for a better world. I don't like the word "Fight," so let's replace it with "Contribute." Why not have faith and trust in God and humanity working together in harmony?

We must resonate with this story of a better world for all rather than the few. Only then will we move toward the fruition of the Divine Plan for humanity's perfection.

How terrible if we were to miss it and remain in the desert of our impoverishment, suffering in the Realm of Disunion, with no way to reach the Realm of Union.

How great if we were to recognize His signs and go through our transition from the Realm of Disunion to the Realm of Union, where we may experience the deepest joy of life possible. A new quality of the divine consciousness that can be established inside and outside of our lives.

This new consciousness needs to be lived if it is to take root and flourish. We must all strive to bring God back into our lives so that we can live with the Holy Spirit and witness the unfolding of the Divine Logos. To get there, we must stop controlling events and people of the world for the interests of the few and instead, concentrate on serving the interests of the whole, always through God, following His will, not ours.

Some people may ask, "But then, how do we figure out the Divine will?" And the answer to this question is simple. We just go inside and outside ourselves, research what has transpired, and, through our feelings and true historical facts, decide what may be coming our way in the future. Then we get together and discuss our findings without any self-interest or conflicts of interest, to benefit the whole rather than the few. Whatever the result, we go ahead with it, as long as it has union qualities and does not include any disunion attributes.

After that, we patiently wait and observe the action that has been taken. If it is not aligned with God's will, it most likely won't succeed. If it is similar, then everything will go smoothly because God's wish is always aligned with the union's wish that follows the Realm of Union, the benefit of all, bringing us lots of support from the universe and its agents.

Let's not concentrate on the wrongdoings of the past. The past is gone, and there is not much we can do about it. But the future is bright if we just come together and let God's Plan unfold as intended. Let's always remind ourselves that the Realm of Disunion was destined to grow, and the elites, with the Jews as their advisors, had to employ certain tactics to keep the stability of the planet while managing the growth of the Age of Disunion.

So far, fortunately, we have all done our parts beautifully, and the Jewish people have fulfilled their mission to facilitate the Divine plan set in motion long ago. In fact, throughout history, we can see the Jews' entire existence affected by their belief that they stood in a unique relationship with God and His Plan for humanity.

Since the Jews accepted their assignment from God, it seems to me that they've been both: 1) blessed by God and entitled to special privileges, and 2) burdened with special responsibilities, some of which have hurt them badly and some have made them super strong and above the norm.

According to Jewish belief, God has guided the Jewish people throughout history, and He will continue to guide them in the Messianic Age, when the universal goal will finally be realized in a political realm of justice and peace.

That's why the Jewish collective has continued to look forward to the future, throughout history, rather than look back to the past, despite all the tragedies that have befallen them. Of course, communal or personal memory is important, but in Judaism, the best is yet to come, and all Jews work toward that perfect day, to be heralded by the Messiah, the anointed one.

We need to help the elites, the Jews, the Persians (e.g., the Bahá'ís), as well as all those collectives who have tried their best to contribute to the accomplishment of the Divine Plan. Now is not the time to weaken each other or humanity as a whole. We must do everything possible to facilitate the coming of the Messianic Age and the difficult task of the Messiah. And we must never rush or procrastinate. We must align ourselves with God and do things according to His will and His pace as we let His Plan unfold as it may.

The next chapter discusses the false Messiah versus the true Messiah.

TRUE VS. *FALSE* MESSIAH

The Lord can do whatever He wishes to do. However, He never promotes the Realm of Disunion and never employs disunion attributes or techniques. In the Divine Reality, everything belongs to the Realm of Union and is done according to the Realm of Union rules and order.

So, for man to sit around and decide what God is going to do, we must understand His Reality, which is the Realm of Union, and do our best to stay in this realm, where He dwells, and Truth resides, to free us from the Realm of Disunion.

Today, there may be around twenty to twenty-five messiah claimants on the planet: one Jewish, sixteen Christians, three Muslims, two Buddhists, one ET-related, and a few others.

These messiah claimants, and many others in the past, honestly believed to be the Messiah and gave their lives to serve God and humanity. These people often contributed to the Realm of Union and humanity's spiritual development. We must honor such people as union individuals and be grateful for their love, dedication, service, and courage in moving us all a step further in our evolution.

We must also accept that, over time, nothing changed except for borders, rulers, and their policies. And that, out of the failed apocalyptic expectations, different religious doctrines arose.

Of course, one of these people, or someone we have not yet known, may be the actual Messiah. No one but God knows! Not even the Messiah! However, it is our destiny to meet the Messiah someday, hopefully soon, through whom God may decide to interface humanity toward the completion of the messianic mission.

When the Messiah finally comes at the end time, as the Lord's representative, he will definitely help us return to God, interface our

Divine Selves, and together establish the Kingdom of God on Earth, where there will be no room for the Realm of Disunion. So, we must study the concept of the messiah and the Messianic Age in the Realm of Union, not in Disunion.

That means: We recognize that it's best to support all messiah claimants and let the natural process of spirituality clear the path for us to see the truth, regardless of whether a person is a true or false messiah. I think we could, if possible, arrange for all the messiah claimants to get together for a conference to discuss various issues related to this topic.

After all, the transformation the Messiah undergoes to reach the Realm of Union from the Realm of Disunion is a spiritual journey every person is destined to take to reach Heaven on Earth. So, instead of prohibiting people from going through this journey, as we've done in the past, and are still doing today, to keep everybody in the Realm of Disunion, why not let people go through this journey to reach the Realm of Union?

Of course, the Messiah comes to make it easier for all of us to go through this journey since he has already been on this path and can explain it to others, but truly, there is no reason others cannot get through it on their own, if we allow it, and not condemn it. It's interesting how most religious institutions have tried to convince their followers to stay away from such a path, fearing that people might get close to God and enter the state of truth where the disunion structure and its people can no longer manipulate them.

When you think about it, what if we realize that many of us are on this path but not sharing our experiences with others out of fear and other disunion traits ingrained in us by the Realm of Disunion? Today, there is no way to know for sure unless we allow people to share their insights and experiences regarding this path of higher spirituality and consciousness.

I'm sure such discussions and explorations will help us all because these messiah claimants and their followers have thought about such issues for a long time, and so, as they come together to find their similarities and differences, they may achieve a better understanding of this topic, perhaps even figure out who the true Messiah is.

When everyone can reach God and become their Divine Self, it would greatly benefit most people to attend such gatherings and conferences to hear what others have to say about it. This sharing of our experiences and insights may help each of us to succeed in our spiritual journey toward God and our Divine Self, which is a projection of God.

Many religions share the concept of the messiah, each giving him a different name. Whether they are referring to the same person or not, the messiah has been portrayed as the anointed one through whom God can guide humanity at the end time, leading us from the Realm of Disunion Hell to the Realm of Union Heaven right here on Earth.

Here, I wish to talk about what we've been told over the years about the true Messiah. Not that I am asking you to believe in any of this, but I feel it's important to address and analyze whatever has been said and or we may believe in this area, considering our knowledge of the Realm of Union versus the Realm of Disunion.

Today, while most religious traditions await end-time events, some, like the Rastafaris, the Ahmadiyyas, the Bahá'ís, the Chabad-Lubavitch, and a few others, believe that such events have already been fulfilled and that their respective founders represent the coming of the messiah or the promised one foretold. In turn, they believe that the spread of their teachings will ultimately bring about a time of redemption and peace.

A few weeks ago, many members of Chabad-Lubavitch gathered and declared that Rabbi Schneerson is the true Messiah.

The followers of the Rastafari movement believe that Emperor Haile Selassie I (1892-1975) of Ethiopia is the Messiah.

Ahmadis believe that Ghulam Ahmad (1835 to 1908), the founder of the Ahmadiyya Movement, is the Mahdi and the fulfillment of the Second Coming of Jesus, the Messiah.

The Bahá'ís believe Bahá'u'lláh (1817 to 1892), the founder of the Bahá'í Faith, to be the end-time figure prophesied in the scriptures of the world's religions.

Zoroaster appears to be the first religious thinker to conceive of an eschatological myth about a future savior who will rescue the world from evil. An idea that may have influenced the development of the messianic concept in postexilic Judaism.

With its limited view of individual salvation in Nirvana, the Buddhist doctrine evolved into the Mahayana doctrine of universal salvation, with the Bodhisattva Maitreya, the future savior of humanity, making a vow not to enter Nirvana until every living being is saved.

Buddhists and other similar religions predict the appearance of Maitreya in the 21st century as the Messiah awaited by all major religions.

Hindus look for the coming of Krishna, and Zoroastrians expect the Messiah to come as Saoshyant.

Judaism developed an elaborate system of law in the Talmud, in which one is guided to conform to God's will, with each person responsible for doing their part to create a better world for all.

Later, in the Kabala, a subtle mystical doctrine, the end of days was predicted with certain events to happen such as the return of the Jewish people to the Land of Israel; the building of the third temple; the coming of the Jewish messiah to guide the Jewish people and the rest of the world and to usher the Messianic Age of justice and peace; the nations to recognize God of Israel as the only true God; and a new Heaven and Earth to come to redeem humanity and return humankind to the Garden of Eden. The Realm of Union. And all these happened before 2240 AD.

The Biblical prophets wrote about various prophesied events as if the temple in Jerusalem were still standing. To some, this was a fulfillment of the prophecies. To others, the destruction of the temple in 70 AD put the prophetic timetable on hold. Therefore, many such believers anticipated the messiah's coming after the Jews' return to Israel and the reconstruction of the temple, not before.

When speaking of the future messiah, modern Jews believe in two potential messiahs: 1) Moshiach ben Yossef (Messiah descendant of Joseph), and 2) Moshiach ben David (Messiah descendant of David). It has been predicted that the messiah of the House of Joseph, a warrior messiah, dies a hero's death after bringing peace and knowledge of God to His people and the world so that humanity will gradually get rid of evil to prepare the stage for the victorious messiah of the House of David, who will rule in wisdom and righteousness, defeat the great powers of the Realm of Disunion world, and establish a kingdom of the Realm of Union in which people can live in peace and happiness.

Under the influence of Greek philosophy and Roman law, Christianity developed a vast system of ritual and doctrine, which shaped the history of Europe and America and extended to the European colonies in Asia and Africa.

Christians believe Jesus to be the Messiah and are now awaiting his return to put an end to evil and bring us all a world of peace where wars, injustice, oppression, sickness, sin, and violence will no longer exist.

It is called "the Second Coming," and Christ himself talked about it. He also mentioned the "Helper or Comforter," who will come in the future to prepare humankind for his second coming.

Jesus' teachings emphasized "Love," an essential attribute of the Realm of Union. As we love, we are free from all attributes of the Realm of Disunion. If most of us were to do that, the world would surely be a better place to live in. When Jesus said, "turn the other cheek," he simply meant that when one is angry, it's best to transform the situation from disunion into union by stepping back from the conflict and trying to resolve the problem, always through God, rather than to aggravate the situation. In other words, the Realm of Union can be reached only through union attributes, not disunion.

Islam, the religion of the Quran, emphasizes creating a just society by submitting to God's will and performing good deeds for others without expecting anything in return. It later gave rise to Sufism by absorbing the insights of many great Sufis from Persia (now Iran, Turkey, Iraq, and Egypt).

Prophet Mohammad (PBUH) said, "I am the seal of the prophets," which means the last. He told the Muslims that the last day of the world would be delayed so that a ruler of the Prophet's family, with the same name, would defeat the evil force and fill the Earth with justice and equity.

The Shiite Muslims identify this ruler as the Mahdi (in Farsi, means the "Guided One") who is supposed to appear to defeat Dajjal, the false messiah or Antichrist, and fulfill the messianic prophesies by ushering in a new era of restoration, reconfirming the validity of God's revelation, and reigning for seven or seventy years before his death, with the aid of angelic armies and assisted by the returned Isa (Jesus).

When I was in Qom, Iran, in 2009, I learned of a mosque called "Jamkaran," where the Shiite Muslims believe Imam Mahdi was last seen and may appear someday again, to prepare and cleanse humanity before Jesus' return to commence the Messianic Age and the establishment of the Kingdom of God on our planet Earth.

At the time, I thought, "Awesome! Jesus and Mahdi are coming together to save humanity from the Realm of Disunion and help us transition to the Realm of Union." I don't know about you, but I have no problem with such a merging of Islam and Christianity. My God, wouldn't you rather have that than what we've got today? A humongous conflict that has been created by the establishment for the benefit of the few! And many are supporting it as if it's real, actually hurting themselves. It's insane. Believe me, without this union, we can never reach the Realm of Union on a collective level!

The Bible tells us that the Prophet Isaiah predicted certain future events and changes, which many Christians believe are true and relate to Jesus Christ's mission as the Messiah.

Isaiah declared that in contrast to the age of war, gloom, and despair of his time, there will come an age when peace reigns universally. It will begin with the coming of the Messiah, the promised future king, so we call it the Messianic Age.

In brief, Isaiah described the Messiah as wonderful, the great counselor, the mighty God (in the image of God), the prince of peace, and the everlasting father (this is the most striking title indicating someone who can produce, direct, and forever maintain.

Most Christians believe Jesus to be the Messiah, the Christ, the child born into the house of David, the Son gifted by God to be the long-expected King, who possessed most of the attributes mentioned above.

However, there is still evil in the world; the Realm of Disunion is rapidly growing toward the possible extinction of humankind on the planet. No sign of the Realm of Union peace in sight!

Thus, the prediction that peace and righteousness would characterize the reign of the Messiah was not fulfilled, even though Isaiah saw the Messiah coming and the conditions of the world order improving. And since peace never came, there was no opportunity to maintain it forever and ever. Hence, the last two attributes were not fulfilled.

Paul said, "The whole Earth will groan, waiting for the day of redemption." Such changes did not occur at Jesus' first coming. So, Christians are now waiting for his second coming, the Great Jubilee, when all major changes will occur.

Most Christians believe that the first advent of Jesus established his identity and that the second advent will establish the Kingdom of God on Earth. When righteousness and faithfulness truly prevail, then the world will transform from the Realm of Disunion into the Realm of Union, its original condition. That is why Christians pray, "Thy kingdom come, Thy will be done on Earth as it is in Heaven."

Many Jews are still waiting for the Messiah, not considering Jesus as the one, because the peaceful reign did not happen during Jesus' life, as was promised by their prophet, Isaiah. They believe that a person now on this Earth, or one yet to be born, will be the exclusive King of the Jews in the Land of Israel.

The Hebrew prophets gave no clue as to how soon all these things will happen or the time sequence of these events, only that they will happen because the Word of God has declared it.

The New Testament tells us that Jesus now reigns above and that Isaiah's vision of a time of universal peace and righteousness in this world will be complete when Jesus Christ returns.

The expected Messiah, whether the Christian Christ, or the two Jewish messiahs (one from the House of Joseph and another from the House of David), or the Muslim Mahdi together with Isa (Arabic name for Jesus), or the Buddhist Maitreya, or the Hindu Kalki, or the Zoroastrian Saoshyant, whoever he may be, or whatever he may be called, if the predictions are true, he will play a crucial role as God's anointed servant at the end time.

After all, he will be ushering in the Messianic Age, as a leading helper and comforter of man, maybe even as God's vessel. Isaiah tells us of God saying, "See, I will create new heavens and a new Earth. The former things will not be remembered, nor will they come to mind. But be glad and rejoice forever in what I will create, for I will create Jerusalem to be a delight and its people a joy."

Some believe that Daniel, the Persian prophet, gave an indication in the Book of Daniel of when the Messiah will come. However, Christians try not to ponder the timing of Jesus' second coming because Jesus said, "But concerning that day and hour, no one knows, not even the angels of heaven, nor the Son, but the Father only."

Hence, no one will know for sure until God decides to use the messiah as His vessel, sometimes during the Messianic Age. When it happens, the messiah may go into shock!

The bottom line is that the Messiah may come at any time during the Messianic Age, so the Messianic Age can begin and grow before the Messiah arrives. The greater the pure energy in and around us, the easier for the Messiah to come.

The reason for this is that the messiah is part of humanity's natural spiritual growth and development, in which caring for greater union leads us all to the messiah, who has already undergone a process of transformation from the Realm of Disunion into Union and is here to guide us to do the same.

The messiah may be the first person in the front of the wave of the Realm of Union, longing for the greater union and letting God guide him to the Realm of Union so that he may then help us to do the same.

That is a spiritual journey of change and transformation from disunion into union, in which the messiah is anointed and trained by the Almighty God to become His vessel, through whom He may guide humanity in transitioning from the Realm of Disunion to Union, personally and collectively.

When you think about it, this whole transformation process can be very simple. So, let us explore it further.

THE MESSIAH'S STORY MADE SIMPLE

The Story of the Moshiach (meaning Messiah in Hebrew) can be very simple and scientific if explained clearly in a unified manner.

In brief, Moshiach comes at the end of disunion as the vessel of Hashem (God) to help humanity transition from Hell to Heaven on Earth.

This process can be summarized as follows:

1. When the Moshiach becomes the vessel of God, he begins to see the universe through Hashem, and so, he sees Hashem in everything and everyone.

2. This closeness allows the Moshiach to feel Hashem's unconditional love for everything and everyone in His creation, including himself.

3. Hashem is in the Realm of Union that is Heaven on Earth. Since the Moshiach is with Hashem, then the Moshiach is also in Heaven and filled with love, kindness, empathy, and other great attributes of Hashem, all of which can bring true happiness.

4. The Moshiach loves Hashem and wants to be with Him, so he is driven to serve Him daily and never grows tired of doing so to meet His needs. That is why the Moshiach remains connected to Hashem throughout his life and is fully satisfied. Nothing can take him away from Hashem.

5. Those who are separated from Hashem are separated from themselves and others. Today, most people are suffering from this separation. I call them "the non-union people" who can be the victims or the disunion people. Regardless, this separation can keep us in bondage and prevent us from meeting our Divine Selves, witnessing the Divine Logos, and fully interacting with it. Moreover, we cannot be in the presence of Hashem and experience Him and His awesome creation.

6. When people meet the Moshiach, they can see the reflection of their soul (their Divine Self, that is, their true self) in the Moshiach's eyes. That can be difficult and painful for most people, reminding them of themselves and their potentialities, which they have forgotten due to their separation from Hashem. Many people despise the Moshiach for reminding them of Hashem and themselves.

7. The Moshiach understands all this and feels compassion for every condition and situation, so he tries to show everybody the way of Hashem, the way to Hashem, and the way to stay with Hashem for good.

8. Since the Moshiach is here to guide us toward our transition from Hell to Heaven on Earth, it's best to support the Moshiach to help us with our spiritual journey. It's best to stay positive (with a union attitude) and not let any negativity (a disunion attitude) slow us down. We must recognize those who are here to delay this process due to fear, doubt, or any other disunion-related factors, and try to neutralize their negative behavior.

9. We must help each other through this spiritual journey (first on a personal level and then on a collective level) that can only be done through understanding the Realm of Union versus the Realm of Disunion and how to differentiate between the two to reach the

redemption of humankind and its every member, no matter the age, race, origin, religion, looks, intelligence, wealth, sex, education, etcetera.

With Hashem, everything can be made simple. When it is not, it means we have not yet truly understood Him or our relationship with Him.

Our understanding of God and His union order can facilitate the coming of the Messiah and the Messianic Age. We may have to follow the Divine will every step of the way for the Messianic Age to unfold naturally. The reason for this is: 1) God always promotes the Realm of Union, not Disunion; and 2) the Realm of Union can solely come to us through the employment of union attributes, never disunion. Thus, we have to learn how to transform every disunion into union.

That is not easy, especially since most of us have not yet learned how to do it. We all tend to use disunion when trying to handle the Realm of Disunion, which does not work, as it adds more disunion attributes that promote the Realm of Disunion rather than Union.

Over the past few years, I have learned to navigate the Realm of Disunion through the Realm of Union and Divine guidance. Believe me, it works, and I do it by continually witnessing the Divine Logos that is here to guide us all. The Logos lets us not only live a life close to God, filled with His miracles, but also protects us against every disunion event that may come our way, so that we may remain in the Realm of Union, enjoying His universe with Him.

The greater the number of people living life this way, the more the extent of manifestation of God on the planet, and the stronger the presence and powers of the Realm of Union in and around us! Naturally, in such a holy place, we feel safe. There is a lesser tendency to live in the past or future, facilitating our innate need to exist in the present moment, where there is no drainage, and thus it is easier to witness the Divine Logos, where God dwells.

At such a state of higher consciousness, when one has no problem seeing the Divine Logos and following the Divine will, then it becomes easier to live spontaneously and let His plan unfold naturally. That is the State of Truth, where we will be able to see everything, including whether a person is a true or false messiah.

Here, I wish to give an example of the enfoldment of the Logos and its Truth.

That's a true story of the day I visited David Copperfield.

On July 1st, 2013, I flew to Las Vegas alone to pick up my two little grandchildren and bring them back to Washington, DC. I got there two days earlier than my daughter and her children were scheduled to arrive.

The next day, on July 2nd, I had one day to spare, so I decided to see some shows. I stopped at a booth to buy tickets. As I looked over the brochure listing all the shows, the young woman at the booth asked me, "What would you like to see?" I said, "Maybe a magic show," pointing to a Chris Angel poster hanging nearby. I then added, "Also, this Cirque du Soleil show honors Michael Jackson."

She turned around and looked at the poster, paused, and then said, "No. I recommend the David Copperfield Show instead." To which I exclaimed, "Oh, yes! That's the one!" Because I had always wanted to see David in person in action. I bought two tickets for later that evening, one to see David Copperfield at 7 pm and the other to see Cirque du Soleil at 10 pm.

At around 6:30 pm, I arrived at the auditorium where David Copperfield was going to perform. Everybody was busy choosing a seat. There were lots of small tables, each table with four chairs around it. I sat at a table to the right and almost in the middle of the auditorium, with two empty chairs to my right and one empty chair to my left. I then placed my notebook on the table and began writing my daily journal.

A middle-aged couple arrived with a young man in his early twenties, all blond, good-looking, and above average in height. The woman asked me to move. She said, "Could you move to the empty seat on your left so that the three of us could sit together?" I said, "I would prefer to sit here for now so that I could use the table to place my notebook on it, making it easier to write my journal." She angrily threatened me and said, "If you don't get up, I will call one of the ushers to force you to move!" I said, "There is no need for that," and moved to the seat on my left so that they could sit together.

I placed the notebook on my leg and continued writing, but with difficulty. Then, I suddenly realized that the incident that just happened may be teaching me an important lesson. So, I tried to be alert, witnessing rather than just watching. By witnessing, I can instantly enter NOW, the Logos, which makes everything sharper and clearer, helping me to see the truth in everything. I have learned how to do this, as I explain in the Chapter, *Witnessing His Logos*, in one of the volumes of this book.

Right before the incident, I was writing about Israel and Palestine and the conflict between the two. I began thinking, "What if the woman and the Jewish collective in Israel have something in common? They both seem to be pushing and pulling to make things happen a certain way."

At the time, it seemed to me that they both preferred excluding others rather than including them. The woman did not want to include me. And the Israelis did not want to include the Palestinians. So, I figured they were probably following their own will, but at the end of the event, I was surprised to realize they were following the Divine will. It was an amazing experience for me because I learned a lot about Logos.

So, let me tell you more.

In the beginning, I thought, "The woman could have embraced my presence as the universe's gift to her and her family and included me in her social circle, but instead, she got confrontational and forced me outside of her circle. Just like the Israelis, excluding the Palestinians."

I was very quiet and didn't say anything to them. I didn't even look at them. I began writing about all this in my journal. The paragraph itself was, "When we have faith in God, we have no fear to live spontaneously, allowing His universe to interact with us, and gradually align us with His will; otherwise, we try to control everything according to our own will. So, we must always have faith in God." The last sentence I wrote was, "We must always have faith in God."

Then, suddenly, everybody cheered. I looked up and saw David on the stage. He was wearing a wonderfully comfortable, light, almost white outfit that looked great on him. "So handsome!" I thought as I closed my notebook and placed it in my jacket's right pocket.

The place was packed, maybe a thousand or more people. After 20 minutes of magic, he said, "Now, I am going to go into the future and bring it back into the present to share it with all of you." He asked a woman from the audience to throw a Frisbee, and it landed on a guy from London. David talked to this Englishman a little and then asked him to face the stage and throw behind him a Red Cross, made of foam wrapped in glowing, soft red satin cloth, but very light, like a Frisbee. The Englishman took the Red Cross and threw it behind him, and it landed on me!

I went into shock. I could hear David calling me to the stage, but I could not get up. I was frozen in my place. A few guys who worked for David came and helped me up. David told me to pick up the cross, which was pretty big, and hold it up. So, I did as I was ushered to the stage. The music was playing, and people were clapping.

On the stage, David asked me, "What is your name?" I answered, "Angel." He smiled and said, "I like that." He then asked me, "Where are you from?" I said, "From Iran." He said, "Angel from Iran! I like that!" He jokingly mentioned something like "Angel can't trust her family," pointing to my small purse hanging around my neck. People laughed.

He also remarked on my notebook, saying, "Angel, what is that in your pocket?" I said, "It's my notebook to write my journals." He said, "Let's not forget to read it at the end." I was so excited; I began dancing to the music. He started laughing and began dancing with me.

He then stopped and asked me, "Angel, we all like to collect things, like stamps; what do you like to collect?" I said, "Stories." He said, "Oh! I like that a lot!" As he continued commenting about stories, saying things like, "I love stories. Stories are important. Words are important," a platform descended from the ceiling, with many strings hanging from it, and at the end of each string, there was a white card with a word on it! He then showed us the words with a camera, each card different from the other, everything projected on huge screens around the auditorium. No word was repeated.

The platform began turning like a flying carousel, all the cards flying in the air while only the white side of the cards could be seen. Then, David showed me how to press a red button in front of me to stop the platform from turning. The music continued playing. As we were both dancing to the music, he took my hand and said, "Dancing with the stars," and then did some hand exercises with me to show me again how to press the red button.

I pressed the button, the music stopped, and another woman, who had been chosen earlier, again randomly, from the audience by throwing the Frisbee, was standing under the platform. She was directed to pull the card that had stopped above her head. On this card, it was written, "GOD!" When I saw that, naturally, I screamed! They showed it on the widescreen. Then, again, the music and some dancing, and David said, "Angel, remember, you are in charge of the music and can stop it at any time by pressing the button."

So, I pressed the button again, stopping the turning platform. The woman pulled another card out above her head with a word on it. This time, "Faith" was written on the card. I screamed again. This time, repeatedly exclaiming, "Oh, my God! Oh, my God!"

He then picked up a huge pair of scissors and cut my hand band, which I had earlier picked up randomly from a basket, one hand band for every person, and on it, under a flashlight, it was written, "Faith!" The camera went around the whole place, investigating all of the hand bands, and no one but me had the word "Faith." I said, "Oh my God!" And he said a bunch of stuff about God and faith, like, "Angel has faith in God, let us all have faith in God!" At the end of it all, I forgot to show him the notebook I had been carrying in my pocket, which he had mentioned during the show.

It was amazing! How did he do it? Especially since, right before the show, I had written a page in my notebook about living in alignment with the Divine Logos and having faith in God.

When I returned to our table, the husband of the woman said, "If we hadn't asked you to move, then the cross wouldn't have landed on you!" So, I began thinking that maybe the woman had listened to the Divine will, which was directing her to make me move to the other seat. I also understood that the Jewish collective may have also followed the Divine will. In about twenty minutes, the Logos had dissolved my mistaken assumptions and shown me the Truth!

After the show, as I hurried to my next show, wondering whether David kept recordings of his shows, I realized my audio journal was on! I had used it earlier, right before getting to the auditorium, and by coincidence, forgotten to turn it off! So, I had my recording of David's magical act, in a way, confirming and blessing my faith in God! I was so pleased! God bless you, David Seth Kotkin (the Great David Copperfield). Thank you, David!

Similarly, why not have faith and trust in God, letting His plan unfold rather than ours?

I tell you, this is how the Messianic Age is going to happen. Through following the Divine will and letting Him direct us to our destination, the Realm of Union, where we go through God for everything, while always keeping in mind that in the Realm of Union, we include, not exclude. The bottom line is to do God's will, not our own.

Here, we have two phases.

The first phase brings us to a state of consciousness in which we let God manifest through each of us, giving birth to our Divine Self. Our true self. As this continues and remains, our personal transformation is complete.

The second phase extends our personal transformation toward collective transformation by bringing each of us together with those who may have undergone personal transformation.

As we come together to experience God in everything and everyone, a holistic integration of all Divine Selves occurs, giving birth to our collective transformation. Our collective consciousness.

The closer we get to this state of consciousness, the easier the transition of every person and every collective from the Realm of Disunion to Union and the smoother the progress of the Messianic Age.

Our transition to the Realm of Union can undoubtedly prepare us to recognize the true messiah and participate in making the world a better place for everyone.

Before I end this chapter, I wish to ask three questions: 1) Can we have many messiahs? 2)Can the messiah be a woman or a non-Jew? 3) How does the messiah become the vessel of God? 4) Can now be the time for the messiah to come?

Let's explore the first question and, if possible, provide some answers. Forgive me for any shortcomings, as this topic, even though simple, has become complex over the years due to the Age of Disunion.

In the past, we have had many messiahs, and in the future, we will hopefully have many more. After all, we all agree that Cyrus the Great was the Messiah; almost two billion Christians believe Jesus was the Messiah; many rabbis and followers of the Chabad-Lubavitch Movement believe Rabbi Schneerson to be the Messiah; etcetera. The reason for all this is that there is not only one messiah in human history. There are many, each instrumental in taking humanity one step closer to redemption.

Then, at the end time, we will have the final messiah, who will help us to finally transition from the Realm of Disunion to the Realm of Union. This end-time messiah is no more precious or important than the other messiahs in history. It's just that this person is the last. Without the previous messiahs, this last messiah could not be! It's like every scientist contributing to the field of chemistry or physics, etc. Each contribution is chained to previous contributions until the climax comes at the end time. That's all!

Let's now talk about the female messiah. Amazingly, all messiahs have been male, even though women have always leaned toward the Realm of Union much more than men.

Looking back at history, the major prophets of the world have been male: Krishna, Abraham, Zoroaster, Moses, Jesus, Mohammad, and Buddha. All these men brought valuable lessons, but why has it always been a man, not a woman, to deliver God's message to humanity?

Let me tell you a story.

Fifteen years ago, I traveled with a Jewish friend, Laurie, an American poet, to Morocco. One day, we were having tea at a rooftop restaurant next to a mosque in Chefchaouen. Laurie began having an interesting conversation with a group of educated Muslim men, a bunch of professors and doctoral students, who were sitting next to us.

Laurie asked them about the mosque, and they told us that their religious leader, who was affiliated with the mosque, was a very knowledgeable and reputable Islamic scholar, indeed, so spiritual and intuitive, beyond belief, as if the Mahdi (the expected messiah in Islam).

Laurie asked them, "Can Mahdi be a woman?" They surprisingly and immediately answered, "No way!" Laurie asked again, "Why not?" They replied, "Because a woman bleeds once a month for one week and is unclean!" Laurie said, "Unclean for what?" They said, "To enter the mosque!" They explained that the Mahdi should be able to enter the mosque at any time, any day, to lead the Muslims. There should be no limitations.

Then, Laurie asked, "What if the woman is old, in her fifties and passed the age of menstruation?" They all looked at each other as if they had never thought of such a possibility. I was amazed, not only because they had never envisioned Mahdi as a woman but also because I, a woman from Iran, had never thought about it!

The whole time I was in Morocco, I saw men relaxing, drinking tea, and having a good time talking in tea houses, while women were mostly covered and busy carrying grocery bags. That's what the women were expected to do when they were outside; otherwise, they had to stay home to clean the house, cook daily meals, and attend to the children.

At the beginning of my stay, I was having a lot of fun, not seeing things. After I heard these Muslim men say the things that they said, I woke up and began seeing everything more clearly. I tell you, it was difficult for me to stand the Islamic discrimination against women, so I left and returned to Granada, Spain, where I lived in an Islamic quarter called the Albaicin, also filled with Muslim women, but living in a much freer and balanced environment.

Later on, I learned that Muslim men in many third-world countries were allowed to beat up women, even kill them, due to a perpetrator's belief that the victim had brought dishonor or shame upon the family name, reputation, or prestige. Although condemned by international conventions and human rights organizations, honor killings are often justified and encouraged by various communities. There is no mention of honor killing in the Quran, and the practice violates Islamic Law. My God, I can go on and on, but this is not the place for it.

The bottom line is that men wrote our history and ancient scriptures for men, not women!

Looking back, it is clear that we once experienced a matriarchal society (feminine energy). A world where people were deeply spiritual and connected to love and nature, living in peace and harmony.

But then, as the Age of Disunion grew, the patriarchal society (masculine energy) took over the planet, leading to male domination worldwide.

I read somewhere that the planet undergoes precession of the equinoxes, taking approximately 26,000 years to complete one cycle through the zodiac.

This cycle goes through feminine and masculine energies.

Hence, humanity has had to come to understand both the feminine and the masculine forces; however, the divine feminine has been forgotten, and spirituality has been replaced by religion.

Ancient healing techniques were abandoned. Women were shunned for their wisdom and cast off as witches, even though the word 'witch' means 'wise woman'.

We have had many female heroes on the planet, like Mary Magdalene and Joan of Arc, but none of these women were considered enlightened messengers or messiahs.

We have been in the Age of Disunion for at least 2,500 years. We had to go through this Age of Disunion because we chose the Realm of Disunion over the Realm of Union, primarily to learn about it and the many faces of evil. During this phase, the Realm of Disunion grew while we maintained the planet's stability. Today, we're almost reaching the peak of the Realm of Disunion.

We need to be rational and realistic. To have focus and discipline. The feminine energy has brought us empathy and nurturing. The masculine energy has brought us stability. But now that the Age of Transformation is replacing the Age of Disunion, we must allow these two energies to merge and balance, bringing us unity.

Fortunately for us, that's exactly what's happening in the universe. We're shifting dimensions into the sacred matrimony of both energies.

Some may understand it as a shift into the higher dimension, where we enter the Realm of Union, filled with infinite possibilities.

As we go through this shift, the universe (Hashem, God, Allah, Jehovah, The Divine, whichever your preference) may send us a messenger to lead us from the Age of Disunion to the Age of Transformation.

The question is: Who is going to guide us to the Age of Transformation, in other words, into the New Age of Aquarius and conscious shift?

Since the Age of Aquarius, or the Messianic Age, as part of the Age of Transformation, is focused on infinite love, spiritual development, intuition, psychic powers, and peace, all toward the Realm of Union, then surely it makes more sense for the messenger to be a woman.

Let's imagine such a possibility, and ask ourselves, "**What would a female messiah look like?**"

Aside from being entirely magical and miraculous, this woman would be armed with a lifetime of experience, wisdom, and caring, and would probably be most unique in her being. A force to be reckoned with, but at the same time, gentle and loving.

She will speak from her heart because she has traveled to the depths of the Divine Spirit. She will relate to people from all over the world because she will be a humble servant of God and His awesome humanity.

Right now, the world needs a woman, not a man, because a woman can bring other women to build a network of strong union people, millions of women, who can nurture and give tender loving care, like comforters and helpers, to the victims of the Realm of Disunion.

 Such women exist all over the planet right now. They are mothers, grandmothers, doctors, writers, teachers, and politicians, my God; it's time to get them all involved in guiding humankind and facilitating our transition from the Realm of Disunion to the Realm of Union.

No doubt, the planet is undergoing incredible changes as humanity awakens and prepares for something big. A shift in the world and every facet of our global society.

It feels as if nature is resetting us for a shift in consciousness and a deeper understanding. New ways of thinking and creating, where a woman of courage, like Esther, is allowed to bring His sovereign plan to completion.

Surely, such an approach will bring many women, hopefully the entire female collective, to play their immense role in transforming humanity from the Realm of Disunion into Union.

Women are used to giving tender loving care and telling tales. After all, the female collective has discovered, through simple common sense, that true morality lies in communion, caring, and giving.

Whenever a mother sees the pain in her child's eyes, whether the cause is emotional or physical, all she wants to do as a mother is to take away that pain, whatever the cost.

As human beings, we have compassion and can be empathic. When we see someone in pain, we want to help. But let's face it. Very few righteous and holy people are at the level where they would be willing, if they could, to take away that pain and feel it themselves. Yet this is how a mother feels any time her child is hurt.

Such feelings, which always come from giving, day after day, night after night, can do wonders.

After all, a woman is accustomed to giving. First, a woman gives her body over to the baby inside her. She carries the baby for nine months, feeling pain, nausea, exhaustion, etc. When the baby is born, there is round-the-clock feeding, rocking, cooing, and diaper changing. As the child grows, the mother has daily and nightly opportunities for giving, like cooking meals, doing laundry, helping with homework, picking up clothes and toys, tending to sick children, and playing—day after day, night after night. Does it ever end? No. As the child grows, the needs change, and the ways of giving change, but the actual giving remains the same.

The story of Esther reminds us that God may seem distant at times, but He is always with us and ready to help us empower the Realm of Union to conquer the Realm of Disunion.

With enough women coming together, standing not just for humanity's material interests but also for spiritual growth, it may not take long to persuade men to be just, moderate, and sociable. Not because God commands it, but because it can make us all happier. Not because we will suffer in hell in another world, but because we will suffer in the Realm of Disunion in this world.

All this considered, some may still wonder, **"Could the messiah be a woman?"** That is a provocative topic. However, when you think about it, it is entirely possible since we're expecting two messiahs. The Messiah of the House of Joseph, who will come first to get everything ready for the Messiah of the House of David, who will be the King of Israel, not a Queen. It's interesting how we know a lot about the second messiah, the Messiah of the House of David, and not much about the first one, the Messiah of the House of Joseph.

There is very little information about the Messiah of the House of Joseph, so this first messiah could be a woman since most past predictions have been about the Messiah of the House of David being a Jew and a King, and not much about the Messiah of the House of Joseph.

Also, this first messiah could be a non-Jew because 1) the Jews were often forced to convert to other religions throughout history so it is difficult to figure out whether a person is a Jew or not a Jew; and 2) the Jewish mission is to bring the Divine Light to all nations of the world, so it may be useful to have one messiah, who is a Jew, and another messiah, who is a gentile, as long as past predictions do not contradict such a possibility. However, I feel that the Messiah of the House of Joseph will also be a Jew. It just makes sense, but truly, who knows?!

The bottom line is that we must keep ourselves open to a male or a female messiah, a descendant of Joseph. After all, God decides who to select as His messiah, what to do with this person to prepare him or her for his or her mission on Earth, and when and how to activate the Messianic Age to bring about the best future for humanity.

So, it is not unthinkable for God to choose a woman, a mother, a grandmother, as His Messiah of the House of Joseph. After all, the world needs a woman like nature—powerful, fearless, ferocious, yet tender, loving, and nurturing. And, God, having our best interests at heart, may decide first to have a female messiah (a descendant of Joseph) and then a male messiah (a descendant of David) rather than two male messiahs, one of Joseph and the other of David.

That's why we need to gather all messiah claimants and let them discuss the Messianic Age to figure out the best way to empower it so that the Divine Will becomes essential in everything that we do, personally and collectively.

Hopefully, we will conclude that it's best to listen to God and honor His will, which may include first selecting and grooming a female Messiah of the House of Joseph, then a male Messiah of the House of David, or bringing them both at the same time, and so on. We must have faith in God and let Him arrange the best possible future for us.

Now, let's explore the next question, "**How does the messiah become the vessel of God?**"

As the messiah continues to serve God and learn from Him daily, a process that never ends, he learns how to walk on the Divine Path of Infinity and act through the Kairos to transform imperfection into perfection. That allows the messiah: 1) to remain in the Divine Presence; 2) to get refreshed continually with the infinite Love and Light of God, and 3) to witness His Logos and properly interact with it to reach spiritual maturity.

As the Messiah shares his life story and explains his spiritual journey, many will wish to follow in his footsteps.

Others' spiritual journey will take the same route as the messiah's, with ten steps, as follows:

1. Denial to be the Messiah.
2. Fear of being the Messiah.
3. Understanding the situation.
4. Acceptance of the assignment.
5. Rejection by others to be the one.
6. Fed up with others' egos, not helping.
7. Realizes the meaning of being a vessel.
8. How to empower the whole and its parts.
9. Becoming one with all, every person a player.
10. Ready to become a vessel in a detached manner.

Just replace "the messiah" and "the one" with "the partner of God," and everything will be the same. At the end of this journey, a person achieves personal salvation, and then, as people come together and build the Divine Kingdom on Earth, they will achieve collective salvation.

Most believers think the word "salvation" means "to be saved from eternal damnation." But it means much more than that.

Jesus told us, "Not everyone who says, 'Lord, Lord,' will enter the Kingdom of Heaven, but only those who do the will of my Father in Heaven."

So far, the Realm of Disunion has succeeded in keeping most of us in bondage and so much drainage that we have no time or energy to bother with the Divine Will. We have accepted the notion that it is our fault to exist in the darkness of the Realm of Disunion because it's easier to accept that once upon a time, we made the mistake of selecting the disunion path rather than the union.

In our Holy Books, there are stories about the Garden of Eden, a period in man's spiritual growth, and God saying, "The man has now become like one of us, knowing good and evil. He must not be allowed to reach out his hand and take also from the tree of life, and eat, and live forever."

But this refers to us knowing good and evil, not necessarily to having the ability to properly discern between the two.

That's why most of us adults often try to control life rather than live it. As a result, we lose our spontaneity, which can help us live in the present. Instead, we live in the past or the future, seldom in NOW, the Realm of Union, where God dwells, and the Truth resides to set us free.

After all, the Realm of Union can help us obtain Divine Energy (His Light) in such abundance that every cell in our body can get fed with enough pure energy never to decay.

As we part ways with the Realm of Union, our ego naturally grows in stature. We venture and live in spiritual denial and arrogance in the Realm of Disunion. With such ignorance, the Realm of Disunion is expected to drain our energy until we die.

If we had followed the Divine will rather than our own will, we would have paid attention and slowly learned from the Divine creation, the Divine Reality, the Logos, how to continually differentiate between good and evil and recognize whether a person, a group or an event is from the Realm of Union or Disunion.

Unfortunately, we decided from the start to ignore the Divine will and continue to do so to this day. Many people don't even realize that it is possible to know and follow the Divine will.

Jesus came and showed us how to do that; how to follow the Holy Spirit. And, if unable to do so, then align ourselves with his holiness so that, through him, we can enter the Realm of Union in an instant.

Unfortunately, most people who follow Jesus' way and enter the Realm of Union don't stay there long enough to gain the necessary pure energy to remain in this awesome realm for good. As they enter the Realm of Union, they get confused and promote the Realm of Disunion, which then takes them out of the Realm of Union.

They often rationalize that it's okay to sin because, no matter what, Jesus will save them, but in the meantime, they end up promoting the Realm of Disunion rather than Union, which can then be very damaging to themselves, others, and humanity as a whole.

The Christians are this way because they don't realize that we can reach heaven while we're still alive, and that we don't have to wait until we die to reach heaven. This misunderstanding has caused people to suffer, surely wasting many lives.

Some may ask, **"What's so special about now for humanity to reach this state of spirituality?"**

Today is a new day. It is the time of Hashem (God) and His revelation for the Jews, who have been waiting for this moment for a long time. It is called "Olam HaBa," or "the world to come," which is an important part of Jewish eschatology.

We're now in the Gregorian year 2022 and the Hebrew year 5782, which is a Sabbath year.

Some people can feel the timing of things and events, and it seems that it may now be the beginning of the Messianic Age and the time of man's salvation. If so, it will be a great time for all of us.

We've been told that humanity is destined to transition from the Realm of Disunion to Union at the end time of the Age of Disunion, when the Age of Transformation has to begin. I strongly believe we're now approaching this point in human history.

In the Age of Transformation, we will learn how to work with God to dissolve the Realm of Disunion for us, both personally and collectively. For this to happen smoothly, we have to reform and reach enough purity to be in God's presence. If we promote disunion, then God departs, and without Him, it is difficult to handle the Realm of Disunion on our own. However, with Him, the Realm of Disunion dissolves, allowing the Realm of Union to appear in all its glory and restore us.

With this restoration, we become whole. A whole person can live through God as a Divine Self, allowing God to manifest in that person. That means he or she can become the vessel of God.

Every person can learn to walk the Divine Path of Infinity and transform from the Realm of Disunion into the Realm of Union, becoming his or her Divine Self and thus a vessel of God. Every person's mission in life is to reach this higher spirituality to become a partner with God. It's just that most of us don't know how to achieve this state, even though we can feel it as a deep potential within.

Knowing all this, the answer to the third question, **"Can now be the time for the Messiah to come?"** is clearly, **"Yes, it's time!"**

TRUE MESSIANISM

The Messianic Age is the age of God's involvement through the Messiah as His vessel in redeeming humankind.

The state of the world reaches such a disunion peak that we're checkmated and ready to embrace the Divine intervention through the Messiah to bring us back to union.

At such a time, we are at a crossroads where we must choose between two paths, one leading us to the Age of Union, the Kingdom of Heaven on Earth, and the other to total Hell. And such an ugly hell that it will be possible not only to crush billions of human beings but also our capacity to be human.

Today, it is evident that many have forsaken what is moral and what makes us human and instead placed personal survival above moral considerations. Everywhere we look, we can see predators preying on others and leaders who have joined the criminal gangs of bullies, ready to steal and kill in the tight solidarity of the good old boys' network.

We can either accept and hope for the best, or we can stand up and say, "Enough is enough!"

Surely, the second path makes more sense, since we will be relying on God, as the Bearer of Burdens, to dissolve the Realm of Disunion for us. We try to follow God's way rather than man's way.

Our readiness to transition from the Realm of Disunion to the Realm of Union is necessary, a prerequisite, for the coming of the Messianic Age, which is a lot like a spiritual movement that is fueled at the end time by God, the Messiah and humanity working in unison, hopefully, every person participating, to heal humanity.

This transformation requires God to work with the Messiah, as His vessel, to guide humanity through the Messianic Age to transition from the Realm of Disunion to the Realm of Union, personally and collectively. The goal is to become whole and balance oneness and uniqueness so that we may live in harmony with the Divine existence to finally reach Heaven on Earth.

Let us explore this spiritual process entailing: 1) the transformation of the Messiah to become the vessel of God; 2) the acceptance of the Messiah to interface with us so that we may learn from him how to become the vessel of God; 3) the salvation of man, first on a personal level for each person and then on a collective level for humanity. These are required steps toward our spiritual maturity.

THE MESSIAH AS GOD'S VESSEL

The Messiah is a messenger of God with unique functionalities, one of which is to become a vessel of God. As the Messiah undergoes a spiritual transformation to prepare for his assignment, he moves closer to God and the Realm of Union, and naturally becomes more alienated from the society that often exists in the Realm of Disunion at such a crucial time.

Since the Messiah has no one but God to look up to and ask for advice, he can become very isolated, indeed, living a very lonely life. Sometimes, a messenger can commune solely with children, nature, and animals, and quietly with God, because no one else can understand him or his essence.

But then, as time passes, the Messiah learns to draw on more pure energy to draw closer to God and His Realm of Union, where his life is so full of God's wonders and miracles that he is filled with joy and delight. This pure energy is so abundant that it can generate enough light to sustain the Messiah and humanity for years.

In the beginning, the Messiah tries to share the joy of his closeness to God with humanity but soon realizes that this is not a possibility until the time is right, so he continues to experience God's wonders and miracles every day, all by himself, hoping that someday, people will be able to relate to him and assist him in delivering God's message and expressing such Realm of Union moments with humanity as a testimony, not to only God's power but His mercy.

The life of the Messiah is never pointless. He is determined to inform everyone that it's best to align with God and His Realm of Union, whether they hear it or not. People may not care to hear the Messiah's recommendations, which may have come from God, but they should try not to remain indifferent to the Messiah's existence, just in case he may be real.

It's time for all of us to see the Messiah as a blessing. It's like when we are sick and under treatment. We try to honor the doctor and do what we're told. So, why not do the same here? The Messiah has come to show us how to heal ourselves spiritually through a healing procedure that the Almighty has recommended. Why would we want to ignore it or not honor it?!

That is our chance to witness God's concern for us as He becomes personal. It is an opportunity for us to see how He cares for us, how He knows inside and outside of us, all of our union and disunion attributes and our need to transition fully to the Realm of Union, and how He may guide His Messiah to serve humanity and His creation in the best optimal way.

The Messiah tries to hold God and Man in a single thought, which is not easy. He gains this ability after years of loving God, while witnessing the magic of life through God and His Logos. The result is a deep-rooted desire always to promote the Realm of Union.

Indeed, the power to see the Divine Logos is of such importance to the Messiah that he does whatever is necessary to serve the truth and its purpose to positively affect others, not as he sees it but as the Divine Logos demands it.

It would be insane to ignore or decline such a great occasion, where a person has practically worked all his life to get ready to serve us in the manner that would please the Creator Almighty, who loves us so.

The Messiah may not know how to do his job well, but as he goes out into the field with outstanding faith, he gradually aligns with and becomes in tune with the Divine will, receives guidance from Him and His agents, and gains the wisdom and confidence to do a good job.

However, before anything can happen, there has to be more trust. With trust, the Divine Energy can flow through and around the Messiah, causing everything to go smoothly and helping him deliver the Divine Message more effectively with the guidance of the Holy Spirit.

At first, the Messiah may be too weak to build this trust if those around him have difficulty accepting him for who he is. However, as he gradually grows in training and strength under God's guidance, a day comes when he realizes that the power of trust can come from above as well as below, with no one's help but God's.

As people begin to feel this trust in him, which may be solely from above, more respect and pure energy can naturally flow through, making it easier for him to deliver God's message.

At the height of the Messiah's development, it is no longer he who delivers; it is God manifesting through him, as His vessel. Every person is equipped to do this as long as there is a strong will to go through the process of becoming one's Divine Self.

Since most people cannot see things clearly and often doubt everything, including God's existence, it becomes difficult for the Messiah to clearly show people the Divine will unless God decides to intervene and directly reveal His will. We need to keep ourselves open to such holy surprises.

When God gives us our mission through His Messiah, He does so because He is dismayed by man's intense greed, even when it stands checkmated as it does today. He loves humanity and His creation equally, wishing for harmony between the two. The imbalance we have created is too unbearable for Him and His universe to stand. There is no other solution but to bring His children to the Realm of Union. The Messiah, as God's lover and vessel, feels His concern and leaves everything behind to understand His message and deliver it to humanity.

As the Messiah takes on the task of conveying the word of God, he lives not only his personal life but also one guided by God's will. He feels God's Heart. And, as he tries to look at the creation through God's

Eye, he learns how to love his fellowmen and every entity in the universe unconditionally through Him.

It is a crossroads between God and man, where God is involved in the life of man, and the Divine mission is not a mere recommendation for man but an expression of the Divine concern, charged with a spirit of disappointment and hope.

God's concern is never with nature or any other part of the universe, which already exists in the Realm of Union, but with human history, totally devoid of balance.

God's mission is not simply the application of timeless Realm of Union principles and standards to a particular human situation but an interpretation of a moment in history and a Divine understanding of a problem urgently in need of resolution.

God's message seeks entrance into the heart of man, calling on the Messiah to communicate it to humanity. A point of no return is reached: the Messiah becomes one with what he says; he becomes so involved with people that his life and soul are at stake in what he says and in what happens afterward. God's involvement echoes, where not only the Messiah but God Himself is engaged in what the words convey.

The Messiah reminds us of humanity's moral state, despite its disunion, marked by lies, disorder, abuse, inequality, and injustice. To us, such qualities seem fine and bearable. To the Messiah, they are inexcusable and dreadful, needing urgent repair of humanity's threshold of existence.

Sin is not only considered a violation of the Divine Law but also a loss to every member of creation, the Realm of Union, and God's presence.

While the world is at ease, intoxicated or asleep, the Messiah is sleepless, feeling the blast from heaven. Few are guilty, but all may be responsible for the structure of the Realm of Disunion, which has almost reached its peak.

But then the Messiah realizes that God is so merciful that He has already forgiven humanity's past sins and is now looking forward to transforming everyone from the Realm of Disunion into Union, so he tries to remain positive.

However, at times, he can't help but challenge most nations, rulers, advisors, managers, compradors, and gatekeepers, always in a Realm of Union way, for he knows that many have distorted what the Lord has demanded of humankind.

To meet and understand the Messiah and hear God's message, we must try to get rid of our disunion habits of judgment and inquisition and detach from the ego and earthly desires. We must also avoid indifference and try to get involved. God is the focal point, and the world is seen as reflected through God.

The Messiah's mission, which is waiting to become everyone's mission, is to return to God. So, he begs people to please forget him, the Messiah, and instead, think of God and His love and concern for humanity. This ability allows him to view everything through the Divine Eye and remain detached as the Divine Plan unfolds.

It is difficult for the Messiah to have to tell people that they are going to die if they don't reconsider. Sometimes, the people and the Messiah have no language in common. Our society tends to cherish appearance, knowledge, wealth, and might. To the Messiah, such fascinations are unworthy and foolish.

And the fact that the Messiah is often unimpressed by such attainments, especially to be the "anointed one," tends to make the situation even more difficult at times.

But the Messiah tries to endure and be the best that he can be.

Being in harmony with the pure essence of everything has prepared the Messiah to endure anything, especially after years of training and wishing to follow the Realm of Union. Thus, we can only ignore the Messiah at the risk of our despair. We must decide whether the ultimate situation is a conflict or a concern.

But then, let us not forget that people usually don't want to be bothered with pondering whether a newcomer is God's Messiah.

No doubt, the coming of the Messiah, or any new messenger of God, can affect people through what their religion supports. And we all know that the Realm of Disunion has infected all major religions worldwide.

Hence, all this can make it difficult for the Messiah and most people to accept the situation as it is and to go beyond the blockages that have come from the Realm of Disunion to prevent the flow of the Realm of Union wave.

That's why it's best to study the Divine Message, proposal, and projects, as described in *And God Said to Angel: How to Transform Collectively*, regardless of the Messiah, and realize that the Messiah is here just in case we may need him to answer any questions we may have.

The key is to follow the Spiritual Formula, detailed in *And God Said to Angel: How to Transform Personally* to obtain the Divine Light, His pure energy and the Divine Love, His full support, to heal humanity, in fact, every human being, to transform from disunion into union, always through Divine guidance.

We need to facilitate our communion with the Messiah and let the Divine Plan unfold. That is why we all must accept the Messiah's strange certainties and tremendous claims at this time of humanity's spiritual development, so that the Messiah can express his feelings and fulfill his fundamental objective: to reconcile God and man.

It's best to welcome all messiah claimants and let them come together to create a group of union individuals who are willing to dedicate their lives to humanity because they care for the advancement of man's spiritual journey toward the Realm of Union. That will surely facilitate the Messianic Age, so why not encourage it rather than go against it?!

At this time, we should be careful to avoid all thoughts, words, and activities that may hinder our spiritual journey toward reconciling our relationship with the Lord.

Why a reconciliation between God and man?

Perhaps because of God's disgust of man's abuse of free will and man's resentment of God's lack of involvement in human history. The latter, of course, is not true, for God has always been involved, but humanity, due to certain disunion attributes and views, has been too blinded to see it.

The key to such reconciliation is to regain the essence of who we truly are and live our own Divine Story, which is part of the Divine Logos intended for each of us. It is then that we can each become the Logos in flesh, through the Divine Self, as Jesus did and guided us to do the same.

Messianism, if correctly understood, is a deep desire for the redemption of this world filled with injustice, lies, deceptions, secrecy, and other attributes of the Realm of Disunion and an intense longing for the Realm of Union accompanied by the knowledge of how to transform from the fragmentary nature of the Realm of Disunion into the wholesome nature of the Realm of Union.

The Messianic Age can begin with a period of teaching and learning how to live in God's reality that is manifesting in the present moment, in NOW, inside and around us, with its infinite love and light. In such a state, all fears disappear. Faith and enthusiasm appear. We start to experience an acute awareness of the transitory nature of existence. We can't help but follow the natural way, which is God's way, rather than our own, and try to learn from Him, every day, everything that is.

When we get up in the morning, we are happy to be alive and eager to witness the Divine Logos. We get to trust Him and His Logos fully, for we can feel His love for everyone and everything, knowing deep inside that His love will always keep intact the universal balance of oneness and uniqueness that protects us all. We try to become Helpers in the Realm of Union, Comforters in the Realm of Disunion, and Servants of God, always promoting the Realm of Union.

We allow God to rule, not us. And when we do that, then naturally there is no room for the Realm of Disunion. No more evil. Just pure bliss!

That is not easy to do. It's easier on a personal level rather than on a collective level, especially since the Realm of Disunion is strong at this time, keeping everybody and everything down and in the darkness where it's difficult to see things.

The main purpose of the Messianic Age is to transform the global structure of the Realm of Disunion into a union structure on a collective level, so that people can begin to be supported by the new union structure and its people on the planet rather than continually attacked by the Realm of Disunion and its people.

In life, when we are in a bad situation heading toward a terrible outcome, we try to leave the path we're on and, if possible, move toward a better future. A future in the Realm of Union rather than Disunion. So, here, we can do the same!

Now that we have talked about true messianism, let's take the time to address its opposite.

Messianism, if misunderstood, finds expression in the political idea that a particular ruler, nation, or collective is invested with a messianic identity to create order in the world without Divine involvement. Not realizing that the Messianic Age can only progress through God's guidance.

Over the years, we've had different collectives try to build various myths and God stories to better compete with other segments of humanity. Sometimes, they've even altered historical facts to continually prove their uniqueness, not realizing that in the Realm of Union we are each created in the image of God and, at the same time, unique and equal to every other person.

Let me explain how two people can each be in the image of God, super unique, where no two individuals are alike, yet be equal.

God has designed everything for a goal. A Divine purpose behind existence. First, to let us grow up spiritually and reach the maturity to know how the Realm of Disunion operates. Second, to guide us to transition from the Realm of Disunion to the Realm of Union.

If each of us were to realize this Divine Design and Purpose, we would come to understand that life has a purpose for each of us: to repair this world and make it into a garden rather than a jungle.

We realize that such attempts to hide or change humanity's past can be very destructive, as they leave no room for exploring our individual or collective identity.

In the past, we've been so accustomed to having our own way rather than His that we've become expert manipulators, always trying to control everything and everyone to a point that we may now be moving toward a state of insanity. That is especially true at the collective level, where we have not yet learned how to witness the Divine Logos together.

Aligning with the Logos individually is one thing, but doing it as a group of two or three, or more, requires lots of practice. Some people don't even know how to do it on their own. The reason for this is our inability to relate to God properly.

Our religions have failed us. Not only have they not shown us the way to God, but they may also have prevented us from reaching the ultimate height of spirituality and living a good life.

A state where we do our best to listen to God and try to figure out His signs for us, where we leave our lives in God's hand, as we try to remain in the Realm of Union.

When we do our best to serve all rather than the few, God will always take care of us, making sure we will not get lost or drained by the Realm of Disunion. He will guide and direct us toward the Realm of Union, which is always the right path.

At this time, we need to realize that the path we selected a long time ago has brought us to the horrible disunion structure we now have in place, draining everyone. That we must gradually (in a union way) put an end to this proactive history of man and learn how to live with God in His Realm of Union according to His will and plan. And that the best way to do this is to align ourselves with our true selves, in other words, our Divine Selves, which can allow God to manifest through us.

It is then that we will be able to experience a gradual transformation of our current structure of the Realm of Disunion into a new structure of the Realm of Union.

Surely, this has been humanity's overall goal all along. To first experience the Mythos and its properties, and then slowly move toward the Logos.

We have to be careful not to interfere with God's plan. What if God decides to assign certain tasks or responsibilities to a particular collective? Then we must honor the Almighty's wish and go along with it, for He always knows best. But remember, whoever is chosen to accomplish a task must continue serving humanity and God and going through God to dissolve disunion, always with union attributes.

We cannot continue polluting the Earth, humanity, and the rest of the universe, promoting disunion attributes in every facet of our lives and our global society. With too much pollution, I assure you, one day, everybody around the world will be so disgusted with the hell of the Realm of Disunion to say, "Enough is Enough!" requesting a change and wanting the Realm of Union.

We don't want things to get so bad to blow up like a volcanic eruption. It's better to have things happen slowly and more naturally so that there is no destruction, just lots of construction for the benefit of all, including the elites, who are members of humanity like everybody else. Also, let's not forget that there are union members in every collective, deserving the best that life can offer.

Every union person plays a crucial role in humanity's spiritual development.

Over the years, all of us union people have been busy promoting the Realm of Union and our many causes, but since the union structure has not yet gained the strength required to properly support everyone, we've been working mostly in isolation rather than united together with the goal and savvy to build a strong union structure and network.

Since the current global structure is the Realm of Disunion, and as a result, many people have become compradors working for the Realm of Disunion and supporting its structure, the network of disunion people is currently larger and stronger than the network of union people.

That's why the disunion structure has grown over the years, increasing the influence of the disunion people on the planet, which, of course, has weakened the Realm of Union and its people. But this is destined to change soon, and the union people and the disunion victims need to become aware of this important aspect of our present global situation.

Today, we're approaching a new era where most of us are getting pretty fed up with the Realm of Disunion, its daily horrors and attacks on people and the planet, its growing degree of lies and deceptions, its ruthlessness and uncaring attitudes toward righteousness and humanity's welfare and its continual need to go to war with the Realm of Union and its people and God, in general.

Humanity is now advancing toward a kind of readiness that has never existed before, at least as far as we know, mainly due to the existing information age, the media, and various digital technologies available to us to help us evaluate our situation, so that we may finally unite against the Realm of Disunion as humankind's enemy.

The key is to recognize the Realm of Disunion for what it is, not as a person or a group or a collective, we may wish to blame for the suffering of man, but as spiritual pollution that has prevented the Divine Light from reaching humanity.

When we begin to see the Realm of Disunion as the sole destroyer of man and how important the Divine Energy can be in dissolving it, then we will be ready to get together to do something about it, and that will set in motion the Messianic Age as part of the Age of Transformation.

Hopefully, one day soon, everybody will come together to build the union structure, and the union network will grow and become as strong and visible as the current disunion structure and network! And our unity will be through God, whereas the disunion unity always lacks God and His awesome, infinite powers!

Imagine the union people gathering in a place and, together, changing it for the better, then moving to another place to change it there as well, and so on, as vagabonds, troubadours, gypsies, and, most of all, avatars, with insights to help humanity.

I hope that as we all get to see the total picture, we will realize: 1) we each have a role to play in all this so we need to become active participants in promoting the Realm of Union, as the children of the light; 2) we can learn from each other and from God to build a better world for all, as we get together with whoever may be interested, to develop a strong union structure and network on the planet that can support all people and their efforts, as long as they promote the Realm of Union; 3) we can share our knowledge and insights with each other to prevent the possibility of the Realm of Disunion deceiving us and making it appear as if we're moving toward the Realm of Union when in reality we may actually be getting more infected in the Realm of Disunion and so weakened by it to gradually die; 4) we can show the disunion people and the rest of humanity, including the disunion victims, why it's in everyone's best interest to promote union rather than disunion; 5) we should act sooner than later to reduce the degree of violence that can affect the extent of destruction, so no reason for a violent ending; and finally 6) if we were to allow the Realm of Disunion to continue with its growth and destruction, in other words, not act soon enough, then it is possible that most of us will be destroyed in the process.

That is important right now, and there is really no reason to delay it.

You may wonder, "What if we use our free will to decide, as a collective, to wait and do nothing or to stay in the Realm of Disunion, even contribute to its growth?" Of course, we could choose these options, but it would be like suicide.

Why would we decide to kill ourselves or wait to take a risk of the annihilation of humankind?

AND GOD SAID TO ANGEL

Three major causes could be: 1) some people getting so greedy and full of themselves that they forget their humanity, 2) our technological advances getting ahead of ourselves, and 3) the rest of us remaining too apathetic to get up and do something about 1 and 2.

When we measure our progress, what should matter the most? Our technological advancements or our humanity? Of course, our humanity. That is the metric we must always use to determine how much we have advanced as a collective. Not by our technological gadgets but by how much of our humanity we have kept.

The key question then becomes, "How should we define our humanity?" The answer is simple and contained in most holy books.

As Jesus said, we must love others as we love ourselves. To care about others as we care about ourselves and our family members. When we make our decisions, we try to think about everyone involved, considering all interests and the benefit of all, rather than our own interests alone.

As this life of realization unfolds, we learn to simply do what is brought to us today and be ready for tomorrow when it comes, knowing that tomorrow will bring tomorrow's instructions. We remember that tomorrow's instructions are not needed until tomorrow comes.

Both the Torah and Jesus told us to live this way because, in the Divine force, there is something vast and powerful that oversees and determines all results.

Can you imagine, just attending to the right side of your body and not the left or your head but not your heart, not realizing that every part of your body must play its part together with other parts for the whole body to function properly?

Suppose we continue with such a limited mentality that aligns itself with fragmentation rather than wholeness. In that case, we're not going to be strong enough to usher in the Messianic Age as it is destined to unfold according to the Divine will.

Below are some possibilities regarding the arrival of the Messianic Age:

- The Realm of Disunion will grow. Humanity will come to a point of annihilation. That will force us to put an end to the Realm of Disunion, which may require a violent ending. The degree of violence may depend on the extent of the destruction. If we were to allow the Realm of Disunion to continue its destruction, in other words, not act soon enough, then most of us may be destroyed in the process.

- But God has given us His promise to safeguard us against such a possibility. So, God will intervene to save us. Such a miracle of God will surely make it easier for us, but whether it brings a peaceful ending will depend on us. If we act proactively in accordance with the Realm of Union and Divine guidance, the ending will be peaceful. If we remain passive or do not act according to the Divine will, we may experience a war, which is never a good thing.

- The Jewish people believe that the Messianic Age will be peaceful and proactive. Every good deed that we do will directly impact the coming of the Messiah and the Messianic Age. The Hebrew Bible tells us that the Messianic Age may come: 1) when and if humanity is ready, or 2) when and if certain apocalyptic events happen. Each time we treat each other badly, we get a negative score. Each time we treat each other nicely, we get a positive score. Then God adds up our collective score. If positive, then we have a peaceful entrance into the Messianic Age. If we want a world of goodness, then we must work toward it. Thus, the Messianic Age is dependent upon every one of us.

- There is one more possibility that is not going to be too good for humanity, and that is the creation of a false messiah acting as a true messiah, all directed by the Realm of Disunion, to move people toward a path of falsehood and greater disunion, but on the surface, making it appear as if everything is unfolding naturally! In other words, more disunion that can keep us all away from the Realm of Union and its truth. We must be careful not to fall for such manipulations of the masses! The best thing to do at such a time is for people to get up and declare their wish to be the Messiah!

Looking at the world today, with all the hatred and other divisions, one can't help but conclude that the Messianic Age may not come unless God intervenes, and it may not be too pretty unless we bring about change soon.

The Bible assures us that God will reach His goal, and based on the resurrection of Christ, I believe it's reliable.

Also, we're told that God will do everything His way, so we must learn to embrace God's logic!

I believe this book has come to help us better understand things. I hope we will all take the time to read it and discuss it, just in case it is for real.

I believe the insights provided in this book have come from God, even though I didn't know how to structure a sentence when I began writing it. That's why it took me twenty-seven years to finish it, and now that it is completed, it may be best for all of us to get together and discuss it so we can improve it, always toward the Realm of Union.

I'm sure any act of genuine caring, wishing to improve things, and moving closer to the Realm of Union, will please God.

On that note, on Sunday, Sept. 24, 2017, many pilgrims and tourists gathered in St. Peter's Square to hear the Pope's Angelus noon prayer, during which the Holy Father focused on Jesus' message about the Kingdom of God.

The Holy Father said, "Jesus told us that there are no idle hands in the Kingdom of God. That all are called to do their part. And, in the end, the recompense for all shall be what comes from Divine justice, not human justice. Happily, here, we're referring to the salvation that Jesus Christ acquired with His death and resurrection. The salvation that is not merited but given, for which, 'The last shall be first, and the first shall be last'."

Reflecting on the passage, Pope Francis said, "In reality, the 'injustice' of the Landowner serves to provoke, in those who hear the parable, an increase in understanding because Jesus does not want to speak of the problem of labor and just wages but the Kingdom of God."

When we get there, we will proclaim, "Yes, Lord. Your plan was perfect. Your ways were and are right. You have made us be like you and made us be ourselves. You have redeemed us from evil and conquered it by the blood of your Son. You have taken our scars and turned them into monuments of your grace. How awesome you are."

When people can care for the collective interest (the union) rather than their selfish interests, they can get closer to the Realm of Union. Most people drain others rather than care for the union because of their own or their family's interests and happiness.

The people who care for the union cannot drain others, so they often end up getting drained by others. When they become weak or poor, they are often considered lesser than others. But to me, they're strong enough to stand up against the Realm of Disunion and not cooperate with it.

The strong people naturally become the leaders of the Realm of Union, with the ability not to get drained at all. That is done through total alignment with God and His will, enabling us to accomplish tasks through Divine guidance.

Our holy books comfort us not to despair, but to hope, because there will come a time when all human suffering ends, and a new age of peace begins, establishing the Kingdom of God on Earth and healing humanity.

Today, some elites argue that the planet is too crowded, which is not the case. There are miles and miles of space everywhere. Even Dali Lama recently said, "What matters is quality, not quantity," when referring to humanity! And the solution, some have proposed, may be "to kill 6.5 billion people" as shown in the monument in Atlanta.

First of all, such an act is irrational and against everything we stand for. If such a mentality is ever supported and/or followed, it will surely be out of insanity, taking away our humanity. Against universal harmony. Extreme Realm of Disunion!

If we were to suggest a lottery with everyone's name in there, all seven billion of us, as a tool to select those lucky half million to remain alive, all done truthfully and indiscriminately, most elites would not go for it, yet they allow themselves to consider such insane ideas.

Let's not be so pessimistic, especially since we now know that it is possible, highly probable, to facilitate the coming of the Messianic Age. Let's keep our optimism for a better world and come together to make it happen.

We must remember that God's will is ready to be manifested in and around every person if we just allow for it.

In the past, we have seen that as God spoke, the object concerned came into existence. Whether in an instant or over a more or less extended time does not matter. What matters is the creative power of the word of God.

Without authority, a king is like any other person. But when allowed to be a king, his smallest word can have awesome effects, with heads rolling, nations prospering, armies marching, and enemies standing powerless. So, why not let God be the Almighty that He is? He is not going to push Himself upon us because He loves us so much, and also, He honors His gift of free will to us. When we promote disunion, He departs because His presence alone can dissolve all disunion. But, if we were to stop our disunion thoughts, words, and deeds and align ourselves with the Realm of Union, He will stay and help us out, always through union transforming disunion.

Seeing the power of words at the merely human level is one thing, but to witness things through the Divine Logos is another kind of experience, where we may finally come to understand the power of God's word in His Kingdom.

There is more to this. So, please allow me to explain. I hope I can make it simple.

An avatar, a saint, or a messenger of God has undergone a process of purification, in which he can see people for who they are and know whether they are disunion people, union people, or victims, because he is pure and righteous, without any attachment to a specific thought system. God is the focal point, and everything in the universe is seen through the Divine Eye.

Such people are no longer limited to one thought system. They can see all thought systems through God without any limitations unless God does not want certain things to be seen. It is truly a blessing to gain an open mind and a way of thinking that allows for such an expansion in both how we view and perceive things.

When a person experiences what it is like to be open, they have gone beyond being closed ever again! A level of spirituality that has been, so far, accessible only to a few, but now that the Messianic Age is coming and the union wave is splashing and overflowing, more of us are going to learn how to acquire an open thought system through the Almighty God.

With an open mind, one day, it is possible to wake up eager to learn from God and His many manifestations in and around us. This yearning to be with Him and continually learn from Him can surely help us become our Divine Selves and remain in the Realm of Union, where there are no limitations on goodness, wellness, love, happiness, and all the other union attributes.

Let's read the signs to recognize the patterns.

The new millennium has passed us by. For all of us who live on this planet, it is an interesting time. It is time to honor our humanity and celebrate its achievements, while recognizing that we are at a crucial crossroads where we must choose between disunion and union.

Those religions that consider their leader to be the Messiah, like the Bahá'ís, originating in Iran; the Ahmadis, originating in India (now

Pakistan); or the Rastafaris, originating in Ethiopia, with millions of followers, can be instrumental in expediting the Messianic Age.

Whether the Messianic Age arrived with their messiah and is now in progress, as they believe, or will arrive in the future, in either case, what's important is their contribution to the Realm of Union and their openness to the Reality of God, His Logos, unfolding as He wills.

No one should ever get stuck in a disunion situation, where the leaders and/or followers of a religious institution or movement act as compradors to bless and aid the theft of resources from other nations by their own home country, or engage in other unrighteous acts, promoting the Realm of Disunion rather than Union.

The founder of religion may be the greatest spiritual servant of God, but the succeeding leaders may have had to cooperate and/or collaborate with the Realm of Disunion that is here to infect every life. We must consider that such leaders often have too much money and power at stake to be truthful to their followers. So, it's best to go directly to God for guidance rather than to someone who is no longer pure or righteous. Of course, there are exceptions!

In some cases, it is difficult to even know for sure. Because they may have thought that they were following the Divine will while erroneously doing the opposite. Sometimes, they may have been forced to collaborate with the Realm of Disunion, either to keep their position or to stay alive!

If and when a messiah claimant appears and is ready to act as God's vessel to usher in the Messianic Age, the leadership of these established messianic movements or other religious organizations may become blinded and go against the person, sometimes convincing their followers to oppose the messiah claimant, all to protect their cushy position. That is not good for humanity. It may even go against God and His plan. And you wouldn't want to be a part of such a disunion act. So, it's best to be cautious!

Just love your spiritual leader and thank him for all of his contributions toward the establishment of the Realm of Union, but don't fool yourself.

Beware of deceptions, and study and understand such frictions as you can. Keep your options open and explore your situation so that you may come to terms with it.

And remember that the reason for the doubts is that the messiah claimants of the past did not reduce evil worldwide, even though they succeeded in attracting many believers and followers during their lives, and even after they died, and many years passed. Others wondered, "If nothing changed for the better, then why are the followers still believing in the person to be the Messiah?"

But this is not aligned with a union viewpoint, where it's best and even necessary to see all past and present messiah claimants as contributors and not drainers unless there is concrete evidence that the person has drained humanity and God's existence, which is very unlikely.

Most messiah claimants gave their lives to helping and comforting humanity, and their contributions were instrumental in advancing humankind toward the Realm of Union.

The key is to rely on God for He has mercy, always guiding us and making sure to reveal His proposal and projects to His messengers and other agents to deliver to us to facilitate our transition from the Realm of Disunion to Union and to show us the best way to reconnect with God so that we may continually live in the Realm of Union, where He dwells.

As we receive a few important lessons in spirituality before the Messianic Age, we will be ready to get involved, for each of us is destined to contribute to it. Such new insights will guide us to become helpers and comforters of man and servants of God. The greater our understanding and support, the easier it will be for the Messiah to usher in the Messianic Age.

By the time the Messianic Age arrives, we should already know how to build a new structure of the Realm of Union on the planet. Let's call it a Realm of Union structure; in brief, "RoU structure." Today, we are in a Realm of Disunion structure; in brief, "Ro∩ structure."

Some insights regarding the RoU and Ro∩ structures:

- Notice that U is a cup that holds things. Thus, in the Realm of Union, there is no drainage.
- Notice that ∩ is an upside-down cup that cannot hold things. Thus, in the Realm of Disunion, there is continual drainage.

The new RoU structure cannot materialize unless we all implement it together. So, from this point forward, the Messiah cannot do the job for us, except for getting involved like everybody else, unless God decides to come through him to interact with us. That is when the Messiah becomes the vessel of God and is very instrumental in the growth of the Messianic Age.

And, as people witness the power of the Holy Spirit, acting through the Messiah and other Realm of Union agents, they begin to perceive God in all things and all things in God.

All this may be difficult to achieve right now but not after we read this book in many volumes and understand its message that directs us to promote the Realm of Union and contribute to the Messianic Age through the implementation of God's proposal and projects, together with other people, hopefully, with the assistance of the Messiah who will come to show us how to become helpers and comforters as well as true servants of God.

The Messiah will act as the vessel of God, through whom we will witness His ways of handling the Realm of Disunion and the Realm of Union, so that we can continue living in the Realm of Union.

Remember that the Messiah needs our support. Even if he is not the Messiah, we can still help him to promote the Realm of Union. There is nothing wrong with that. No risk whatsoever as long as we don't put the Messiah or anyone else on a pedestal and we keep "WE THE PEOPLE" in charge!

I tell you, humanity has always had a habit of looking at great leaders in awe and putting them on a pedestal. That is not a good thing to do. It can be dangerous.

When the Messiah comes, we must respect and thank him for what he has done for us, and surely hear his insights and opinions, but we should never let him rule us! The Messiah may guide us, but that's about it! If the Messiah tries to rule rather than serve, then this, in itself, can be a sign that he is not the true Messiah! No one but God should be allowed to rule! The rest of us, including the Messiah, shall serve Him!

Moreover, this approach to life must continue throughout the Messianic Age and afterward when pleasing God becomes our highest priority. Right now, God is pretty upset and tired of all of the lies, deceptions, caballing, and killing, just for the sake of money!

He wants us to wake up to His Realm of Union and try to help each other to leave the Realm of Disunion, in which we've existed for a long time, habitually busy satisfying our own will to wonder about God's Will for us.

We must each try to connect with God in His way, not ours! Relating to God does not require any holy book, because the Realm of Union is in the heart of every man, with all the signs of God, but our holy books are here to give us examples that can guide us.

Some questions may arise: Why did we have to wait for our collective salvation? Why did we have to wait for the Messiah to come and explain the way to us rather than know it ourselves? Why did we have to wait for the Realm of Disunion to reach its peak before getting tired of it?

No doubt, we could have each reached salvation personally, for Jesus came to show us the way, but to do it collectively, we had to wait. We couldn't have done it early on in our spiritual development because every person had to learn how to go through a process of transformation from every disunion into union, where the Age of Disunion had to show us the many faces of evil and allow for the completion of our necessary tools as an extension of humanity to finally put an end to all evil, as mentioned throughout this book.

First, we must understand that even some of the disunion people who contributed to the disunion structure, in whatever manner, may have been permitted to do so. That is something we should not bother to figure out right now. In the future, as we enter the Realm of Union, with the truth all around us, we will come to see the purpose behind such things.

Second, as we explore the Realm of Union path, which can be defined as a reflection of the age of caring, many paths will open before us, all leading to the same destination: the Realm of Union. The actual path itself may differ from one person to another, one collective to another, one culture to another, one nation to another, etc., because we are all different with unique backgrounds, abilities, and preferences.

Surely, with God and His universe being infinite, this should be expected and really shouldn't be a problem. It's time to celebrate God and His universe, always trying to accommodate our varied tastes, by rejoicing and allowing everyone to investigate the many paths potentially available to humanity, so that we are free to learn from each other. The more paths from which to choose, the better for all of us, just like having many fruits, vegetables, or trees available to us.

Who knows? We may want to explore one path for a few years, then another for a few more as we grow in spirituality. Surely, this should be okay as long as we follow the Divine will and study specific events that could move us toward self-actualization and help each other do the same. The key is to facilitate the unfolding of the Messianic Age, which should take us all to the Realm of Union.

Third, it's okay to expedite the coming of the Messianic Age, if done through the Realm of Union and its attributes, but not through the Realm of Disunion, because disunion brings more disunion, never union. However, union always brings more union, never disunion, if done through God.

The problem people often encounter is that they employ union attributes, but because they do so without God, they become blinded and easily deceived by the Realm of Disunion, leading them astray. So, all this takes some time and practice!

Fourth, the disunion people may try to bring disunion thoughts, words, and/or acts to promote the Realm of Disunion, one crisis after another, so that we remain too drained, confused, and/or disoriented to work together toward the Messianic Age.

Now, there is a new tactic of involving celebrities, giving them money to set up different humanitarian foundations and causes so that they appear as a union hero and then, later, paying them off to generate different disunion words and acts that everybody can next talk about for weeks or months while the global structure is coming down on us!

I guess, the disunion people have gained some smart realization that staging too many terrorist attacks and killing school children around the world may be moving the masses toward a volcano eruption, which I talked about earlier and so, why not just create stupid dysfunctional incidents and events that the masses could talk about among themselves and that way, they could keep busy doing what they love to do, which is to talk and gossip about celebrities.

It's time for the masses to also gain some insight into the activities of elites regarding proactive history.

Also, the Iranian government has been complaining about the oil fiasco and wanting to put an end to it, asking Russia and China for help, and the takers of oil have been creating so much chaos and insanity around the world, not to allow the voice of the Mullahs to be heard! The problem with all of this is that some people take advantage of the situation and commit horrible acts, knowing that the authorities will not come after them because they hide their unrighteous acts! So, many compradors are busy backstabbing and blackmailing each other! And the people at the top don't know what to do about it!

Fifth, the disunion people may try to attack the Messiah, saying he is power hungry and should not be trusted! Also, since the elites have often leaned toward proactive history, there is an option open to them to groom a person as the messiah with the code to save us all, but, in reality, use him to control the masses!

We must never fall for such idiotic scenarios where the messiah claimant is disrespected, or the global disunion structure creates a made-up messiah!

In such a situation, we should demand the opportunity to freely communicate with the messiah to ask him our valid questions so that he may give us valid answers. If this does not happen, we should not follow such a closed, made-up state of affairs that prohibits people from asking questions.

It's best to move toward an open state, where all messiah claimants are supported and encouraged to contribute their lives to serve God, His Realm of Union, and humanity! I would love to work with such people to bring true democracy to the planet. Why not? Since no damage can be done, and after a while, we shall all come to recognize the true messiah, because that's how the Realm of Union works!

At such a time, the best thing to do is for everyone to stand up and declare, "I wish to be the Messiah," just like in the movie "Spartacus," where every gladiator claimed to be Spartacus to save Spartacus' life! But here, we each want to become a messiah to save the messiah's life and humanity's life, so that we can all work together to make the world a better place for all.

We must do whatever it takes to help everybody end up in the Realm of Union, surely knowing how to employ union attributes and also how to minimize the elites' disunion attributes and efforts against union heroes, as they've often done in the past.

But, at the same time, we must be careful not to generate any disunion that may promote the Realm of Disunion. We must weaken the Realm of Disunion, not strengthen it.

For instance, we must take the time and effort to engage in dialogue, cooperate, and/or collaborate to find solutions that benefit our world, thus all of humanity.

If we want to move forward together toward a better world for all, then we need to resolve our conflicts, many of which happen to arise from our religious differences, as well as racial and class discrimination.

The reason for our religious differences is that the Realm of Disunion often uses religion as a tool to abuse humankind. Such religious exploitations have existed in the past and will continue in the future unless we get together and declare, **"Enough is Enough!"**

We need to help each other look beyond the stereotyped images our media conveys. We must reclaim the power of interpretation to better understand ordinary citizens, their hopes, and their concerns. We need to express our diverse heritage in innovative forms and aesthetics.

We need to figure out what God may have wanted from and for us over the years and what he may want from and for us today, which, I'm sure, has a lot to do with humanity trying to leave the Realm of Disunion so that we can live together in the Realm of Union where God dwells.

And God Said to Angel: Toward the Divine Plan explains this further, telling us about the Divine Solution and how to bring it about by establishing Jerusalem as His City and doing our best to let holiness unfold in His City as the start of the Messianic Age and then for every collective to come forward and participate in witnessing the Divine Logos, personally and collectively, to obtain Divine guidance on how to spread this holiness to cover the Earth.

Next is the conclusion, which summarizes what's happening with humanity and how the Realm of Disunion keeps us in darkness, so we may never reach the Divine Light and Love that can dissolve the Realm of Disunion and lead us to the Realm of Union.

CONCLUSION

So far, we've been in the Age of Disunion, supporting the disunion structure, knowingly or unknowingly, but always praying and hoping for the best. That can be said pretty much for everybody.

Now that the Age of Disunion is ending and the Age of Transformation is beginning, it is time to wake up and figure out a way to satisfy the Divine Plan and, if possible, expedite humanity's transition from disunion to union.

To achieve this goal, we must raise awareness that people must unite to help each other understand the disunion structure and how it operates, while building a union structure on planet Earth that can support us all.

We're in the dark mainly because we've been promoting disunion far more than union attributes over the years.

Imagine every person doing this daily for centuries. I tell you, it can pile up, and it has. That's why we're now in darkness, even though the Divine Light is in abundance and accessible to everyone, always through union attributes.

I compared union versus disunion attributes in this volume, and I tried to do so spontaneously through channeling, without much effort or control, as God wanted me to. Here, in this conclusion, I'm going to provide a summary of what I've seen in my life regarding the disunion structure. If every person were to write a summary of their life experiences and share it with others, we might, together, have enough data to see and monitor humanity's movement through time and space.

Everything in this volume came to me primarily as a stream of consciousness. In such an effort, there is no room for ego.

As I wrote this volume, I watched my ego disintegrate. As it grew lighter, I was able to deepen my spiritual connection to all that serves the Realm of Union.

Today, I try to embrace the Divine manifestations in everyone and everything. I live in the Buddha State of NOW, where I can experience God's truth and gain the knowledge and wisdom I need to handle the Realm of Disunion, always through the attributes of the Realm of Union and Divine guidance.

It feels great to stand free of all fears, doubts, and sufferings and observe everything that passes through me with no attachment to the Realm of Disunion. Surely, I sometimes experience pain, but with the total awareness and support of the Realm of Union.

I believe that this state of life with God, which is the Realm of Union, is the highest spiritual level attainable by man and that our prophets, sages, and other union people must have experienced it and tried to tell us about it.

So, I'm not unique in seeing the Realm of Union versus the Realm of Disunion and how these two realms can affect one's life. Many have seen all this, but they've been quiet about it, not knowing how to explain it. People have asked me, "Angel, since you have a message from God to humanity, then are you a prophet? Could you be the Messiah?" Let me answer these two questions.

I BELIEVE: Every person can witness the Divine Logos and learn to interact with it in a way, where he or she can become the Logos in flesh, as Jesus succeeded to do and directed us to do the same, to become our Divine Selves, each Divine Self, a vessel of God, through whom He can manifest in the person, continually guiding the individual to achieve personal salvation. As we each achieve personal salvation, we will come together to help each other achieve collective salvation, which humanity has not yet reached but is destined to experience soon, when the time is right, according to the Divine Plan. The Christians believe this will happen at Jesus' return.

The bottom line is that we must honor every individual's spiritual journey to this higher state of spirituality. Otherwise, we will be holding people back from reaching the Realm of Union and becoming their Divine Selves, which goes against God and His wish for us to know Him so that we can live in Heaven on Earth.

The Messiah undergoes this spiritual journey to become his Divine Self, defined as oneness with God. It is through this oneness that God can manifest His will to the Messiah to properly guide humanity. When the time comes for the Messiah to become a direct representative (or representative) of God, through whom He may communicate to humanity, a direct connection between God and humanity is established, with the Messiah becoming God's vessel. At such a time, if we're awake and living in the Realm of Union, it will be clear to us who the Messiah is, but until then, no one but God knows. So, we shouldn't wonder, "Who is the true messiah?" Instead, we try to live in the Realm of Union as we wait for the Messiah to become the vessel of God.

The day we determine, one hundred percent with no doubt, that someone is truly the Messiah, then we honor the individual as God's representative and support the person fully to achieve his Divine mission on Earth.

That is pretty much the process the Messianic Age will take to establish the Kingdom of God on Earth. Remember that the Messiah will come during the Messianic Age. Most likely, we will have to empower the Realm of Union and prepare for the coming of the Messiah; otherwise, the Messianic Age may not get enough momentum to unfold as intended.

All this means: we don't ask Angel or anyone else, "Are you the Messiah?" Because she has no idea!" No one knows. She is just doing her best to serve God and share her insights with humanity. That's about it! And who cares who is the actual messiah? The Messiah will surely not care. All he will care about is for humanity to listen to God and follow His will, which we've been shown how to do, over and over again, throughout history.

So, let's say we all do our best to promote union attributes to empower the Realm of Union; naturally, the Messianic Age will unfold and soon bring us the Messiah to guide us. Any other way but this won't work. Any attempt to expedite this process through our made-up messiah(s) or other agendas is going to damage the messianic process. We must let the Messianic Age and the coming of the Messiah unfold naturally, as God has intended for us.

There is no reason we cannot honor and support all people who wish to follow in the footsteps of the Messiah, especially since such a path will help many clean up their lives and evolve toward the messianic consciousness, which we are all destined to embrace during the Messianic Age.

Let's say, we end up having a million people sharing their insights about this whole process and a few hundred individuals suspecting themselves to be the Messiah. That shouldn't be a problem and is really a no-brainer. We just support them all and let them figure it out. I'm sure, after a while working together and achieving more and more of the impossible, this group of messiah claimants will gradually come to see who is the true Messiah and let us all know. If not, then so be it; we just help each other get the job done.

Because of the Age of Disunion, most of us don't have the time or energy to be creative and imagine the unimaginable. We are often driven by what we can see, not by what we cannot see. That's why materialism has won over spiritualism. But the Age of Disunion is scheduled to end soon.

As we approach the Age of Transformation, materialism will no longer be an end in itself. Spiritualism will dominate materialism worldwide, bringing Divine knowledge and the understanding of the natural way to all people.

Furthermore, with spiritualism comes a revolution of consciousness, in pursuit of Divine knowledge and presence, filled with creativity, daily miracles, and insights.

All this will help us stop our Disunion behaviors and begin promoting the Realm of Union so that the spirit may begin to dominate matter, as God intended.

God has told us that the Messianic Age will come just as in the days of Moses, when God intervened with His miracles and helped His messenger guide His people out of Egypt. That means God will help us move toward the Messianic Age.

We will come to realize that every good deed that we do will directly impact the coming of the Messiah and the Messianic Age. If we want a world of goodness, then we must work toward it. Hence, the Messianic Age is dependent upon every one of us.

Such miracles of God would surely transform us to know that we're here to serve Him. Spiritual emancipation to change the world, and this time for good!

So, what is our role in this? Surely, our collective mission can be summarized as humankind uniting to increase our acts of goodness and kindness and follow the voice of good and balance rather than the selfish voice, like the butterfly effect, where one little act can change things and bring incredible transformation, as Rosa Parks, the black woman, did.

Our mission can be summarized as every person or collective taking the time to witness the Divine Logos and how to interact with it to receive guidance from it to know what to do every day to live a better and fuller life, according to his or her purpose in life, to better serve God and His Realm of Union.

After a while of sharing such information, I'm sure it will get easier to conclude a set of signposts to get us to our destination, which is the Realm of Union. I will include a guide at the end of this book that shares my own insights on this matter.

The bottom line is that we are here to serve the Divine Plan for humanity. Toward this goal, we must acknowledge that we can no longer afford to let a bunch of doubting gatekeepers do whatever it takes to keep us all away from the Realm of Union.

We must come to recognize the Realm of Disunion as our true enemy and work together to reach the Realm of Union. Believe me, most people would rather live in the Realm of Union than Disunion. They just don't know how to reach such a state of spirituality and often need assistance. That is true about everybody, even the elites and the global managers of the planet.

Humanity's spiritual journey should continue as a part of the Messianic Age. We should all take it seriously and help each other through our personal transformation, detailed in *And God Said to Angel: How to Transform Personally,* and our collective transformation, detailed in *And God Said to Angel: How to Transform Collectively*.

I'm convinced no one wishes to be in the Realm of Disunion, including the disunion collective.

Let's all contribute to a global discussion that tries to analyze where we are, how we got here, and what we must do now to reach the Realm of Union, first personally and then collectively, to build a union structure on the planet that will support us all.

Below are my insights as a contribution.

A GUIDE TO DISUNION SIGNS

I wish to share some of my insights as signposts to facilitate our personal and collective spiritual journey. Don't worry if you cannot relate to a bullet and its text. You can always go back to it later.

Hopefully, someday, it will all make sense to us. For now, just read it and let it sink in as you do your best to stay positive. Remember, we can no longer afford any negativity whatsoever.

So, with the Spirit of Love and Aloha, here are some insights we may decide to keep as our signposts:

- Today, the Realm of Disunion has almost reached its peak. It has become strong, nearly fragmenting every life. Fragmentation naturally breeds confusion, making it hard to see the whole picture and figure things out. In such an environment, falsehood spreads alongside secrecy and continuous drainage of energy.

- As we each add to disunion attributes daily, polluting the spiritual realm, mainly due to our ignorance and inability to recognize union versus disunion, the disunion structure gets stronger and spreads around the planet. The disunion structure always tries to control everything and everyone as much as it is possible.

- Those who support the disunion structure have learned how to stay in control through the Realm of Disunion and its many disunion attributes and techniques. The disunion structure is driven to keep everyone in bondage and below their potential.

- Most people will ridicule you and try to stop you when they see you living your life heroically, pursuing your potential. The reason is that they don't want to admit they're living their lives below their potential, sometimes not even to themselves.

- The disunion structure has developed a system of propaganda over the years to confuse us and not let us see that we are in bondage.

- That's why most of us don't know we're living in darkness. We remain confused by a lack of intuition that keeps us victims of the Realm of Disunion, and mostly drained. Without the Divine Light, there can be no other place but darkness, where we are blinded and unable to witness Divine Reality, His logos, and interact with it to receive our daily instructions. Yet we are here to experience the Logos, the Realm of Union, where God dwells and truth resides to set us free.

- We must realize that we can either contribute to the Realm of Union or the Realm of Disunion and that as we depower one, we empower the other. The Chapter, *Union versus Disunion*, in *And God Said to Angel: How to Transform Personally*, tries to explain all this. I hope it does a good job.

314

- The universe follows certain laws, rules, and regulations to keep the overall harmony. We must live in the Realm of Union to remain aligned with this harmony. If we are not aligned with it, then we end up in the Realm of Disunion, where we promote disunion attributes and techniques and cause damage to ourselves and other members of this awesome universe of God.

- You can reach happiness only through the Realm of Union, never Disunion. So, righteousness and happiness are truly tied together. You cannot promote disunion and expect to be in harmony with yourself and your surroundings. It doesn't work that way.

- God has shown us how to be righteous through employing union attributes. All messengers of God came to take us toward the path of righteousness that is the Realm of Union.

- The reason most of us have failed to stay on this path of righteousness is that we have not yet learned how to balance oneness and uniqueness.

- Oneness is the ability to look at the world through the Divine Eye, where we connect to everything and everyone solely through Him.

- Uniqueness is the ability to live life, not through our egos, but through our Divine Selves, where God can manifest through us, i.e., through our Divine Selves.

- The balance of oneness and uniqueness is a process. If we allow it to unfold, it brings us closer to God, helping us gradually get to know Him and our Divine Selves.

- Every Divine Self has a distinctive identity. So, no two are alike. Each person must find his or her true identity and try to follow it through God and His will for the individual, which is a part of the Divine Logos. This process will surely facilitate our spiritual journey.

- When someone says, "God is not answering me!" they are not calling God as we've been directed. It's time to learn how to do it right! We cannot employ disunion attributes and techniques and then call on Him to help us with it. We have to stop our disunion activities and then call on Him. Moreover, remember that He knows what you're thinking, saying, and doing at all times. Of course, it is often not possible to stop the disunion activities around you, but you, yourself, can do what it takes.

- The disunion structure tries to weaken the Realm of Union. It has done this for centuries, and we have allowed it to happen. We have not done anything about it. But today is a new day, where we will finally learn how to do it. Of course, it's not going to be easy, and it's not going to happen overnight. It will take some time and effort, but it's all doable.

- The key is to learn how the disunion structure works. We must try to examine the various disunion techniques and teachings that have been developed to weaken different collectives and humanity as a whole.

- We must go deep inside and outside ourselves and determine how the Realm of Disunion has weakened us and our lives, and try to talk about it. It is only through sharing our personal and collective experiences and discussing such information that we can see the many faces of evil in our community and on our planet, and finally put an end to it. It's time to reduce the Realm of Disunion's influence upon our loved ones and us so that we can reach the Realm of Union. Every person can surely do this to reach his or her potential and then come together to achieve our collective potential.

- We must categorize this information and, together, classify the different faces of evil around the planet, affecting each person, collective, and humanity.

- For instance, one of the areas where the disunion structure has done a number on us is the way it has always tried to bind the female collective. In every culture, we can see this. Some cultures suffer more than others. In the Islamic culture, we can see how women have been forced to cover themselves for years, not letting them participate properly in society.

- I was in Morocco a few years ago. After a few days, I realized that only men were having tea in teahouses, enjoying the sunshine and each other's company, while women were mostly covered, carrying groceries home to cook for the family and to attend to the kids. It was so painful watching this that I had to leave early.

- In such cultures, women are being abused physically, emotionally, sexually, mentally, and spiritually, with no way to escape this horrible treatment of the feminine side of society.

- Think about it. When women are abused and weakened, it affects the whole society. Moreover, this abuse is not just in Eastern societies. It can be seen in the West as well, in different ways.

- How can we bring balance to humankind when half of its population is being maltreated? And this disrespect for women can affect men as well, as they do not know how to treat women properly. So, the most basic unit of our global society has been damaged, and most of us are too blind to see it.

- Of course, those who are aware try to do something about it, like the Me Too Movement, but they usually don't get too far because the disunion structure wants such abuses to continue, weakening humanity. As long as the disunion structure is stronger than the Realm of Union, we're going to see similar results. That's just the nature of the beast!

- Furthermore, when a movement begins, it often goes through a period of wonderment, excitement, and hope, but then it sizzles down because humanity is not allowed to know the truth. Often, we lack proper discussions and investigations to find out what's going on.

- When a union person or group seeks the truth and promotes the Realm of Union, the disunion structure strives to stop them.

- The disunion structure solely supports the Realm of Disunion and its people. They don't support the union people or the victims.

- As the disunion structure grows, it naturally needs to recruit more disunion people to support it, so the disunion collective grows larger over time.

- The disunion structure teaches every disunion person how to promote the Realm of Disunion and weaken the Realm of Union.

- The disunion people love to drain others (the union people, the victims, and also the disunion people, so even the members of their collective). They must do this to obtain energy from others because they don't know how to get pure energy from the Source. Over time, more and more people become ghouls (like monsters), driven to find ways to drain others daily.

- When we obtain energy directly from another person rather than from the Source, it becomes polluted energy that can build up in the spiritual realm, bringing spiritual darkness that can prevent us from seeing things clearly.

- It is possible to obtain pure energy from the Source, directly or indirectly (through another person), so it is crucial to know how to get our energy the right way, as I explain in the Chapter, *The Energy Transfer*, in *And God Said to Angel: How to Transform Personally*.

- Every disunion thought, word, and act can add up to pollute the spiritual realm, so the lesser the better for the Realm of Disunion. When it does happen, in other words, a disunion event occurs, then it's best to transform the disunion into a union as soon as it is possible. Today, we see the opposite: we're continually broadcasting disunion everywhere, copying and spreading it.

- The goal in life is to strengthen the Realm of Union that can naturally weaken the Realm of Disunion and its effects on us by gradually dissolving it through Divine presence and guidance so that we can live comfortably in the Realm of Union. We must learn how to do this. There is no other way!

- As we empower the Realm of Union and gradually make it stronger than the Realm of Disunion, life's struggles begin to diminish, allowing us all to live better lives.

- The key is to learn how to employ union attributes and techniques rather than disunion. We must learn to cooperate rather than compete, to love unconditionally, and not to have expectations, etc. Every union thought, word, and act can add up to take us closer to the Realm of Union and away from the Realm of Disunion.

- There is a threshold in the spiritual realm beyond which there is too much pollution for humanity to co-exist with other entities in the divine creation. If we persist in adding disunion to the accumulated pollution of humanity's spiritual realm as we are doing today, we will reach this threshold and get dissolved. In other words, we will gradually break down and kick the bucket!

- On the other hand, if we each add union attributes to the spiritual realm daily, we will slowly reduce pollution and even purify ourselves. The purer and holier we become, the easier it will be for all of us to reach the Realm of Union.

- Remember that God knows you and your intentions at every moment. So, if you make mistakes while trying your best to serve Him and His creation, He will come to your rescue. Have faith in Him!

- The Realm of Disunion and its people cannot stand the Realm of Union's purity and beauty, for it reminds them of how polluted they have become. So, naturally, they try to go against every union attribute and stop every union person.

- It is difficult for the union people and the victims to succeed in today's disunion structure. If you see a union person getting ahead and living comfortably, remember it hasn't been easy. Most people try to sabotage it. They suffer from disunion attributes that keep them from making things easier for themselves and others.

- When we surround ourselves with union people, life can get easier and better, for they don't compare themselves to others and wish the best for everyone.

- Every disunion attribute residing in a person, a group, or a collective can prevent them from supporting the Realm of Union and its people.

- For instance, we compare our religions rather than see them as steps toward humanity's spiritual development.

- Those who envy can't help but be happy when they see others suffer. This horrible attribute can even drive some people to intentionally damage others to prevent them from achieving their goals.

- Those who want others to succeed try to help, not harm. They do it because they love the Realm of Union and realize that by promoting the Realm of Union, it will get easier for all of us to succeed and reach the Realm of Union.

- The disunion people prefer to be in the Realm of Union, working extremely hard to be in customized heavens with their loved ones, but when it comes to others, they don't care. They try to keep others in the Realm of Disunion. Not realizing that this is not how it works. If you promote disunion, then you're in disunion. You cannot promote disunion and then be in the Realm of Union (heaven) yourself.

- Please learn to recognize union versus disunion people and the victims. Many people pretend to belong to the union collective, but it can all be a facade. They may be ashamed of who they've become. It's best to check things out to see if they're for real. Usually, you can tell by tracing their money (how they fund themselves and their projects)! But this must be done lovingly, for we can no longer afford any disunion.

- We should never use disunion attributes that can take us toward the Realm of Disunion. We must be careful always to employ union attributes that take us toward the Realm of Union. That's why our great leaders have always directed us to keep the peace when dealing with the Realm of Disunion.

- But such leaders have seldom explained to us the details of how to do this because they didn't know much about it themselves. I hope this book can show us how to do it.

- It's simple and comfortable for union people and victims to live in a union structure because God supports the Realm of Union, allowing people to belong to it and promote it. The key is to stand near God, where there is less struggle and drainage and more creativity and productivity because of His Light and His Love, both of which are infinite.

- We must build a planetary union structure in a union manner that can gradually and peacefully replace the current disunion structure. But to achieve this goal, we must learn to rely solely on union attributes. No disunion whatsoever because the union structure cannot be built upon any disunion attributes. It just can't, for this is the nature of it all!

- We must figure out where we are, how we got here, and what we must do to reach a better place for humanity. And you better believe that the disunion structure will use some of its disunion techniques to keep us from reaching the Realm of Union.

- For instance, the disunion structure has learned how to weaken people by dividing them and creating all kinds of conflicts to keep them from getting along and possibly coming together. These conflicts are unreal, so the disunion structure must continually fuel them to keep them real. Otherwise, these conflicts can slowly vanish.

- The disunion structure encourages people to join the disunion network by bribing them and, if not possible, threatening them and their families. I've even seen the disunion structure kidnap people and put them under mind control to force them to comply! But it's best not to blame anyone for this because this is the nature of it all!

We cannot afford any disunion attribute. We have to learn how to resolve issues through union attributes with divine guidance.

- The disunion structure creates false entities that appear to be in the Realm of Union but are aligned with the Realm of Disunion (often promoting misinformation). That way, there are disunion people spread globally across every field, ready to sabotage any movement toward the Realm of Union. Some of these people don't even know what they're doing or how the Realm of Disunion is using them.

- In every field, every organization, and every religion, we can see the disunion people getting promoted by the disunion structure to keep humanity down.

- The disunion structure has developed mind control programs all over the world to hijack the minds of people, like children in schools and social services, soldiers in the military, patients in different designated hospitals, and many others, instead of protecting them.

- The disunion structure is always monitoring people and trying to recruit those who may be succeeding. If such people are willing to come on board, the disunion structure guides them, funds them and their projects, and even helps them reach their goals. But if they decide not to join, they won't support them, even making it difficult for them to succeed. That's why many people go along with it!

- As the Realm of Disunion grows, polluting more of the spiritual realm, the disunion structure grows stronger, darker, and more fragmented until we cross the threshold of disunion, where we dissolve. Every person can affect this threshold by employing union attributes to convert a disunion into a union. But if everybody does the opposite out of ignorance or selfishness, then there is not much a single person can do about the melting away of humanity. However, together, as we recognize the Realm of Disunion as our true enemy, we can empower the Realm of Union to dissolve it.

- Most people prefer to be in the Realm of Union, but they don't know how to get there. They're scared of the Realm of Disunion hurting them and their families, especially since the disunion structure tends to trick and/or force people to join the disunion structure and continue supporting it, even though in bondage.

- Today's disunion structure has built a network of disunion people who will do whatever it takes to stop the union people. But since the Realm of Disunion is internally very weak and lacks support from the divine universe belonging to the Realm of Union, there is a way to gradually move humanity toward the Realm of Union.

- We can each build a union environment for ourselves and our families and try to help our friends and extended families to do the same. Every family living in the Realm of Union can help spread the Realm of Union and its attributes on the planet. That is something we can all do. After all, the Divine Pure Energy is everywhere. We can easily obtain it daily to make ourselves, our families, our collectives, and humanity strong again. That is what Cyrus the Great tried to do in the Persian Empire, for which he was highly regarded by many leaders worldwide.

- Many of the forefathers of the United States of America sought inspiration from Cyrus the Great through works such as Cyropaedia. Cyrus has been a personal hero to many people in history, including Thomas Jefferson, Mohammad Reza Pahlavi, and David Ben-Gurion.

- On a collective level, however, since we're all living in the disunion structure, it can get difficult right now to bring a change for the better unless we follow God and His Plan for humanity, as explained in detail in *And God Said to Angel: Toward the Divine Plan and Heaven on Earth*.

- This volume, which you now hold, reminds us not to generate any disunion attributes whatsoever, but to always employ union attributes. Please try to remain appreciative of things and stay positive. That way, you empower the Realm of Union. Otherwise, you will promote the Realm of Disunion, which we can no longer afford.

- At the same time, try to learn about the current disunion structure and its many disunion techniques, which have been put in place to stop us from ever reaching the Realm of Union. The disunion structure doesn't want us to clean up the mess we've created. We're not supposed to tamper with the way things are.

- But don't let it discourage you or stop you. Just try to recognize the disunion techniques detailed in And God Said to Angel: How to Transform Collectively, and act smart about it. Try to love all disunion people and be kind to them. They don't know any better. They do need our help.

- Get busy building your network of union people, and work with the union collective to help every victim become a union person. That is truly the key to heaven's door.

- Please learn to obtain pure energy daily, as it will help us all increase the planet's overall pure energy. The greater the pure energy globally, the easier for each of us (all of us) to do what we must do to strengthen the Realm of Union.

- Do not ever entangle yourself with the Realm of Disunion. Let God handle the Realm of Disunion for you. In And God Said to Angel: How to Transform Personally, the Chapter "How to Rely on God" explains this approach to life.

- Remember never to tag anyone, saying they are a disunion person or a victim. It's best just to help the person transform into a union person.

- Most people at the top of our current disunion structure know what's going on. But they cannot talk about it. They are afraid, and so they remain silent. I'm sure many joined the disunion structure without knowing the details. The Realm of Disunion probably tricked them. So, they need our help.

- That is why we need to promote the Realm of Union and let it support everyone, including the disunion people, who are often tired of the Realm of Disunion and prefer the Realm of Union but don't know how to get out of it. Of course, the disunion structure has helped them achieve success, but at a high price, and they know it. In some ways, they're not too happy about it.

- Of course, some people at the top have succeeded without getting entangled with the disunion structure, but such individuals are rare and incredibly lucky. I know a few of these fortunate people. I worked with them when I was busy building my encryption company. They are utterly amazing people belonging to the union collective.

- Some people, as they try to reach the top of the disunion structure, agree to do certain projects to promote the disunion agendas and, in return, get ahead, but then, after they complete their tasks and are ready to be rewarded, they often find themselves and their projects forgotten by the disunion structure. That's when they realize that the disunion structure can't always remain loyal to people.

- After all, as the disunion structure changes, older people retire, and new people take control. Things get dropped on the floor with no one interested in caring and/or bothering with old promises and expectations. And since many deals are done secretly, under the table, if the original contact is no longer around, there is no one to complain to.

- Today, many people are suffering from such abuses of the disunion structure. Of course, these people are not too happy to be left alone. But there is not much they can do about it.

- Those who have not been affected by such disloyalty within the disunion structure are happy and amazed to be at the top, giving us all huge grins as their bank accounts are filled with billions of dollars. Sometimes, not because they earned the money, but because they were given the money as trusted entrepreneurs willing to support the disunion structure and become effective gatekeepers.

- These gatekeepers know "who can enter" through the gate, so they try to help those who are willing to support the disunion structure while keeping others out! That way, the top of the disunion structure, and right beneath it, are filled with disunion people, with a few exceptions, here and there! The non-disunion people (i.e., the union people and victims) are often kept down in the structure.

- I knew a CIA friend who was a lawyer and an accountant. A long time ago, he told me about off-the-book accounting and how some people were given a lot of money and other goodies to become supporters of the global disunion structure. Some people were given a few billion dollars!

- The reason I always say "nobody is at fault" is that the structure is flawed. We need to build a new union structure on the planet that can gradually replace our current disunion structure, which has always leaned toward the Realm of Disunion, which is our true enemy!

- Most people at the top are concerned about humanity. They know that everything is falling apart. If you listen to them carefully, you can sometimes hear each person's unique plea. Often, they do their best to communicate in ways that can't get them in trouble.

- Some elites think that they can continue employing disunion techniques to rule humanity, but the situation is changing. The Age of Disunion is ending, and the Age of Transformation is coming, where the old ways will stop working.

- Some elites realize all this and would prefer to promote the Realm of Union and its methods, but they're isolated and often surrounded by a bunch of disunion people who are busy satisfying their self-interests.

- The bottom line is that most of us are in bondage. Very few are free. That's why the union collective is still ridiculously small compared to the disunion collective and victims. That can complicate things. But I still have hope because I genuinely believe that God is in charge and eager to guide us to transition from the Realm of

Disunion to the Realm of Union, especially since it is now time to go through this process both personally and collectively.

- **The key to humanity's success is for all of us to:** 1) not blame anyone for our failures or humanity's failures, and try to see the disunion structure as the cause of everything and everyone going away from union toward disunion; 2) acknowledge our successes and failures, but empower the positive in everything and everyone, never the negative; 3) appreciate every collective's struggle with the Realm of Disunion and contribution to the Realm of Union; 4) realize that the elites have been instrumental in keeping the stability of the planet, especially since it's never easy to predict the future; 5) care about the elites, their advisors, and their compradors for keeping us all safe; 6) never employ disunion attributes to get things done, i.e., never support the possibility of hurting one of humanity's collectives, including the elites; 7) trust in God and His Realm of Union way by always relying on Him to dissolve the Realm of Disunion for us, through union attributes and techniques; 8) do whatever possible to get close to God so that we can get to know Him; 9) it is only by satisfying His wish to be known that we can reach our wish to be in heaven on Earth; 10) let God show us the way to our transition from disunion to union; etcetera.

- I have talked about this book and these signposts to some of my friends and family. So far, I have not received the proper support, except from a few truly awesome individuals. I'm sure God will reward them appropriately for their contributions.

- The reason for this is that I'm surrounded by the elites of this world, who don't know what to do about our current situation. They're afraid of the Realm of Union promoting the benefit of all when they've been used to supporting the benefit of a few. They can't comprehend the Realm of Union or the possibility of peace for humanity, especially since they have often promoted divisions and conflicts to confuse everyone and stay at the top. But remember, they've done this because that is all they knew how to do at the time.

- We must never forget that we've been living in the Age of Disunion for more than two millennia, ever since Alexander the Great conquered the Persian Empire. Western civilization was destined to follow the Greek rather than the Persian teachings and ways because we had to go through the Age of Disunion. That naturally forced many elites to keep plugging away throughout history, hoping for the best.

- Some elites and their advisors have been instrumental in maintaining the planet's stability during the Age of Disunion's growth, and we must thank them for their struggles and achievements. After all, they kept us safe until now; hopefully, the time for our transition from the Realm of Disunion to the Realm of Union. It is surely a miracle!

- But for a miracle to appear and then succeed, we must first believe in miracles! That is true about everything in life.

- Thus, we must help each other see that we're now at a great place, a miraculous position, and try to take advantage of this miracle of God by learning how to work with Him.

- Otherwise, we will remain in this disunion structure where the global establishment will continue coming up with new schemes to drain our energy, damage every member of humanity, take our money, and weaken us in any way possible to control us. And the funny or sad part is that most people, from the top to the bottom, would rather not be in such a horrible situation: the peak of the Realm of Disunion.

- Look around you; every few months, we've got a new crisis, all made up pretty much by the global establishment as part of a proactive history that began a long time ago. They try to do whatever is possible to deceive us all. Of course, most people in the structure know what's going on but don't know what to do about it. Some are ignorant, wondering what's going on. Poor humanity!

- Let me talk about a few schemes, just in the past few years, in 2020, 2021, and 2022, to open up your eyes.

- Take the last few months, for example, when all these companies are calling senior citizens to offer them goodies from Medicare. I was one of these people. For a few years, I was harassed by different companies calling me every day and asking me to switch my Medicare Plan to this program that would save me a lot of money. As I began investigating it, a friend of mine who works for the intelligence community warned me not to switch for reasons I cannot explain here. The bottom line is that they plan to cut the entire Medicare program, so they want everybody to switch to make it easier to achieve this goal. Naturally, I kept my Medicare.

- The whole coronavirus gradually became a fiasco that could aid the disunion structure to scare people and force them to comply with a program of insane control through vaccination. It has been proven that this was patented by one of the companies involved in the fiasco. A few months ago, a friend of mine, a scientist working for the US intelligence community, told me in confidence that the coronavirus contains certain DNA sequences and structures that may be harmful, and I just read an article that confirmed it. Can you imagine the insanity?!

- We're now having another war, this time with Russia, abusing and killing people. Why? God only knows! However, I'm praying that it is not because of a bunch of idiots who can't see straight, thinking, "Let's set up the Gog and Magog War to expedite the coming of the Messianic Age." Some include this in the Great Reset!

- Any war involving superpowers can keep people on edge and in bondage, not allowing any monitoring of what is truly happening on the planet.

- Every time one fiasco ends, and people regain peace and calmness, another fiasco begins, and if there is any delay in setting up the new fiasco, there are a few killings here and there on the planet to raise the public's feelings of fear and hopelessness to get people all wrapped up in discussions that usually don't get us anywhere!

- Unfortunately, most people working in the disunion structure cannot come out and report to everybody else what's going on. They're scared, and truly they should be for being involved in such an abusive, exploitive, and conniving structure of the Realm of Disunion.

- Believe me, all this is not going to get better. It's going to get worse, unless we all wake up and put an end to it, not through destruction but construction, as explained in this book and recommended by God.

- THROUGH CONSTRUCTION means we don't touch, confront, or sabotage the global establishment, the current disunion structure, or the disunion people, because we would then be contributing to the Realm of Disunion. Instead, we must try to build a new union structure on the planet, through the Almighty God and His guidance, which can dissolve every disunion and turn it into a union, in support of every person, including the disunion people. That is an urgent matter because we're approaching the threshold of disunion.

- God is calling us all to read this book and learn about the Realm of Union, the Realm of Disunion, and how to differentiate between the two. It is then that we will finally come together and establish the new union structure that will facilitate our collective transition from the Realm of Disunion to the Realm of Union. *And God Said to Angel: How to Transform Collectively* shows us how to build a union structure on the planet by giving concrete examples of projects, some of which have been recommended by the Almighty God.

- The Divine Projects have miraculous powers, so we must study them and implement them as necessary.

I can go on and on, but I think it's enough for now, especially since other volumes of *And God Said to Angel* detail various drainages and drainers.

I must emphasize that I'm not attached to any of the above insights (bullets). I spent twenty-seven years of my life writing this book series primarily to please God. Not to please anyone else.

Believe me, I was directed to do it, and really, I had no other choice. Now that I've done it, I'm just trying to figure out some of the possibilities facing humanity, like everybody else interested in this messianic process.

Thank you for being here, and I'm so grateful for your support.

THE AUTHOR

MY NAME IS ANGEL
I AM A UNION MESSENGER

Angel Fereshteh Bailey (also known as Youssefi, meaning Ben Yosef in Farsi) was raised by French Catholic nuns and her Iranian parents at the Shah's Palace in Tehran. She came to the United States in 1965 as a teenager, grew up in Alexandria, Virginia, with her mother and siblings, married an Irishman in 1975, and became the mother of two sons and a daughter, now adults living their lives. She is an award-winning scientist, inventor, filmmaker, and screenwriter best known for her encryption and authentication technology, which became the industry standard worldwide. In 1992, at the height of her business success, while running her telecom security company, she became terminally ill with cancer. In 1996, she left the Washington, DC area for the Blue Ridge Mountains to heal herself. A few years later, and to her amazement, she found a way to cure herself and potentially heal humanity. She believes her insights come from God to help her guide humanity back to wholeness. This book details how Angel regained wholeness to better relate to the Creator, His Creation, and His wish to be known, and how every person and/or collective may do the same to reach heaven on Earth.